THE DIARY OF A JOURNALIST

BY SIR HENY W. LUCY

SIXTY YEARS IN THE
WILDERNESS
Some Passages by the Way

SIXTY YEARS IN THE
WILDERNESS
More Passages by the Way

NEARING JORDAN
Being the Third and Last Volume
of "Sixty Years in the Wilderness"

THE DIARY OF
A JOURNALIST

BY SIR HENRY LUCY

LONDON
JOHN MURRAY, ALBEMARLE STREET, W.
1920

192/229

K:Hyt: 92

FIRST EDITION . *October* 1920
Reprinted . . . *December* 1920

PREFACE

In volumes published during the last five years telling the story of a journey of *Sixty Years in the Wilderness* there were given occasional entries from my Diary. The form of continuous narrative was found more in accordance with the design of the work, and the notes from the Diary were few and far between. The habit dominant through many years of daily noting interesting events coming within personal observation, yielded a collection personally, politically and historically interesting.

Sir George Lewis somewhere writes, " Journals entered day by day have this advantage over memoirs. They exhibit faithfully tneir impressions of the moment, and are written without knowledge of the ultimate result." This Diary, fulfilling the conditions of being entered day by day, may claim the advantage indicated.

H. L.

CHAPTER XIV

CHAPTER XV

CHAPTER XVI

CHAPTER XVII

CHAPTER XVIII

CHAPTER XIX

CHAPTER XX

CONTENTS

THE DIARY OF A JOURNALIST

CHAPTER I

November 13, 1885.

THIS morning's post brought me a wrathful letter from Chamberlain, betraying his deeply rooted animosity to the Conservative party and all their works. I take it he wishes me to deal with the matter in my London Letter to the provinces. His born and trained enmity towards Conservatives is fully reciprocated in Parliament, on the platform, and in the Press. The virulent personal attacks directed against Bright and Gladstone during the last twenty years are to-day concentrated upon Chamberlain. So far from disheartening him, they inspirit him. Single-handed against a host, he gives as good as he gets.

The danger ahead of him does not lie in the hands of his enemies. In the near future it is his political friends who may put a spoke in his chariot-wheel. He has just returned to town after spending the recess in carrying through the country the flaming cross of an ultra-Radical programme of legislation. It is a barely disguised bid for support of the masses in a plot for the supercession of Gladstone as Leader of the Liberal party. It has already dealt a damaging blow to the Cabinet. Harting-ton threatens resignation if Chamberlain is permitted to retain his seat at the table. The prospect would daunt an ordinary man. But Chamberlain is not an ordinary man. I have a strong conviction that, whithersoever this critical turn in his public career may lead him, he will come out at the top.

" DEAR MR. LUCY," he writes under yesterday's date, " I think you may be interested to know the following circumstances, which throw a light on the character of Birmingham Toryism that may be new to Londoners.

"A week ago I informed Messrs. Rowlands & Co., the solicitors of the Tory party, that Messrs. Horton & Redfern, the Liberal solicitors, would deal on my behalf with any communications they had to make. I heard no more of the matter until last night, when at half-past eight o'clock I was personally served with a subpœna to attend the Birmingham Police Court at ten o'clock this morning by a person who gave me a card of which the enclosed is a copy, and which I think is well worthy of publication.

" The subpœna was dated the 8th instant, and I am unable to avoid the conclusion that the service was purposely delayed in order to cause me the greatest possible inconvenience, while the method adopted was clearly intended as an insult. The facts will no doubt be stated in the Police Court to-day, but in the meanwhile, you are at liberty to make any use you please of the statements contained.

> "Yours faithfully,
> " J. CHAMBERLAIN."

The card, copied in Chamberlain's handwriting, which like his speech was translucently clear, bears the name of a London " Confidential Agent," who undertakes to have " inquiries carefully made in divorce, libel, loss, fraud, robbery, and all family matters requiring secrecy, discreetly investigated ; and the movements of suspected persons or friends watched, in town or country, by male or female agents."

November 17.

At Edinburgh, chronicling the latest Midlothian campaign for the *Daily News*. At Lord Rosebery's invitation drove over to Dalmeny for luncheon. Only a small party—Lord and Lady Rosebery, Mrs. Gladstone,

Mary Gladstone, a Gladstone son whom I don't know, Spencer Lyttelton, the Countess of Spencer, and a pretty, charming young wife, daughter of Sir John Lubbock. I sat between her and Lady Spencer, and had interesting conversation with the latter, chiefly about Ireland.

Gladstone came down half an hour late, and was rallied by Lord Rosebery upon his unpunctuality. Reminded him of something he had said about punctuality at luncheon time. Gladstone took up the question with as much energy as if it were one of Randolph Churchill's accusations in the House of Commons. Finally he drew from Rosebery the admission that he had been in error, that Gladstone had never said anything about being punctual at luncheon, but had recommended the desirability of absence of formality—that anybody should drop into luncheon as they pleased and sit where they liked.

G. was in the liveliest spirit, talking throughout the meal in a rich musical voice with delightful humour. I sat immediately opposite to him, with a fern in a silver cover between us. This he presently removed for easier converse. He talked about the *Punch* staff, being much interested in what I told him about the Wednesday dinner.

After luncheon, Lord Rosebery proposed that we should go and see the castle, an old ruin he has rebuilt on the sea coast, which bounds one side of Dalmeny park. (Omitted to say that Lieutenant Greely was of the party. Very quiet at luncheon. A tall, narrow-chested, delicate-looking man, with bushy, black whiskers, and spectacles, more like a student than an Arctic explorer.) Lord Rosebery walked with me to the castle, Lady Spencer went on before, with Sir John Lubbock's daughter, whose married name I did not catch. Presently Greely arrived, and afterwards Gladstone.

It is a charming place, full of old furniture and precious memorials, chiefly belonging to the Stuart time. There are also many old books. Gladstone was still in the highest spirits, talking incessantly. He picked up one of the books and, dropping on to a broad window seat, began reading and discoursing about it. We spent a good half-hour here walking through the rooms. At four o'clock, much after his usual time, Gladstone went off for a walk with Lady Spencer and Lord Rosebery. Lieutenant Greely walked with me to my hansom waiting to take me back to Edinburgh, and we had a long chat.

March 15, 1890.

Dined to-night with Gladstone in St. James's Square —a house he has rented for the season—a big roomy, gloomy mansion, built when George I was king. On the pillars of the porch stand in admirable preservation two of the wrought-iron extinguishers in which on nights gone by the link-boys used to thrust their torches when they had brought master or mistress home, or conveyed a guest. Inside, hideous light-absorbing flock papers prevail. One gets a sight, rare in these days, of the gloominess amid which our grandfathers dwelt. Gladstone has brought some of his portraits to town with him. The dinner-table was as loveless in appearance as everything else about the hired house, evidently sore lack of the delicate taste that knows how to fling flowers about and make tables bright with chastened light and dainty colour. There was a central candelabra, in which blazed eight candles without a shade; on either side stood two others making hideous bare light over the almost squalid table. It was more than even Mr. G., presumably accustomed to this kind of thing, could stand. After a while he ordered the smaller candlesticks to be removed.

He talked with unbroken flow of spirits, always having more to say on any subject that turned up, and saying it better, than anyone else. His memory is as amazing as his opportunities of knowledge have been unique. In and in Ireland still current, meaning of brogue is the stout coarse shoe worn by the peasant.

One of Labouchere's best stories told in the House of Commons bearing upon his diplomatic career is staged at Washington. Seated one day in the office of his chief, a Britisher bounced in and insisted upon seeing His Excellency. As he could not be got out of the outer office, he was handed on to Labouchere, who told him that the Minister was not in. The Briton was not to be put off by idle subterfuge of that kind.

" Then I will wait till he comes in," he said.

" Very well," said Labouchere, " pray take a chair."

The bland *attaché*, his invitation accepted, continued the writing interrupted by the arrival. At the end of an hour the visitor, still fuming, inquired whether the Minister was expected back. " Oh, certainly," said Labouchere. Another hour passed, the morning caller evidently growing increasingly impatient.

" Do you think he will be back before lunch ? " he asked, looking at his watch.

" I think not," said Labouchere in his sweetest manner. " The fact is, he sailed for Europe on Wednesday, and can scarcely yet have sighted Queenstown. But you know you said you'd wait till he came back, so I asked you to take a chair."

Labouchere, an experienced story-teller, did not spoil his narrative by saying what response the visitor made.

January 5.

After many years working in the front rank of a kindred profession, Du Maurier one morning last year woke to find himself famous as a novelist. The United States and Great Britain closely competed in the race to do the fullest honour to *Trilby*. Here the book is in its eighth edition, an exceedingly rare distinction for a three-volume novel at its absurd nominal price of a guinea and a half. In America, published at a sum

2

equal to five shillings of our money, the press can scarcely keep pace with the demand. The author looks upon this rush with such philosophy as he can command. He sold the book outright to the American publishers, and has no share in the golden shower raining on their coffers. He reckons that had he retained royalty rights on the American publication he would have been richer by at least £7,000. In other ways he profits by his good fortune in having become the fashion of the hour at the libraries. He tells me he has just had an offer made to him on the part of an enterprising American magazine of £200 for a short story. He flies at higher game, and is already meditating a novel which is to exceed the success of *Trilby* in measure as *Trilby* outstepped *Peter Ibbetson*.

For the theatre managers the book has turned out even a richer gold mine than it proved for the publisher. The shrewd American who secured exclusive rights for the play in the United States has for some time been netting a profit of £2,000 a week. In this country Du Maurier sold the acting rights of the book to Beerbohm Tree, who will on an early day place on the stage his own adaptation of the piece. He is naturally attracted by the part of Svengali, which might have been conceived for him. The difficulty here, as in the United States, is to find a satisfactory Trilby.

January 13.

A gentleman already far at sea has sad and startling news awaiting him at his journey's end. This is Mr. George Baxter, Writer to the Signet, who has been acting as editor to the new Edinburgh edition of Stevenson's works. At the beginning of last week he took ship *en route* for Samba, carrying with him splendidly bound copies of the first two volumes of the Edinburgh edition. They were designed to delight the eyes of the author, who took an almost feverish interest in the fortunes of this monumental enterprise. Five days after Mr. Baxter sailed came news of the death of Stevenson, of the closing of the eyes that will never look upon the volumes prepared for his pleasure with tender care. It is curious to learn how Stevenson's later days were clouded with apprehension that he had lost his hold on the favour of the public. The success of the Edinburgh edition ought to have convinced him that this was an idle fancy. Published at something like a fancy price, it was immediately subscribed. Had the number been less strictly limited there would have been no lack of purchasers.

CHAPTER II

RANDOLPH CHURCHILL'S stormy life closed at break of day in the stillness of long unconsciousness. Six weeks ago his case was recognised as hopeless. He was the last to be convinced, and it was only after long and dangerous delay that he was induced to give up his cherished hope of shooting big game in India, and the desire, still nearer his heart, of seeing "Burma, which I annexed." His sudden cutting-off in what, as the almanac reckons, is the prime of life has touched the public with an unusually acute pang. Like—in most ways unlike—Disraeli and Gladstone, his personality has been fascinating to the populace. To them he was always "Randolph," as if to each he had been a school-fellow or kinsman. To hear of him coming home on Christmas Eve to die in his mother's house saddened many a Christmas board, though to those who sat round it he was personally a stranger.

Those coming in contact with him have at least been prepared for the inevitable event. All through last year it was evident he was fatally stricken. It was characteristic of his dauntless spirit and imperious character that, almost up to the time when he was carried ashore from the steamer that brought him to Marseilles, he talked and acted as if he were suffering from a passing indisposition, and would be quite ready when the session opened to take his old place and play his familiar part. Before he started on a journey planned on imperial scale it was still more difficult to convince him that things were strangely altered since the time when he was wont to command the attention of the listening Senate, and to delight enthusiastic meetings gathered in great halls in the provinces. An affection of the tongue, precursor of the paralysis that finally declared itself, prevented his clearly articulating. Even in private conversation it was difficult to follow his meaning, the situation being rendered additionally embarrassing by the fact that within the past twelve months his sense of hearing, never very acute, grievously failed. Whilst he was still in fighting trim it was curious to note how he and an adversary almost double his age had precisely the same gesture when following debate. Gladstone on one side of the House, and Randolph Churchill on the other, were often to be found at the same moment sitting in the same attitude—leaning forward with right hand behind the ear, endeavouring to catch the drift of some ill-spoken sentence.

None were more surprised at the long struggle Lord Randolph maintained against the sure advance of death than were the doctors, who since his return from the East have been in daily and hourly attendance. They knew that beyond all hope he had come home to die. Dr. Keith, who accompanied him in his professional capacity on his journey round the world, felt that great things had been achieved when he brought him alive as far as Dover. There were some anxious moments when he reached Marseilles, the end seeming imminent. Such was the strength of his constitution that he rallied, and during the past five weeks made a succession of revivals that astonished the doctors. The flicker of vitality never deceived them. Great skill and tender nursing, helped by what was left of a strong constitution, day after day averted the fall of the blow. It was known to be inevitable and irresistible.

The remarkable demonstration of public concern and sympathy evoked by his peril was, till he finally became unconscious, made known to Lord Randolph, and touched him deeply. It was doubtless by accident that after his arrival in Grosvenor Square, Lord Salisbury and Arthur

Balfour delayed to join the throng of daily inquirers. The omission was marked in the sorrowing household and warmly resented. The relations between Lord Randolph and the titular head of the Conservative party have not, since Lord Salisbury assumed the Premiership, been of a particularly friendly character. The Leader of the Fourth party was ever a thorn in the side of his respected chief. When, chiefly by his activity and generalship, Gladstone was turned out of office, Lord Randolph was not lacking in peremptoriness in his demands as to the distribution of the spoil. Still, in the shadow of death such things are forgotten and cannot be supposed to have influenced Lord Salisbury's movements. As for Balfour, he to the last maintained those intimate personal relations commenced in Fourth party days.

To those who recalled his parliamentary triumphs, it was acutely painful to see Lord Randolph addressing the present House of Commons. It is, happily, doubtful whether he ever fully realised how hopelessly deep and wide was the gulf fixed between the Lord Randolph Churchill of 1880-86 and the parliamentary prodigal who, two years ago, in the opening session of the new Parliament, came back to the old familiar scene. When, early last spring, he returned to London from a political campaign, taking Bradford on the way to Scotland, he told me he had never addressed such large and enthusiastic audiences. He was elate with conviction that having tried his capacity by the severest test he had shown that he was as good as in his primest days. A friend who accompanied him on the tour assured me, in a voice broken with emotion, that it had been the most pitiful failure. There had, indeed, been crowded halls, filled by the magic of Lord Randolph's name. People who had never seen him in the flesh, or heard his voice, eagerly availed themselves of the opportunity of looking upon a famous man. Before he had spoken a quarter of an hour the buzz of conversation rose in the hall, then shuffling of feet was heard, and the audience rapidly melted away. They could not follow what he was saying, and soon grew tired of the effort to solve the mystery of his strange inarticulation. He nevertheless went on to the end, beating his hands together, thumping the desk, uplifting his voice in denunciation of argument, just as he used to do when he held the House of Commons with light, firm touch, playing upon its passion and its humour with master hand.

When last session opened, he had evidently made up his mind to resume his old position in the front rank of the Conservative party. He spoke frequently, always with result that made his friends miserable for the rest of the sitting. Those who were present will never forget the scene on a Friday night early in the session, when he stood at the table for half an hour vigorously declaiming inarticulate ramblings, whilst by his side sat his old subaltern, Arthur Balfour, with face buried in his hands, shutting out the painful sight. There was a time, not severed from that night by many years, when Balfour, an inconsidered stripling, was ready to fetch and carry tumblers of brandy and soda for Lord Randolph's refreshment, what time the Leader of the Fourth party fulminated against Gladstone and all his works. Now Arthur Balfour was Leader of the Conservative party, with the Premiership in certain view, whilst Randolph Churchill talked to a House whose emptiness was here and there relieved by a few faces that looked on saddened at evidence of so great and hopeless a fall.

The first time I noticed Lord Randolph in the House of Commons was on a May day in 1875. Charles Dilke, pursuing what threatened to be an annual crusade against unreformed corporations, made merry at the expense of Woodstock, then represented by one who was known in the parliamentary arena simply as a cadet of the ducal house of Marlborough. From the third bench behind that on which Ministers ought to have been sitting—whence, unmindful of the portent whose fulfilment had a vital interest for some of them and for the Conservative party, they were absent—rose a well-groomed young man with protuberant eyes, pale face, and a ponderous moustache, with which as he spoke he nervously toyed. Members asking each other " Who's this ? " learned that it was the Member for Woodstock rising to defend the corporation of the borough that sent him to Parliament.

Though assisted by notes, on which the speech was fully written out, the young Member was so nervous, his voice so badly pitched, his delivery so faulty, that there was difficulty in following his argument. But here and there flashed forth a scathing sentence that made it worth while to attempt to catch the rest. When he sat down Lord Randolph had made his mark, had established himself as an interesting personality, in an assembly in which within ten years he was predominant.

Three years later he justified the promise made in this casual speech. In March 1878 he appeared in the rôle, subsequently familiar, of candid friend of a Conservative Ministry. Mr. Sclater-Booth, President of the Local Government Board, brought in a County Government Bill, whose main object was to transfer the government of counties to boards elected partly by county magistrates, partly by boards of guardians. The rejection of the Bill was moved by Mr. Rylands, a fussy Radical who, through successive sessions, was, like Martha, troubled about many things. To the astonishment of the House Lord Randolph Churchill rose from the Ministerial side to second the amendment. The personal conjunction was piquant enough to attract attention. Lord Randolph's speech held it in close grip.

" I do not," said the Member for Woodcock, as Jacob Bright in solitary unpremeditated flash of humour called him, " want to say anything disagreeable ; but I have

ransacked the whole arsenal of denunciatory phrases
and have not found any that adequately express
my estimation—or rather lack of estimation—of this
measure." Failing full success in that direction, he
characterised the Bill as " Brummagem make, stuffed
with all the little dodges of a President of the Local
Government Board when he attempts to legislate upon
a great question."

This brought him to the President of the Board, seated
massive, apparently impassive, on the Treasury Bench,
over which Randolph threateningly towered.

" Remarkable," he murmured, contemplating the back
of Sclater-Booth's head, "how often we find mediocrity
dowered with a double-barrelled name."

" I have no objection," he continued, " to the President
of the Local Government Board dealing with such questions
as the salaries of inspectors of nuisances. But I do
entertain the strongest possible objection to his coming
down here, with all the appearance of a great lawgiver,
to repair, according to his small ideas and in his little
way, breaches in the British Constitution."

In these later years frank criticism by private Members
of their pastors and masters, on either Front Bench, is so
common as to attract little attention. In 1878 it was
not altogether unknown below the gangway on the
Liberal side. It was quite new with Conservatives.
As Randolph spoke the Ministerialists sat silent in pained
amazement ; whilst the Liberals, gleefully watching
Sclater-Booth, bolt upright on the Treasury Bench,
with head slightly thrown back, one leg crossed over the
other, hands clasped across his portly figure, an unwonted
flush on his stolid countenance, laughed and cheered.

The sheaf of notes held in Lord Randolph's right hand
testified to careful preparation. At this time, and
for some years later, he was in the habit of writing out
his speeches, learning them by heart and reciting them.
Amid the excitement of his attack on Sclater-Booth his

notes got inextricably mixed up. He attempted to sort them by arranging them between the open fingers of either hand—a device that had comical result. Waving his hands about in the heat of oratory, the action suggested that he was playing with what schoolboys call clappers. Happily the laughter and cheering from the delighted opposition was so persistent that he had time and opportunity to find successive clues, and triumphantly proceeded to the close of a speech that established his position as an original, daring debater.

Having joined a turbulent Radical in opposing the measure of a Conservative Government, Lord Randolph proceeded to make things increasingly unpleasant for right hon. friends on the Treasury Bench. He denounced the Bill as " this most Radical and Democratic measure, this crowning desertion of Tory principles, this supreme violation of political honesty." There was, in the peroration, further echo of Disraeli attacking Peel. " I have," he said, " raised the last wail of the expiring Tory party. They have undergone a good deal. They have swallowed an immense amount of nastiness. They have had their banner dragged along many a muddy path. It has been slopped in many a filthy puddle till it is so altered that nobody can recognise it."

After this outburst the young Member for Woodstock, to the relief of Ministers—more especially of the hapless President of the Local Government Board—practically retired from the scene. It is true that the following month he, with characteristic audacity, stirred the deep pool of the Irish Education question. But his attendance was rare, and thereafter his silence complete. It seemed as if he had finally relapsed into the state of indifference to political ambition and parliamentary allurements that marked his earlier manhood.

It is a coincidence notable in view of subsequent events that on the threshold of their careers Arthur Balfour nd Randolph Churchill were alike indifferent, even inimicable, to a parliamentary career. By further coincidence, it was accidental vacancy in a family pocket-borough that led both to Westminster and a place in history. In the autumn of 1873 Mr. Balfour took counsel with his uncle as to what he should do with his young life. It happened that a vacancy was pending in the representation of the family borough. "Why not sit for Hertford?" Lord Salisbury suggested. After some hesitation the future Prime Minister accepted the invitation. Lord Randolph was almost driven by his father into the parliamentary seat of Woodstock. Hertford and Woodstock have gone the way of all small boroughs lying in the pathway of a Juggernaut Reform Bill. The names of their representatives elected to the Parliament of 1874-80 will live for ever.

It was accident that brought Lord Randolph finally out of his shell. By fresh coincidence the same episode was the occasion of Mr. Balfour's emerging from the condition of Philosophic Doubt with which hitherto he regarded the assumed privilege and pleasure of membership of the House of Commons. In the haze that gathers round events even so recent as fifteen years ago, it is generally understood that Lord Randolph devised the Bradlaugh difficulty—that thin edge of the wedge inserted with fatal result in the framework of the great Liberal majority in the earliest stage of its existence. This is an error. It was Sir Henry Wolff who first raised objection to the Member for Northampton taking the oath. He was discouraged, his action discountenanced, by Sir Stafford Northcote. Sir John Gorst, not yet knighted, rallied to his side; some of the country gentlemen, scenting sport, began to cheer the grave and reverend champion of Christianity. It was on May 3, 1880, that Bradlaugh raised the controversy by presenting himself at the table claiming the right to affirm instead of taking the oath. It was not till May 24 that Randolph Churchill appeared on the scene.

With characteristic acumen and industry he had spent the interval in studying Bradlaugh's published writings. He brought down with him a copy of one pamphlet entitled *The Impeachment of the House of Brunswick*. Having read a passage, he flung the book on the floor and stamped upon it. This reminiscence of Burke and his dagger, in analogous fashion used to punctuate a passage in impassioned speech, momentarily took away the breath of the crowded audience. When it was recovered, Ministerialists loudly laughed. In the end, as we know, it proved no laughing matter for them. As Lord Morley testifies, in his *Life of Gladstone*, the controversy thus begun " went on as long as the life of the Parliament, clouded the radiance of the party triumph, threw the new Government at once into a minority, and dimmed the ascendancy of the great Minister."

Incidentally the Fourth party was created. Various explanations of the origin of the historic name are current. Some find it in the fact that it was composed of four persons, " which," as Euclid emphatically remarks, " is absurd." In his *Life* of his father, Winston Churchill suggests its origin in an interjected conversation in debate. A member affirming that there were two great parties in the State, Mr. Parnell called out " Three." Lord Randolph, going one better, cried " Four." That incident may have contributed to the vogue of the phrase. It actually had its origin in a passage in a speech by Mr. Frank Hugh O'Donnell, who, alluding to a condition of things at the time prominent in the French Legislature, named the Irish Nationalists " Le Tiers Parti." The suggestion of a Fourth party thereupon becomes obvious.

Absence of premeditation in connection with an epoch-making combination was attested by the circumstance that when Henry Wolff and John Gorst, seated on the Front Bench below the gangway, opened the Bradlaugh business, Lord Randolph had settled himself on the

third bench above the gangway, corresponding with
the place occupied by him during his first Parliament.
Warming to the work, he found it desirable to be in
close communication with his new allies, and accordingly
changed his quarters. His supremacy was speedily
asserted. Paul Drummond Wolff might have planted
the sapling; Apollos Randolph Churchill watered it
so effectually that its proportions spread till they over-
topped the trees of the forest. Within a fortnight of
his appearance below the gangway Lord Randolph
was the acknowledged leader of the Fourth party.

According to long-established tradition, broken only
in the case of Parnell, who cherished inflexible scorn
of all precedents of a Saxon Parliament, leaders of
sectional parties, however minute, must needs hold a
corner seat from which to address the House. At a
time when Lord Randolph assumed leadership of the
Fourth party, seated all in a row on the Front Bench
below the gangway, the corner seat was held by Beresford
Hope, an old much-esteemed Member whose Batavian
grace Disraeli in an historic passage recognised. For
the greater part of the session of 1880 he remained in
near neighbourhood with the lively group. Approaching
a dazed condition, he remembered the fact that though,
as a matter of practice, the bench flanking the table
to the left of the Speaker is reserved for ex-Ministers,
Privy Councillors have equal right to share its accommodation. One afternoon to the surprise—when they realised
the situation to the delight—of the House, Beresford
Hope passed his accustomed seat, and crossing the
gangway found quarters on the front Opposition Bench.

"They made it too hot for me," he whispered in the
sympathetic ear of Sir Richard Cross, whom Lord Randolph,
scornful of spotless respectability, was accustomed to
snub. The Leader of the Fourth party personally
succeeded to the vacant seat, jumping upon it and boister-
ously waving his hat when, five years later, his work

in Opposition was done, his triumph complete in the
downfall of a Ministry which in 1880 came back from
the polls apparently impregnable.

During the more or less tumultuous five sessions
that limited the life of the Parliament elected in 1880,
Randolph increased in esteem of Parliament and the
country day by day. Having once put his hand to
the plough, he, to the surprise of old friends, showed
no sign of turning back. On the contrary, he stuck
to his post with a constancy that left no opportunity
neglected. He had the advantage, attractive in the
House of Commons, of being the impartial critic alike
of Ministers and ex-Ministers. On the whole, he paid
more deference to Gladstone than to his nominal leader,
Stafford Northcote.

Once, to the huge delight of the House, Sir Stafford
turned and rent his tormentor. Interposing in a controversy between the two front Benches, Lord Randolph
moved an amendment which, if carried, would have
extricated Ministers from a difficulty. "The action
of the noble lord," said Sir Stafford, "reminds me of
the practice of the confederate of the thimble-rigger
on the racecourse. 'A bonnet' he is called, I believe ;
his business being, whilst concealing personal knowledge
of the operator and complicity with his game, to assist
it by egging on the public to take a hand."

No one enjoyed this double-edged stroke more than
Lord Randolph. Possibly his delight was increased
by the fact that Sir Stafford of all men had managed,
without being called to order by the Speaker, to liken
Mr. Gladstone to a thimble-rigger. Sir Stafford's com-
bativeness was exhausted by this flash of barbed wit.
Once, early in the session of 1883, he wrote a private
letter remonstrating with the Leader of the Fourth
party upon the appearance of what he regarded as an
inspired paragraph in the morning papers, announcing
that in a certain contingency they would act against

the Front Opposition Bench. The reply he received did not encourage further correspondence.

Lord Randolph had no personal animosity towards Sir Stafford—one of the sweetest-natured, highest-principled men who ever attempted to breast the masterful tide of political life. He honestly believed that his leadership of the party in the Commons was fatal to the interests and prospects of the Conservative party. He was, accordingly, almost brutally implacable in his pursuit, finally succeeding, against the heart's desire of Lord Salisbury, in driving him out of the Commons. When the end of the Gladstone Government was in sight, someone asked Sir Stafford, " What place will you give Randolph when your Government is formed ? "

" Ask, rather," replied the veteran statesman, " what place will he give me ? "

The words were spoken in bitter jest. As the proverb affirms, many a true word is spoken in jest.

Another occupant of the Front Opposition Bench whom Randolph couldn't abear was Sir Richard Cross. His native mediocrity, made more prominent by a certain pomposity of manner familiar in chairmen of Quarter Sessions, rankled in his bosom. With W. H. Smith he was somewhat impatient. But " Old Morality's " modest manner, concealing sterling merit, disarmed animosity.

There was an amusing scene in the House in the session of 1882 illustrating this little prejudice. An amendment to a bill before the House was moved without notice, and carried. Gladstone, in charge of the bill, moved a consequential amendment. Naturally, it was not on the printed paper, and Lord Randolph, discussing it, was at a loss to recall the precise phraseology. Sir Richard Cross, above all things a man of business, made a note of the amendment as it was read out from the chair. With shrewd idea of propitiating the terrible young man below the gangway, he, with engaging smile, handed him his note. The consequences were akin to what followed in the case of a man who, fleeing from a grisly bear, remembered he had a bun in his pocket and stopped to present the refreshment to his pursuer. Poor Sir Richard was snapped up, body and boots. " A pretty pass we've come to in the House of Commons," said Lord Randolph, with dainty repugnance holding the sheet of paper between finger and thumb, " when we have to consider amendments passed about from hand to hand on dirty bits of paper."

The smile faded from Sir Richard's countenance. He, G.C.B., ex-Home Secretary, trusted lieutenant of Benjamin Disraeli, had condescendingly gone out of his way to pay attention to a young and unofficial Member, and had been rewarded by public accusation of harbouring a dirty piece of paper.

Lord Randolph and his merry men were always ready for a lark at the expense of portentous personages on the Front Opposition Bench. One night, the business on the paper approaching conclusion, Sir Stafford and his colleagues seized the opportunity of going off to bed. " Come along," said Randolph to Drummond Wolff, and crossing the gangway, followed by two-thirds of his party, he seated himself in the place of the Leader of the Opposition. Thence he raised debate *apropos de bottes*, which the three kept going for an hour, to the increasing anger of junior Ministers necessarily kept in their places, and the amusement of a small body of Members on both sides who had agreeably dined.

Lord Randolph's often successfully concealed admiration for Gladstone was based upon intellectual sympathy. If gratitude played any part in politics, which it notoriously does not, his esteem would have been supported on personal grounds. Having once devoted himself to political life, he was irresistible, his goal assured. It was Gladstone who gave him a good send-off at the start, sparing no pains to keep him going. With the generous instinct of a noble nature, the veteran statesman, at the outset recognising the capacity and genius of his ruthless assailant, missed no opportunity of paying tribute to it. He habitually conveyed what to an un-official Member is the compliment, rare for a Prime Minister, of following him in debate.

Towards the close of the long campaign terminating in ministerial disaster, mainly consequent on Lord Randolph's action, he instinctively, doubtless unconsciously, addressed his argument not to the Leader of the Opposition, but to the young man toying with his moustache on the corner seat below the gangway. Lord Randolph was not slow to perceive the advantage thus secured for him. It would have been fatal to his aspirations and plans to have been severely ignored. When by accident approach to that calamity was indicated, the Fourth party proceeded to " draw Gladstone," as they put it.

Committee, wherein a Member may speak as often as human patience will endure, was their favourite field for this sport. Lord Randolph would lead off, drawing that child of Nature, Gladstone, into lengthy reply. When the Premier resumed his seat, Drummond Wolff rose, and with profuse declarations of deference asked for information on another point. Up got the Premier, brimming with energy and another speech. In this the subtle mind of John Gorst discovered a flaw which he did not doubt arose from misapprehension of what his hon. friend the Member for Christchurch had said. On this he laboured for a quarter of an hour or more, Mr. Gladstone intently listening, whilst his colleagues on the Treasury Bench, conscious of the snare, tossed about in despair. The temptation to instruct three guileless young men, evidently searchers after truth, certainly most deferential in their recognition of age and experience, was too much for the Premier, who eagerly sprang to his feet with a third speech. Thus did Lord Randolph's strategy, excelling the bedstead

3

in the village inn known to Goldsmith, contrive a treble
debt to pay. It wasted the time of the House; it undermined the authority of the Premier; and it kept the
Fourth party well to the front.

With the formation of Lord Salisbury's second Government, consequent on the rout of the Home Rulers at
the poll in 1886, Lord Randolph reached his zenith.
Chamberlain, friend and ally in spite of what happened
consequent upon the Aston Park riots, was so moved
that he made rare incursion into the Latin tongue.
Writing on June 18, when the composition of the new
Government was practically complete, he exclaimed:
"What a triumph! You have won all along the line.
Moriturus te saluto." The Marquis of Salisbury, installed
as Prime Minister, was the nominal, of course the ultimate,
dispenser of ministerial prizes. Lord Randolph was the
absolute bestower of patronage.

Having selected his own position—Chancellor of the
Exchequer and Leader of the House of Commons—he
did not forget comrades in the fight that resulted in
splendid victory. He wrote to Lord Salisbury saying
Drummond Wolff ought to be made a Privy Councillor
and John Gorst appointed Under-Secretary to the India
Office. Whether in this last suggestion he was influenced
by consideration of the fact that his ancient animosity,
Sir Richard Cross—who, he insisted, should leave the
House of Commons solaced with a peerage—was to
be head of the India Office, is not known. Certainly
quick-witted, sharp-tongued John Gorst was exactly the
man to buzz unpleasantly about the ears of arch mediocrity.
His famous speech upon what is known as the "Manipur
incident," his chief being during its delivery seated in the
Peers' Gallery, of itself fulfilled any possible expectation
of fun cherished by the prophetic soul of Lord Randolph.

Lord Salisbury looked after his nephew, making him
Secretary for Scotland, thus completing provision of
the Fourth party. That was natural and expected.

Where astonishment deepened to consternation was on the pitchforking into the Home Office of Henry Mathews, a gentleman not only untrained in administrative affairs, but new to parliamentary life. Lord Randolph highly esteemed his capacity, proved in the professional conduct of his case when he carried into a court of law his charges against Chamberlain in respect of the Aston Park riots. If Mr. Mathews were not made Home Secretary Lord Salisbury was told he must be prepared to get along without Lord Randolph.

The new Parliament met on August 5, 1886, and was prorogued on September 25. The period was short. It sufficed to reveal a new phase of a many-sided character. At no period of his parliamentary career did Lord Randolph display such high qualities as shone upon an astonished House during his term of leadership. His uncurbed temper, his imperious manner, abruptly changing to one of boyish recklessness, seemed fatal to success in the dignified office to which at the age of thirty-seven he was called. The poacher had been made head-game-keeper. Nowhere was the experiment watched with more nervous trepidation than on the Treasury Bench. That Lord Randolph himself felt the difficulty and delicacy of the situation was shown by his nervous manner when following Gladstone in debate on the Address. He speedily recovered full command of himself, and remained master of the situation. As Winston Churchill truly says, "Lord Randolph knew the House in all its moods. He humoured it, offended it, and soothed it again with practised deliberation. Yet he always appeared to be its servant." The general verdict on his conduct was expressed in a much-prized autograph letter addressed to him by Queen Victoria on the eve of the prorogation. "Lord Randolph"—she wrote, in the third-person form of address with which Majesty approaches meaner mortals— "has shown much skill and judgment in his leadership during this exceptional session of Parliament."

This fresh start in a career he jocularly said would lead to the Premiership and Westminster Abbey, closed in a blaze of triumph. He was as popular as he was powerful. Everyone, save perhaps disappointed claimants for office and ministerial colleagues whom he contemptuously called " the old gang," rejoiced in his prosperity. The shock was the greater when, exactly three months to a day after receiving the Queen's gracious letter of congratulation, there appeared in the *Times* an announcement that the Chancellor of the Exchequer had resigned office. The occasion of the Cabinet quarrel rose out of circumstances now familiar. Lord Randolph, pledged to economy, had framed a Budget made impossible by the demands of the Army and Navy. Lord George Hamilton, First Lord of the Admiralty, yielded to the extent of modifying his demand by £700,000. W. H. Smith, with a tenacity as unexpected as it was admirable in one of his mild and modest manner, was implacable. He declined to reduce his estimate by a penny. Lord Salisbury, eloquent with apology, stood by the heads of the spending departments. Lord Randolph resigned.

There is no doubt he did not count upon his withdrawal from the Ministry becoming effective. Regarding the persons seated round the Council table he felt he was indispensable. There was, he thought, none among them who could stand up against Gladstone, either as Leader of the House or as Chancellor of the Exchequer. Unfortunately for him, for the Conservative party, and for the country, his gaze did not extend beyond the walls of the dingy house in Downing Street. He " forgot Goschen."

Winston Churchill throws doubt on the existence of this forgetfulness. As I gave currency to a phrase since become historic, this may be a convenient place for stating my authority. It was Lord Randolph himself. " A little less than a week after I had written to Lord Salisbury resigning the Chancellorship," he said, in

words of which I made a note at the time, " I was walking
up St. James's Street when I met——" (mentioning the
name of a lady well known in political and social circles).
" She was driving, and stopped the carriage to speak
to me. She asked how things were going on. I said
I thought they were doing nicely. Hartington had
refused to join them, and whom else could they get ?
' Have you thought of Mr. Goschen ? ' she asked in
voice and manner that indicated she knew more than
the innocent inquiry indicated. It all flashed on me
in a moment. I saw the game was lost. As I confessed
to her, I had forgotten Goschen."

Shortly after this conversation I met the lady, happily
still with us, and mentioned Lord Randolph's statement.
She confirmed it with the curiously graphic remark :
" Driving up St. James's Street, I never pass a certain
lamp-post without thinking of Randolph—of the sudden
change that came over his face when I mentioned Mr.
Goschen, and the abrupt salute with which he passed on."

He had played his game, laid his last treasured card
on the table, and it was trumped.

When Parliament met for the session of 1887, under
the leadership of W. H. Smith, there was reiterated
rumour of reconciliation and return. Gradually it ebbed
away, and Lord Randolph lapsed into the position of a
private Member. His personal influence was, however,
scarcely less powerful than when in office. His every
movement in and out of the House was watched
with keen interest. His lightest word was reported.
At an early stage of the new situation there were indications of a coalition between himself and Chamberlain.
For a while they dreamed the old dream of a Central
party free from the vices and weakness inherent to
political partnership, a brotherhood where none were
for a Party but all were for the State. Like earlier
projects, since and before the time of Macaulay, it came
to nothing. Presently hasty words spoken on both sides

brought about a coolness in the relations of two men attracted to each other by certain similarity of character.

Then came rupture. Lord Randolph held a safe seat
in Paddington, but he had no sympathy with villadom,
and yearned for a great constituency that would appreciate
his democratic Toryism and strengthen his position
as its apostle. Opportunity hailed him from Birmingham.
John Bright was dead, and Central Birmingham, where
by the irony of circumstance arising out of the Home
Rule Bill the once ultra-Radical had been supported
by the Tories, was looking about for a successor. Lord
Randolph, whose personal popularity in the Midland
metropolis was barely exceeded by Chamberlain's, eagerly
accepted overtures inviting him to stand. On April
2, 1889, a deputation representing the Tories of the constituency arrived at the House of Commons with formal
invitation. Lord Randolph's course seemed so clear,
his mind was so joyously made up, that pending the
striking of five o'clock, the hour at which he was to receive
the deputation, he instructed his friend, Louis Jennings,
to draft an address to his Paddington constituents,
severing his connection with the borough, and another
to the electors of Central Birmingham accepting their
invitation to contest the seat.

As at an earlier crisis he forgot Goschen, so now he
left Chamberlain out of his calculation. The blending
of the Liberal Unionist element with the main body
of the Ministerial forces was still so far from being complete, that there existed an understanding whereby certain
seats should be reserved for Liberal Unionists. Chamberlain claimed Central Birmingham as one. Even whilst
the deputation were approaching Westminster, assured
of the success of their mission, whilst Louis Jennings
was penning the two election addresses, whilst Lord
Randolph was preparing to receive the emissaries,
Chamberlain was at work. He saw Hicks-Beach as
representative of the Government, and warned him that

Lord Randolph's candidature would mean disruption of the Unionist alliance. He dragged the unwilling figure of Lord Hartington to his side. In despair Sir Michael saw Lord Randolph and explained to him the peril of the situation. With that loyalty to his former colleagues which, on several critical occasions since he quitted the Ministry, gave an air of irresolution to his actions, Randolph left the matter in the hands of his old friend. The old friend loved him as a father loves a favourite son. But he loved his party more, and knew that it remained in office by sufferance of its arbitrary ally from Birmingham. Lord Randolph was accordingly sacrificed.

This was, I think, the hardest of the many knocks that were battering out the still young life. He felt it even more acutely than the sudden halt in his ministerial career at its most brilliant hour. I happened to be in the Lobby on this critical afternoon when he came out of the Whip's room, where doom was spoken. He was so altered in personal appearance that for a moment I did not know him. Instead of the familiar swinging pace, with head slightly bent but with swiftly glancing eyes, he walked with slow, weary tread, a look on his pallid face as if tears had been coursing down it. No one who knew him only in the fierce struggle of public life would have imagined him capable of such profound emotion. It was a blow from which he never recovered, though there was temporary rebirth of the ambition to represent something other than the *bourgeois* of Paddington, when, little more than a year before his death, he announced his intention of standing for bustling Bradford.

Eleven months later another incident befell which again wounded him to the heart. When Lord Salisbury's Government announced their intention of appointing a Royal Commission to inquire into the *Times* allegation against Parnell, Lord Randolph, generously mindful of the peril into which his old colleagues were blundering, drew up a reasoned protest addressed to W. H. Smith. Amongst State papers it is distinguished by keen insight, clear argument, and remarkable prescience. Ministers took no heed of counsel coming from this quarter, and affairs went on to the appointed end. When in March 1890 the report of the Commission came before the House of Commons, Lord Randolph, in conjunction with his *fidus Achates* Louis Jennings, drafted an amendment in which censure was strictly confined to the procedure of the *Times* in the matter, ignoring the action of the Government. Jennings was in his place, prepared to move this amendment, expecting in accordance with custom that on resumption of the debate the Speaker would call upon him.

But Lord Randolph, in his wilful way, had changed his mind, and in his imperious manner disregarded the claims of others, even though one might be his most intimate and faithful friend. To the astonishment of everyone, not least of Louis Jennings sitting on the bench behind him, he rose and delivered a speech in which he made an uncompromising attack upon the Government. When he sat down the benches began to empty. Interest in the situation was exhausted. Promise of Louis Jennings' amendment had crowded the House, because it was understood, correctly, as we know, that it was actually Lord Randolph's, and that he would support it by speech. On the contrary, he not only displaced the priority of the amendment, but delivered a speech wholly contrary to its spirit, being a bitter indictment of the Government. Wounded in the house of a friend, Louis Jennings straightway severed his connection with one to whom for some years his services had been chiefly devoted. Lord Randolph, even as he sat down, perceiving how matters stood, tore off scraps from his copy of the Orders on which he pencilled pathetic little messages, and had them passed on to Jennings, seated midway on the bench behind him. They met with no response, not

even that of an angry look. " Jennings has taken
the needle," Lord Randolph said, coming up to me
in the Lobby shortly after his speech. It was a quaint
phrase I never heard before or since. It lingers in memory
over the waste of years.

The episode had a personal bearing which brings
into strong light one of the marked features of a strange
character. Lord Randolph was a delightful person
as long as he was pleased with his company or his surroundings. But he could not stand anything in the way
of difference from his expressed opinion. Slightly to
vary the characteristics of the little girl of fable, when
he was pleased he was very very nice, when he was crossed
he was 'orrid. In the course of time he quarrelled with
all his intimate co-workers, with the exception of Hicks-
Beach, Ernest Beckett, later Lord Grimthorpe, his
brother-in-law Lord Curzon, and Henry Wolff. John
Gorst and Henry Mathews were amongst other former
friends and companions dear whom he ruthlessly cut.

My personal acquaintance with him, ripening into
warm friendship, began early in his public career. It
certainly was not nourished by monotonous adulation.
In *Punch*, in the " Cross Bench " articles in the *Observer*,
and elsewhere, I wrote of his parliamentary phantasies
with freedom untrammelled by private intimacy.
He seemed to enjoy rather than resent the criticism.
During the session of 1886 there appeared in the *Daily
News* a leading article commenting rather sharply on
a speech made by him the night before in the House.
I was not the writer of the article, but chanced at the
time to be editor of the paper. Visiting the Lobby of
the House of Commons, I was accustomed to stand by
the chair of the chief doorkeeper, and Lord Randolph
passing in or out invariably stopped for a friendly chat.
On the evening of the appearance of this article he looked
me straight in the face as he passed and walked on without
a word.

Naturally I said nothing then or later, and for four years we were strangers. At the beginning of the session of 1890 Louis Jennings several times approached me with intimation that Lord Randolph wanted to make up the quarrel. In the end I said that he had deliberately cut me as I stood in my usual place in the Lobby, that I should be there every day after Questions, and if he came and spoke to me conversation would proceed as nearly as possible in continuance of what we were saying the last time we spoke. On the next evening Lord Randolph came up with outstretched hand and beaming face. There was no apology or explanation, only the old friendship was renewed, not to be broken again save by the hand of death.

He wrote to me:

February 22, 1890.

DEAR MR. LUCY,

Very many thanks for your letter. I much regret that our former friendship should have been interrupted for so long, but I like to think that it is now renewed.

It may amuse you to know that that part of your article in the *Speaker* which referred to Balfour was inserted prominently in the Birmingham Tory paper, but the part which referred to me was omitted.

Believe me to be,
Very sincerely yours,
RANDOLPH S. CHURCHILL.

What difficulties the Government have got into. But Gallio (i.e. Randolph) cares for none of these things.

In the old familiar way he asked me to dine with him at the Junior Carlton on the following Sunday to meet some friends—an invitation I was delighted to accept. Among the guests was Louis Jennings, greatly pleased at the result of his friendly offices. The date of the dinner was Sunday, March 31. On the following Tuesday happened the event recorded in connection with the Parnell Commission. Passing through the Lobby, having announced his intention of not moving the amendment, Jennings said to me, in tones whose bitterness testified to his hurt, " It's an odd thing Randolph has just as many friends to-day as he had a week ago. He has regained you and he has lost me."

The rupture was final. Lord Randolph made several attempts to recapture his old friend. They were sternly, stubbornly ignored. Three years later, Jennings, one of the truest-hearted men that ever breathed, died, not having in the meanwhile broken the pained silence that brooded over blighted friendship.

In 1890, the Salisbury Government being in a parlous state, there seemed prospect of Lord Randolph's being called to its assistance. Hicks-Beach, probably not altogether easy in mind, recollecting the part played by him in the matter of Chamberlain's repulse of Lord Randolph in his candidature for Birmingham, personally urged Lord Salisbury to recall the strayed reveller. But the Premier, small blame to him, had had enough of the company in the Cabinet of his intractable young friend. Perish the Government rather than resuscitate Lord Randolph ! Accepting what he regarded as the closing of his political career, Lord Randolph set out for South Africa in search of gold and big game. The former he found ; the latter, in the person of a lion, nearly found him. He came back early in 1892 improved in health, his interest in politics quickened by the circumstance that the Unionist party was now in Opposition. At Arthur Balfour's request he seated himself among his old colleagues on the Front Opposition bench.

Thence he rose to take part in debate on the second reading of Gladstone's second Home Rule Bill. The appearance of the House testified to the deathless interest he commanded. Every bench was filled, a crowd of members, unable to find seats, thronging the Bar. The stars in their courses fought against Sisera. It was arranged that he should resume the debate immediately after

Questions. Had that been possible all might have been well. But someone raised a question of privilege, discussed for a full hour, through which Lord Randolph sat fuming. He had at the proper moment taken some drug designed to " buck up " his frail body through the hour he intended to speak. When the hour had sped the tonic effects of medicine were exhausted. It was a decrepit man with bowed figure and occasionally inarticulate voice that at length stood at the table—a painful spectacle, from contemplation of which members gradually withdrew. The Chamber, which once filled at the signal " Churchill is up," was almost empty when he sat down. Yet Bryce, who sat attentive on the Treasury Bench opposite, and heard every word of the speech painfully read from MS., assured me it was a cogent argument, admirably phrased, illumined by happy illustration, in these respects falling nothing short of earlier successes.

Lord Randolph was an habitual diner-out, even more enjoying opportunities of giving dinners. At the end of the session of 1880, when the Fourth party had succeeded in making themselves an organised power in the House, they, gravely mimicking the prevailing custom of Ministers, dined together at Greenwich. They invited a single guest—Labouchere !

Lord Randolph was rather a trial to hostesses, none being quite sure in what mood her festival might find him. It came to pass in time that he acquired the habit of royalty, commanding that the list of guests should be submitted to him before he replied to an invitation. The first time I met him at table, precursor of many delightful foregatherings, was at a farewell dinner Colonel Fred Burnaby gave on the eve of my departure on a journey round the world. Burnaby told me that, showing Lord Randolph the list of guests, he asked him whom he would have as companions. He named Frank Burnand, then editor of *Punch*, and one of his contributors. And a very jolly night we spent seated on either side of him.

In the height of the Fourth party campaign I was several times privileged to form one of a quartette driving in a four-wheeler from the House to dine at Connaught Place. On such occasions, Lord Randolph, Drummond Wolff, and John Gorst were like boys just let out of school, not only speaking disrespectfully of their pastors and masters, but ruthlessly chaffing each other. I never met Balfour at these symposia. Lord Randolph frequently gave little Sunday-night dinners at the Turf Club, where one occasionally had the felicity of meeting those renowned Irish wits, Dr. Nedley and Father Healy.

The dinner party that turned out to be the last at which Lord Randolph and Louis Jennings sat at the same table, was memorable in other ways. The invitation was " to meet H.R.H. the Prince of Wales," later King Edward VII. The fact leaking out that among the company was Dick Power, the popular Whip of the Irish Nationalist party, complaint was sounded in Unionist circles that Randolph was plotting to bring H.R.H. and the official Home Rulers together. What the host chiefly had at heart was to draw round his Royal guest a cheery company, an effort in which he was successful. Of other persons present I remember Harcourt, seated on the host's right ; Lord Morris on the Prince's left ; on other chairs Frank Lockwood, Louis Jennings, and George Lewis, not at that time knighted.

The last time I dined with Lord Randolph was on what proved to be his final appearance in the character of Amphitryon. Contemplating a journey round the world, he bade to his mother's home in Grosvenor Square a score of old friends, whose names testify to the wideness of his range of personal sympathy. On his left hand sat Arthur Balfour, in old Fourth party days a private under his command, now his successor in the leadership of the House of Commons ; on his right was Henry Chaplin, from whom in the early 'eighties his vagaries had compelled grave reproof. Round the table sat David

Plunket, afterwards Lord Rathmore, Rochefort Maguire, Labouchere, Edward Dicey, George Lewis, Henry Calcraft, of the Board of Trade, Edward Hamilton, sometime Gladstone's private secretary, Edward Lawson (the late Lord Burnham), Hicks-Beach, Algernon Borthwick (Lord Glenesk), John Morley, Henry Arthur Jones, the dramatist, and Sir Francis Knollys, secretary to the Prince of Wales.

Lord Randolph told me he had asked three others, whose presence would have further diversified this notable gathering. They were Sir William Harcourt, detained at home by a dinner engagement ; Asquith, on Home Secretary's duty at White Lodge in anticipation of the birth of an heir to the Duke of York ; and Henry Irving, engaged on theatrical duties.

The host was not in talkative mood, but kept a watchful eye on the comfort of his guests. One noticed how nervously his hand beat on the table as he gazed around. After dinner he talked to me with eager interest of his coming journey. As on his visit to South Africa he sent letters to a London paper, he had now accepted a commission from a Paris journal to write descriptions of his tour, intending to fill them chiefly with narratives of his shooting expeditions. But he did not reach India, and Burma never looked on the face of the statesman who, in his brief tenure of the India Office, added the glow of its rubies to the splendour of the English crown.

This dinner took place at 50 Grosvenor Square on June 23, 1894. At Christmas time—following once more a memorable epoch in his life—Lord Randolph was hurried home and carried a mere wreck into his mother's house. At early dawn of this new day he died unconscious of his surroundings. He was in his forty-sixth year, the very prime of life as years are counted.

CHAPTER III

March 7, 1895.

THE latest trouble in Rosebery's Cabinet has been the demand made by members of all parties in the House of Commons for Campbell-Bannerman to be Speaker in succession to Arthur Peel, whose retirement from the chair is pending. He is Secretary of State for War, one of the ablest men in the Administration, certainly the most popular on the Treasury Bench. Had he been available for candidature, the tangle about the Speakership would have been forthwith unravelled, and the desirable end reached of unanimous election to the chair. Harcourt, however, put his foot down, and declared that Campbell-Bannerman could not be spared. His election to the chair would necessitate the reconstruction of the Ministry, not to speak of the loss of a vote deducted from an exceedingly narrow majority. Campbell-Bannerman, in yielding, sacrificed a long-cherished aspiration at length within his grasp. I believe he was finally moved in this direction by a personal appeal from Lord Rosebery, who more than hinted at the impossibility of his holding on if deserted in the Cabinet by the colleague upon whose loyalty and fidelity he chiefly leans.

At dinner the other night, talking on the subject that comes up whenever two or three House of Commons men are gathered together, Gladstone said, " The most remarkable thing in the controversy is that, as far as I know, no one has mentioned the name of the man best suited for the position."

" Who is that ? " was eagerly asked.

" Harcourt," he replied, in that deep voice he employs when moved by strong conviction.

March 12.

Buckingham Palace is again in the hands of the work-man. That is practically the normal state of the Royal palaces. There being a fathomless purse in which to dip, the luxury of patching and improving is not limited, as in the case of the common householder. There are two Royal palaces in the personal occupation of Her Majesty which are maintained out of the Imperial Ex-chequer. These are Buckingham Palace and Windsor Castle. Iindeed, when the account comes to be made up, small items are thrown in, such as Adelaide Lodge in Windsor Home Park, the kitchen gardens at Windsor, Frogmore House and grounds, and the Royal Mews in Pimlico. These are not so immaterial as they look, since last year for the Royal Mews alone the House of Commons voted a sum of £2,220 for maintenance and repairs, with a trifle of an additional £580 for new works and alterations. St. James's Palace is regarded as " partly in the occupation of Her Majesty," though I do not remember when the Queen was seen there. The building is down for £1,305 for maintenance and repairs, with £800 spent last year for furniture, doubtless in con-nection with the new household of the Duke of York. Marlborough House cost the nation last year £1,785, a decrease of £600, as compared with the expenditure of the previous year, when £600 was spent on new works.

On the whole, the maintaining of the Royal palaces costs a trifle under £40,000 a year. Of this amount Buckingham Palace is responsible for nearly £7,000. This is above the average of the years, and is largely due to the fact of expenditure on drainage works. The Palace was built over what in the time of the Stuarts was known as Tye Brook, a silver stream gurgling from the northern heights of London to the Thames. In these prosaic, overbuilt days, Tye Brook is a sewer, whose proximity is regarded with reasonable anxiety by the housemaids and footmen who for 360 days out of the year are the sole denizens of this costly fabric. In the time of the late Government pressure was brought to bear upon the First Commissioner of Works to induce him to undertake a complete overhauling of the drainage. It was estimated that the work would cost £8,500, and it is the expenditure of this money that is responsible for the tumbled appearance of the courtyard of the Palace, and for the coming and going of the army of workmen.

March 16.

Chamberlain, whose facial resemblance to the great Pitt is in profile most remarkable, has established another claim to the company of statesmen in general, and of Pitt in particular, by developing tendencies to gout. His attendance at the House through the week has been more than usually fitful, and his face shows traces of the suffering accompanying a frailty usually regarded as the birthright of the " gentlemen of England." Gladstone never had the gout, Disraeli was subject to its inroads. The late Lord Granville was a martyr to it, the closing years of his otherwise happy life being primarily devoted to warding off the enemy. He had a natural and cultivated taste for wine, and to the last his table was lavishly supplied with rare vintages. They were for the guests, the host being permitted only to look on with his gracious smile, enjoying other people's pleasure, since participation in it was forbidden to himself. I remember his telling me one night that if he but wetted his lips from a glass of wine he felt the immediate effects, and would be chained by gout to his chamber for several days.

March 18.

To those familiar with the general character of Sydney Cooper's works, few excluding from their composition three acres (more or less) and a cow, there is something delightful in the idea, which evidently possesses the veteran artist, that in his ninety-second year he is starting out

4

upon quite a new style. I am afraid his pictures, once popular enough, are now somewhat of a drug on the market. To all appearance he is happily unconscious of any declension of the popularity of his brush. A dozen years ago he endowed Canterbury with a gallery of art, in which many of his pictures are on view. There is a more precious legacy in store for the institution. He makes no secret that in his will he has provided that the work upon which he chances to be engaged at the time of his death shall be added to the gallery, and that the brush falling from his hand, and the palate he will never more use, shall be exhibited to coming generations.

April 8.

To-day Mr. Peel for the last time stepped out of the chair to which, through eleven years of stirring interest, he added dignity and power.

Gladstone had the highest opinion of his conduct in the chair. During his visit to Kiel on the *Tantallon Castle*, the ex-Speaker, a guest on Sir John Pender's yacht, came aboard to pay his respects. When he left, Gladstone in conversation with me said, " Mr. Peel " (it was hard for one who had known him all his life to drop into the new style and talk of Lord Peel) " should for ever hold a high place in the list of Speakers of the House of Commons, if it were only for a single event. He once interposed to save the House of Commons from a position into which, had it fallen, it would have been eternally disgraced." Then, with gathering fire shining through flashing eyes, in a voice that might and doubtless was heard across the tender in which we were seated, he recalled an event in the early history of Joseph Gillis Biggar. He had made use of an expression which the Speaker denounced as a breach of order. In his dogged way he refused to retract and apologise. He was " named," and the usual motion followed that he be suspended from the service of the House. The debate was adjourned, and at the next sitting Biggar, yielding to the advice and entreaty of some of his friends, withdrew the offensive expression and offered his apology.

At the time the Member for Cavan was, not undeservedly, an object of especial contumely and scorn on the part of the Conservative Members. They declined to accept the proffered apology, and noisily insisted upon carrying the motion for the suspension of the errant but judiciously repentant Member. Then it was the Speaker interposed, and suggested that Biggar, having made an apology, penal proceedings should not be carried further.

" It was a bold, courageous step for the Speaker to take," said Gladstone. " But it was a great thing to do, and it saved the House of Commons from a lamentable position. It will be an evil day for the House when it comes to pass that an apology offered by a Member for an offence is not promptly accepted as absolute amends."

Three weeks before his retirement, the Speaker addressed to me the subjoined letter :

March 18, 1895.

MY DEAR MR. LUCY,

I have in the course of my official life received much kindness from you—both in public and in private— and it would be strange if I did not seek an opportunity of acknowledging it.

In times of trouble you have sympathised with me, and sympathy at such a time is never forgotten. In ordinary times you have dealt with me with a humour that conveyed real and searching criticism ; but whatever the occasion, I have never failed to find a partial and friendly monitor.

And now, as the hours of my authority are numbered, I recall many instances of your favourable verdict, and if I have at all deserved this last and best proof of your good opinion [the reference is to an entry in the " Diary of Toby, M.P.''], it is a satisfaction to me if I may think that it is in any way deserved. But leaving the decision on that point to others, I cannot but cordially thank him from whom the praise comes in such generous and ample measure.

With very kind regards to Mrs. Lucy and yourself,

I remain,

Most truly yours,

ARTHUR W. PEEL.

April 9.

In the following letter " John Oliver Hobbes," with charming frankness, describes and contrasts two eminent statesmen :

OLD PARK, VENTNOR, I.W.

March 31, 1895.

MY DEAR MR. LUCY,

I must write and tell you how much I enjoyed your delightful dinner the other evening. I thought Mr. Balfour charming, *but* he does not convince me. Curzon may have less tact, but I swear he has more ability. What he knows he knows thoroughly ; and his judgment in State affairs is astute to the last degree. When he is merrier and happier, and in a comfortable home, we shall see what we shall see ! He has not had much of an opportunity yet. The weather here is delightful ; so bright and sunny. I am not doing a stroke of work, and I am having " a good time." My head is rather painful, but I attribute its soreness to my fight with Balfour's book !

With kindest regards,

Yours always faithfully,

PEARL CRAIGIE.

April 12.

Revisiting the Viceregal Lodge, Dublin, after an interval of two years, one finds still in force the boycotting of the Lord-Lieutenant. For a political party who were loud in their denunciation of similar practices on the part of the peasantry when aimed at the landlord, this is a little illogical. Remembering that Lord Houghton is the direct representative of the Sovereign, it is, from " the constitutional party," a little unexpected. These are, however, considerations that have no weight with the ladies and gentlemen who systematically treat the Viceroy

with insolence not always veiled. They refuse to attend
his levees, would sooner starve than dine either at the
Castle or the Viceregal Lodge, and when the representative
of the Queen appears on public occasions in state or
semi-state, they ignore him.

In these circumstances Lord Houghton might reasonably hope to find compensation in the enthusiasm
of the Nationalist party. The homage the loyalists
decline to pay to the representative of the Queen, might
be expected to be shouted by the popular voice when
the representative of the party that has sacrificed everything in the effort to realise the national aspiration
is caught sight of in the streets or on the public platform.
Here also expectation is falsified. On Easter Monday
there was held, at a place some ten miles distant from
Dublin, a race meeting, at which were gathered all sections
of Dublin Society, the lower class predominating. Lord
Houghton, who does everything *en prince*, drove out
to the races in an open landau, with postillions riding
the splendid four-horse team, in itself a spectacle sufficient
to move the heart of an Irishman. As he drove along
the crowded country lanes, passing the multitude tramping
or driving out to the races, he here and there met with
respectful salutation. When the equipage drew up
at the crowded grand stand, a score of hats were raised
to greet His Excellency, who, by the way, had contributed
to the attractions of the meeting a silver cup of the value
of £100. To think what would have happened if, in
analogous circumstances, the representative of the Queen
had appeared at Epsom or Doncaster, was to make one
feel sick and sorry.

Lord Houghton, though he has scrupulously refrained
from displaying political colour, is the colleague of
Ministers who have attempted to give Ireland Home
Rule, and who still mean to do it. The vast multitude
on the course chiefly belonged to the class who
claim Home Rule as a birthright. It might have

been supposed that they would eagerly seize such an opportunity, accidentally presented, of making a demonstration in favour of their champion. They did nothing of the kind, the chilly atmosphere of the grand stand being unruffled by storm of welcome from the populace who flooded the course.

This is a situation which in its curious complexity makes the post of Lord-Lieutenant one of peculiar difficulty. It could be mastered only by a man of imperturbable temper, inflexible patience, and inborn tact. Happily such a one is found in Lord Houghton, who by his administration of Viceregal functions amid such surroundings performs a supreme national service. What it must cost him smilingly and graciously to go through the petty annoyance of a single day no one can say. On that point he is silent.

April 14.

As the artist for *Vanity Fair*, whose fortune the portraits by " Ape " did much to make, Pellegrini had the run of the Lobby of the House of Commons, where he used to study the subjects for successive drawings. It was pretty to watch him stalking his man, even more delightful to observe the object of the flattering attention. " Ape " never asked for a sitting. All his sitters were, in fact, standers. He liked to shoot Folly or Wisdom as it walked about, presumably unconscious that it was serving the purposes of a popular artist. It was wonderful how men of all conditions played up to the comedy of unconsciousness when Pelligrini was studying them. He brought out neither pencil nor paper. His notes were mentally made. Having fixed upon his man he viewed him from all positions and distances, watching him as he walked, as he stood, as he talked, as he reflected.

The Lobby of the House of Commons is not large in area, and at certain hours of a sitting is crowded. It was always easy to tell whom Pellegrini had in hand at a particular time. With stealthy tread he followed his man round and round and all about, looking him up and down from head to heel, the Member trying with delicious lack of success to look as if he didn't know what business was to the fore. If Pellegrini had thus comported himself in a public place in his own beloved Italy he would doubtless have been swooped down upon by the police, and haled to prison under suspicion that he had a stiletto in his bosom, and was watching for a favourable opportunity of plunging it up to the hilt in the back or breast of the man whose steps he dogged. But it was only " Ape," with no design more deadly than that of making a caricature portrait of a more or less well-known M.P.

April 26.

From Sir Henry Campbell-Bannerman

April 25, 1895.

MY DEAR LUCY,

Alas! Tuesday is a day when my Committee on the Relief of Distress from Non-employment revels in its hideous details, and I have to sit in the chair curbing the impetuosity of Mr. T. H. Boltonparte, listening to the lispings of Mr. Isaacs Mantalini, and bearding the Keir Hardie in his den.

Your dinner party would have given me better employment, no distress from Hardie, and relief from Mantalini ; but the British soldier knows what his duty is, and he does it—with a d—n.

Yours,

H. C-B.

T. H. Bolton, one of the Members for Derbyshire, known to the readers of the "Diary of Toby, M.P.," as Boltonparte, was so named in allusion to a lock of hair carefully curled over his forehead in support of a supposititious but cherished resemblance to Napoleon. "Isaacs Mantalini" was "C.-B.'s" own happy invention of a name that suggested marked personal characteristics of the Member for Walworth.

CHAPTER IV

May 1, 1895.

LAST night Sir Henry Wolff, home from Madrid on brief holiday, was entertained at dinner at the Senior United Service Club by Lord Ashbourne. The guests were in main of the straitest sect—the bluest blood—of Toryism. Of a gathering of twenty, including a famous General and an equally well-known Admiral, there were only two Liberals, one being Lord Russell of Killowen. It was a pretty illustration of the best side of English politics to see the great advocate who destroyed Pigott and the case built round that burly but insubstantial form, sitting at the festive board, shoulder to shoulder with Lord Londonderry, the incarnation of hostility to Home Rule.

The Marquis, though still a young man, is perhaps the stoutest pillar of Unionism in Ireland. Under the late Tory Government he was Lord-Lieutenant of Ireland, working hand-in-glove with Arthur Balfour whilst that equally young man gave Ireland a taste of resolute government. The ex-Viceroy has set the seal of his approval upon the fashion of high Society in Dublin of boycotting the representative of the Queen at the Castle because he happens to have been nominated by Gladstone. Lord Londonderry and Lord Houghton are old friends. Londonderry is too stern a patriot to permit personal feeling to sway his actions in matters where the integrity of the Empire is concerned. He likes Lord Houghton much; but he loves his country more.

Happily, he has hit upon an arrangement whereby he keeps his friend and does not lose his self-respect. As long as Lord Houghton remains in Ireland, whether

46

at the Castle, at the Viceregal Lodge, or on tour in the country, Lord Londonderry will not call upon him, look at him, or touch his hand. Often Lord Houghton runs over to London, and never does so without finding, and accepting, warm invitation to dine at Londonderry House.

Like Henry Wolff, Chauncey Depew chances to be in London just now, and formed one of the guests at last night's dinner. He is perhaps the most popular man in America ; is certainly the most welcome and effective speaker, whether on the platform or at dinner. He has brought the art of after-dinner oratory to its highest pitch. In London it is not yet the custom for toasts and speech-making to find a place in the menu of private dinners, whether given at the club or at home. But the opportunity of hearing Depew was rare, and not to be foregone.

Lord Ashbourne managed to bring about the speech with a skill and touch of humour that appropriately led up to it. When the waiters had withdrawn, the guests were astonished, some appalled, to find the host on his feet alluding to the pleasure with which he welcomed Lord Londonderry and Sir Henry Wolff, seated respectively on his right hand and his left. It was naturally thought he was about to propose their health, and that they must needs respond. Londonderry's face at this moment was a delightful study. He had come out for a quiet dinner in choice company, and here he was being let in for a speech ! When his face had grown almost anguished in expression, Ashbourne, suddenly turning aside, called upon Chauncey Depew to respond for His Excellency and the noble Lord.

Depew was as absolutely taken by surprise as were the rest of the company. It was an ordeal sufficient to try even his trained capacity. He proved equal to the occasion. Rising without a moment's hesitation, he spoke for ten minutes—a gem of a speech flashing with wit, rich in apt illustration, and lightened by a story that seemed made for the occasion—as possibly it was.

May 8.

The Duke of York [His present Majesty] is taking to the business of public speaking as a duckling takes to water. He thoroughly enjoyed himself last night at the meeting of the Royal Literary Fund, over which he presided. It is presumable that he has assistance in the preparation of his speeches, but the delivery is entirely his own, and is excellent. He has the slightly guttural accent of his father, without the *soupçon* of German accent more marked with H.R.H. in private conversation than in his public speech, but distinctly recognisable in both. In other respects our next-King-but-one strikingly resembles his father, of whom he might be taken as a slightly reduced replica.

His aptitude for public speaking, and his almost boyish pleasure in taking part in public functions, is a considerable relief to the ever-increasing duties imposed upon the Prince of Wales. Last night father and son were out on duty, the Prince of Wales presiding at the festival of the Printers' Pension Corporation. The Duke of Teck sat beaming at the left hand of his son-in-law, who was always punctilious, when commencing his speeches, to turn towards his father-in-law, addressing him as " Your Highness."

Lord Houghton delivered a speech which, unfortunately, the etiquette of newspaper reporting has done slight justice to. The Duke of York being reported verbatim, and the night being elsewhere a busy one, a very meagre report is provided of a speech full of sparkling point, imbued with fine literary flavour. George Wyndham's speech, brightly conceived and charmingly delivered, made it more than ever a mystery how it is he has not succeeded in catching the ear of the House of Commons.

May 15.

A trip to the Baltic is arranged in connection with the opening of the Kiel Canal, an event upon which the German Emperor is concentrating his fearful energy.

He intends to make it as memorable as was the inauguration of the Suez Canal a little more than quarter of a
century ago.   He will not emulate the oriental hospitality
of Ismail Pacha, who made Cairo one vast hotel for
the entertainment of guests bidden to the ceremony.
Short of that modern chapter of the Arabian Nights,
the festivities of next month will be on an imperial
scale.   All the nations of the world will be represented
by their fleets, and, as far as they go round, by members
of the Royal families.   The Duke of York will appear
for the Queen, and it is expected that a member of the
Government will be deputed to attend.   There is likely
to be some competition for the appointment, as, given
fine weather—surely due in mid-June—the spectacle will
be magnificent and the assembly most interesting.   Sir
Donald Currie is going out in the finest vessel of his fleet,
and has issued invitations to something like a hundred
Members of the House of Commons.   Fortunately,
as usually happens in these social engagements, the
invitations are pretty evenly distributed among political
parties, making it possible to arrange for pairs.   Otherwise the pleasure of the errant Members might be disturbed
by receipt of a telegram announcing defeat of the Ministers,
imminent dissolution, and hurried General Election.[1]

May 17.

There is something dismally tragic in the thought of
Oscar Wilde in his prison cell, whilst two London theatres
are crammed with audiences, delighted with the clever
situations and light persiflage of plays from his pen, in
the full tide of their popularity when his career was
abruptly cut short.   The situation was a little awkward
for the manager of St. James's Theatre, where *The
Importance of being Earnest* is played, and for Messrs.

---

[1] This actually happened.   On arriving at Gravesend on the return
voyage the guests on board the *Tantallen Castle* purchased the morning
papers announcing defeat of Lord Rosebery's Government, and the
consequent dissolution of Parliament.

Waller and Morell, who had arranged to continue at the Criterion the successful run of *An Ideal Husband*. They have attempted to meet it in a measure that is problematically wise, but indubitably mean. They keep on the plays, but have struck out from the bills the name of the dishonoured author.

May 25.

Rarely out of Golconda or the De Beers Compound have there flashed so many diamonds as sparkled amid the company that thronged Brook House on Saturday night in commemoration of Queen Victoria's birthday. In other respects it was exceptionally brilliant as to costume. Her Majesty's principal Ministers had, in accordance with custom, been banqueting, their guests being in court, ministerial, military, or naval uniform. The stars of many nations, gifts of kings and emperors, flashed on manly breasts. When the Ameer's son arrived with his suite, he succeeded in hiding behind an impassive countenance any feeling of surprise or delight he may have felt at discovering that Western civilisation is not absolutely incompatible with oriental magnificence. Two of his suite, less well trained, were in a state of amazement delightful to watch. One in particular, a man who for fully sixty years had seen life in Afghanistan, looked as if he were walking in a dream. As his black eyes rolled round, possibly thinking with Blücher what a place London would be to loot, his lips parted, literally gaping with wonder.

The Shahzada, heir to the Ameer's throne, is, it must be said, a most unsatisfactory person to cater for in the way of amusement. Nothing he sees causes his eyes to brighten or his swarthy cheek to flush. It would not be exact to say he preserves throughout the day and the week a bored expression. To be bored implies some impulse of emotion. The Shahzada is not bored. He only stares out into space with absolutely impassive countenance.

It should be remembered that his lot is not altogether

a happy one. For a mere lad, not quite half-educated according to our notions, to go through the day's work appointed for him by his English hosts is no light task. There is not a soul near him, save his personal suite, with whom he may converse in his native tongue. To the interpreter who accompanies him he talks Persian, and, it is said, talks it very badly. Yet going to and fro, a central figure in elaborate pageants, he must say something to the personages with whom he comes in contact. He has already mastered the, to him, novel accomplishment of shaking hands. He does it with a flourish, watched with keen interest by the brilliant company that thronged the staircase at Brook House.

It is quite possible that being initiated it may speedily become the fashion. " The Shahzada shake " may take the place of that absurd pawing at the outstretched hand of an acquaintance which long enthralled London Society with its grace. I do not know whether the fashion ever extended beyond our four-mile radius. Within it, among the feebler folk, it was long prevalent. Instead of frankly grasping the hand of a friend the trick was to raise the elbow nearly to the level of the shoulder, and thrust out (not too far) extended fingers. The acquaintance did the same ; the hands wagged at each other in utterly tired fashion, and the greeting was over. The Shahzada has a more picturesque way. He half raises his hand as if about to salaam, and, pausing half-way, brings it down with a slam on the outstretched hand of his acquaintance.

This gesture, of oriental origin, only shows how small the world is. Here, on our transpontine stage, when the burly farmer, or the home-sped tailor, or the benevolent solicitor, meets an acquaintance, he takes the extended hand in his left, holding it underneath, and brings his right hand down with respondent thump indicative of the heartiest welcome and the most abundant friendship. The Shahzada greeting the Prince of Wales on the stair-

case at Brook House, of course stopped far short of that
energetic action.   But the drop of his right hand into
the friendly palm extended had in it something remi-
niscent of the stage greeting familiar to us in boyhood's
days.

June 22.

This is the very height of the London season, and Her
Majesty the Queen is rusticating at Balmoral.   To the
intelligent foreigner it must seem a curious arrangement.
Here it has come to be so much a matter of course that
it passes unnoticed.   It is well known that if Her Majesty
were not at Balmoral she would be no nearer London
than Windsor or Osborne, and in this case a hundred
miles more or less makes no difference in the practical
bearings of the situation.   Not an extra dress would be
ordered, not the slightest ripple shown on the stagnant
waters of trade.   Her Majesty is due to-morrow week
on the return journey from Scotland.   She goes straight
to Windsor, resting there for three weeks as a preliminary
to passing on to Osborne, where she will stay till the end
of August, returning to Balmoral for a more prolonged
sojourn.   Visitors from distant climes discover that if
they want to catch a glimpse of the Queen of England
her capital is the last place to which they should repair.
Taking the year through Her Majesty does not sleep in
London seven nights, which seems an inadequate reason for
keeping Buckingham Palace in a condition to receive her.

This habit on one occasion led to a threatening interlude,
of which Mr. Speaker Denison gives a graphic account in
his diary, printed for private circulation.

In May 1868 an acute ministerial crisis developed.
The Government were at a single sitting twice defeated on
critical points in the Scotch Reform Bill.   That it was the
opening of the London season did not deter the Queen
from arranging a long visit to Balmoral.   The political
crisis, which on constitutional grounds necessitated her
presence in London, was not more effective.   Within a

few hours after its occurrence she set out on her journey northward.

This was too much for the sorely tried patience of the House of Commons. The following notice was handed to the Clerk at the Table, with the object of having it placed on the notice paper for May 21 : "To ask the Prime Minister, as the Queen's health appears to be so weak that she cannot live in England, whether he has advised her to abdicate in favour of the Prince of Wales."

The Speaker ruled the question out of order. Notice of it appearing in the papers fluttered the dovecotes at Balmoral. The Queen hurriedly communicated with Disraeli, asking that he should "say something" in the House of Commons. In a letter addressed to the Speaker, Disraeli asked whether it would be in order, if notice of the question were persisted in, for him to move that it be not received at the Table, and take the opportunity of saying what might be said in extenuation of Her Majesty's conduct. This suggestion did not commend itself to the judgment of the Speaker. A day or two later the question was orally put. Disraeli sat silent and the incident passed over, but doubtless had some measure of effect, if only temporarily, in the quarter towards which it was directed.

Fortunately for the interests concerned, the Prince of Wales is tireless in the discharge of functions pertaining to royalty, and of late has found a loyal and efficient deputy in the Duke of York. As far as playing the host goes, the Prince of Wales is too polite and too dutiful greatly to exceed the practice of the Queen in this matter. In the course of the year Her Majesty entertains at Windsor or Osborne a few Ministers and ex-Ministers. They go down one day and return the next, having dined and slept. The Prince of Wales occasionally gives snug little dinners on Saturday night at Marlborough House, where are gathered a company in the main more notable for brains than titles. Better known is his dinner on the eve of the Derby; most enjoyable of all are the late autumn parties at Sandringham. The garden party at Marlborough House presents opportunity for wider recognition of friends and acquaintances much prized by London Society.

July 9.

Amongst the many congratulations Sir Henry Irving has received upon his knighthood, none pleased him more than the supper spread for him last night by the Arundel Club. In response to the toast of his health, he delivered a charming speech, full of fancy, warm with kindly remembrance, spoken with a grace which, if displayed in the House of Commons, or on a public platform, would be irresistible. It is a pity it was not reported verbatim in the morning papers. It would have introduced a gleam of sunlight into the cloud of political screeds just now filling the columns of the Press.

Nothing was more pleasant than to see round the table the gathering of actors and managers, unless it were to hear the kindly words in which they paid honour to their chief. It is one of the most striking testimonials to the nobility of Irving's nature, the sweet healthfulness of his character, that whilst, starting out of obscurity, he has outstripped all competitors on the stage, not one scowl of envy, not a syllable of detraction mars the pleasure of his success. Last night actors young and old came on from their work to pay him honour. Among those present were Charles Wyndham, Beerbohm Tree, George Alexander—at present the youngest manager of London theatres—and Forbes Robertson, who is about to enter the field and will commence with nothing less than the direction of the Lyceum Theatre, leased during Irving's tour in the United States.

Wyndham, in the course of a speech in response to the toast of the drama, recalled an interesting episode in the joint history of Sir Henry Irving and himself, when, as he put it, they cooled their heels outside the stage door of a theatre in Liverpool, looking for an engagement. Brighter days have dawned on both, and it is pretty to see how friendship commenced in earlier days with Henry Irving deepens as the years pass.

August 8.

Electricity has at length invaded Westminster Abbey, performing a fresh wonder under the ancient fane. At all the services the congregation are first startled and then witched by bursts of music, played by unseen hands, coming from the south transept furthest removed from the organ-loft. The secret was out last evening, when Dr. Bridge invited some of his friends to a private recital in the Abbey. The Abbey was dark throughout, save for a single gaslight flickering in the nave, and another in the organ-loft, where might be seen shadowy figures as the organ pealed forth, or as one of the boy choristers stood up to sing " Angels ever bright and fair." Suddenly the big organ that seemed to shake the Abbey roof with its thunderous peal was hushed, and out of the darkness at the remote end of the Abbey there stole forth the softly played notes of the prelude to *Parsifal.*

> Music, that gentlier on the spirit lies
> Than tired eyelids upon tired eyes.

This last result of science is known as the Celestial organ, a fine instrument presented to the Abbey by Mr. Clarke. It is placed in the triforium of the south transept, above the tomb of Handel, entirely hidden from observation by the congregation seated below. Though in all respects a separate organ, complete in itself, it forms a part of the grand instrument in the choir, which still includes some of the stops on which Purcell played two hundred years ago, when he occupied the post now filled by Dr. Bridge. By means of an electric cable two hundred feet in length, the new organ is connected with the old, is controlled from the same console, may be played of itself, or may be used in conjunction.

5

CHAPTER V

TROUBLE in high quarters is given by the Shahzada. Soon after he arrived in this country he began to show signs of weariness, and there were doubts whether he might not, some fine morning, bolt, leaving the ordered programme of the junketings and journeyings unfulfilled. Indications of this intention were found in his abruptly breaking engagements, leaving robed mayors, anxious aldermen, and expectant town councillors waiting forlorn at railway stations for trysts His Highness ruthlessly disregarded. Now even more pressing trouble is occasioned by the effort to get rid of him. Long ago he took leave of the Queen, and later said good-bye to the Prince of Wales. He has outlived the Ministry that brought him here, Sir Henry Fowler having gratefully handed him over as a legacy to the new Secretary of State for India, Lord George Hamilton.

The mystery of mysteries is the attraction that induces him to outstay his welcome. No longer on visiting terms with Royalty, unnoticed by mayors, lord mayors, and corporations, he spends whole days in seclusion at Dorchester House. He has fallen so low as to be glad to accept an invitation promising an evening's recreation at a shilling exhibition. This strange behaviour succeeds in making ludicrous what was intended to serve as a stroke of State policy, and does not promise much for the substantial results of an undertaking that has cost India a pretty penny.

November 8.

An intimate friend of Parnell tells me his premature and almost sudden death was contributed to by actual poverty. He was so short of cash that at the time of his illness there was in the house no food suitable to his condition, nor means of obtaining any. Certainly the desolate couple were unable to raise the fee of an eminent specialist, who, had he been promptly brought down to Brighton, might have saved Parnell's life. This is a story on the face of it so incredible that I would not mention it save on the authority of an intimate friend. Mrs. Parnell was legatee to a large amount under the will of her aunt, Mrs. Wood. The will was disputed, and, pending settlement of the case, distribution is withheld. Still it is hard to think that even in such circumstances the legatee would be left in a state of penury.

Parnell, though not a wealthy man, had a patrimony which, in quieter times, sufficed for his needs. A few years before the crash came he was the recipient of a princely money gift, the offering of the Irish people at home and abroad. It amounted to a sum of £38,000. The money, being banked, was drawn out in a single cheque, armed with which a deputation went down to Avondale, a little awestruck with the magnitude of their mission.

One who was present told me at the time how effectually Parnell relieved them from all embarrassment. Being themselves only mortal they expected that a man to whom £38,000 came in this fashion would exhibit some signs of emotion, might even overwhelm them with evidence of gratitude. When the cheque was held out to him Mr. Parnell simply said, " Thank you," much as he might have done had someone passed him a light for his cigar. He carelessly thrust the cheque into his pocket, and silently waited to see what topic of conversation his guests might be disposed to start next.

As far as outside observation went, the cheque might have remained in Parnell's pocket uncashed. He lived no more expensively than before. It was understood amongst his friends that the money was sunk in the quarry he worked at Avondale—an industrial enterprise in which sacks of sovereigns had earlier disappeared. But Parnell was not a communicative man, and not even Mr. Biggar, to whom nothing else was sacred, presumed to ask him questions.

November 10.

Tyndall's house stands on the crest of a hill, on the high road leading to Hindhead. Compared with houses of more recent structure it is a commonplace villa. But the view it commands is magnificent, albeit closed in on one side by a curious structure, something between a turf-stack and the battlements of a stage castle. This is the famous structure put up by the irascible man of science to hide from his view a house which a presumptive person had dared to erect between the wind and his nobility.

Tyndall owned a large stretch of land in this quarter. One patch, a little way down the hill, two or three hundred yards from the house, was held by another, who, perceiving morbid anxiety on the part of his neighbour to possess a clear prospect, held out for a prohibitive price. Tyndall declined to be bled to that extent. The unspeakable man ran up a villa, Tyndall making the retort, more grotesque than courteous, of building a dead wall at the end of his garden, which not only obscured from his indignant gaze his neighbour's house, but shut off the upper view from his neighbour's eyes.

The thing has been skilfully done, the bare dead wall being turned upon the obnoxious householder, whilst for the Tyndall community the asperities of the situation are softened by a lining of brushwood and heather. In addition he planted a row of trees, hoping that in time they would serve as a screen. But they had not grown beyond the proportion of saplings before the angry eyes were closed to the loved scene from the hill-top, and the weary Professor was at rest.

November 17.

As long ago as the present generation remember, " Lady A.," otherwise Maria Marchioness of Ailesbury, whose

death is announced, has been a foremost figure in London
Society. Her appearance in any room was certain to
attract attention, since she dressed unlike any other
woman. Disdaining modern fashions, she wore quaint
frocks, crowned by a wig apparently as old as herself,
with corkscrew curls flattened down by the side of her
face. Her vivacity and energy found a parallel only in her
contemporary Gladstone. Perhaps even more than he
she was perpetually on the go. Of late years, save when
critical divisions are pending in the House of Commons,
Gladstone makes it a rule to be in bed by midnight.
" Lady A." being out for the night (as she generally was)
stayed up as late as any one, appearing at luncheon
next day as if she had enjoyed her beauty sleep.

Amongst the stories told to account for her phenomenal
vivacity is one to the effect that on a day of each
week she remained through the twenty-four hours in
bed in a darkened room, closely shuttered from noise
without. Here she renewed her youth like the eagle.
Whereinsoever lay the secret, her tireless energy seemed
miraculous. For some people the end of the season comes
as a relief, providing opportunity to retire into quiet
quarters from the rush of dinners and the riots of routs.
For " Lady A." the end of the London season was the
beginning of a tour of visits to country houses, where she
was as blithe as a lark. She was a great favourite not
only with Queen Victoria, but with the Prince of Wales—
a very different thing.

Perhaps the most remarkable thing about this *grande
dame* was her belief in, and admiration for, Gladstone.
London Society has always been on the other side of
politics. Personally and politically they detest him.
" Lady A." not only had her private prejudices, but had
an exceedingly frank way of expressing them. It was
refreshing, amid the lisping of a fashionable assembly,
to hear her far-reaching voice setting forth a few home-
truths. If it be true that she kept a diary, and has

jotted down in it her recollections and impressions in the frank way she was accustomed to utter them, we have in store one of the most interesting books of this half-century. She intimately knew Canning, Palmerston, Macaulay, Earl Grey, Melbourne, Brougham, Lord John Russell, Sir E. L. Bulwer, Derby, Disraeli, and, to the last, Gladstone. She saw Macready act, heard Newman and Pusey preach, knew Charles Dickens in the bloom of his fame, and possessed the First Edition of Tennyson's early works.

November 20.

Divers versions are enshrined in history of the circumstances under which old Nathan Meyer Rothschild, founder of the family, obtained the earliest exclusive information of the battle of Waterloo. One of the favourite stories is that he accompanied Wellington's forces disguised as a sutler, and as soon as the fortunes of the day were decided, posted off to London, where he made the best of the markets.

One of his grandsons, a partner in the London house, tells me the true story, which, he adds, has never been published. His grandfather, who settled in London whilst his eldest brother Anselme remained at Frankfort, and his second brother Salomon opened a branch of the bank at Vienna, established relations with the English Government, acting as their agent in buying gold, much needed to carry on the campaign against Napoleon. For the purposes of his business, Nathan Meyer had in his pay a swift-sailing lugger, which kept him in correspondence with his brothers and other friends on the Continent. One day in June 1815, the captain of the lugger, fresh from a trip across the Channel, came upon Rothschild. He had, in quite a casual way, put in his pocket a Dutch newspaper. Looking it over, Rothschild found an account of the battle of Waterloo, brief, but so unfaltering and evidently authentic, that he straightway went on 'Change and bought Consols by the bucketful.

They were on this particular day beaten down lower than ever, the last news from the seat of war not coming down later than an account of the affair at Quatre Bras, represented as a check to Wellington. When, later, the Government received official dispatches describing Bonaparte's rout, the Funds went up by leaps and bounds, and the fortunes of the house of Rothschild were established on a princely scale.

November 22.

A fortnight ago I met Sir Robert Peel at the house of his brother, the Speaker, whither were bidden the company gathered at St. Margaret's Church for the wedding of his niece, the Speaker's daughter, to Mr. Rochfort Maguire. Yesterday morning his servant, entering his bedroom, found Sir Robert lying dead. Hæmorrhage of the brain is the explanation given by the doctors of this sudden cutting off of a striking personality. One is surprised to be reminded that Sir Robert on Saturday last celebrated his seventy-third birthday. His well-set figure, his springy walk, his ruddy countenance, and his lively talk, proclaimed a much younger man. It must be admitted, on review of the career of the son of the great statesman who gave the people cheap bread, that it fell short of reasonable expectation. He began well under the most promising auspices, but after a lively time in the House and in office, he long ago disappeared from the political arena.

November 28.

A. M. Sullivan, the eloquent Member for Louth, as Gladstone once called him, used to tell a delightful story about that *rara avis* in Ircland, during the 'eighties rarer than snakes—a loyalist mayor. Having occasion to propose the toast of Queen Victoria at a local banquet, he said :

" Gentlemen, I give you the toast of Her Majesty the Queen. She is populous at home ; she is populous abroad ; she is populous with the rich, she is populous with the poor ; and, gentlemen, what is a truer test of good womanhood, she is populous in her family."

Another story from this side of the Channel shows that the Irish mayor has not the monopoly of unconscious humour. Early in his elevated career, the mayor of a small town in Lincolnshire was called upon to preside at a banquet. The list of toasts being submitted to him, he was advised that in proposing the health of the King and Queen, it was not necessary or desirable that he should expand his remarks. Profiting by this advice, when the time came he said :

" Gentlemen, I will ask you to join me in drinking a toast to the King. I am told, and I am sure you will agree with me, that the less said on the subject the better."

The toast duly honoured, he rose again.

" And now, gentlemen," he said, " the King being drunk, I give you the Queen."

November 29.

The death of Rustem Pacha removes a familiar and popular figure from London Society. No one talking to the Turkish Ambassador as, in the short season of this broken year, he sat at the dinner-table or moved about a crowded drawing-room, would guess that he had long passed the limit of fourscore years. In the season, certainly up to the present year, Rustem dined out nearly every night, and on most nights went on swift tour through a succession of drawing-rooms. Short of stature, spare of figure, his pale, grave countenance was ever ready to light up with a smile at the approach of a friend. The unwonted warmth of Lord Salisbury's reference to him, when already he was in the shadow of the valley of death, testifies to his personal attraction. He could be silent in seven languages, and upon occasion was. Seated after dinner in congenial company, with his precious little pipe filled, he was a delightful companion.

He shared with Charles Keene a curious fancy in the matter of pipes. C. K. had a collection dug up from

under the walls of ancient London, the bowl of each
not bigger than the top joint of a lady's forefinger.
These he filled incessantly, and smoked radiantly.
Rustem Pacha had a pipe somewhere about the same
size, though more akin in style to the Japanese. He kept
it in a handsome case, and when, after dinner, cigars
went round, produced it, solemnly filled its infinitesimal
proportions, and serenely smoked.

In his semi-military frock-coat, on State occasions his
chest adorned with orders, Rustem was distinguished
in whatever throng he sat or stood. He always wore his
fez, even at the dinner-table. On big nights through
the parliamentary session it invariably lent a bit of
colour to the Diplomatic gallery in the House of
Lords.

November 30.

One of the most striking things in the moving story of
Jabez Balfour is the sudden collapse of public interest in
his case. On the eve of his trial elaborate preparations
were made by the London newspapers to rise to the
occasion. Special staffs of reporters were organised,
with intent to supply a verbatim record of the proceedings,
whilst picturesque writers were put on to preface and
supplement the shorthand report by description of the
scene in court. The rush of the public for places on
the opening days taxed alike the cubical capacity of the
court and the patience of its janitors. Before the third
day had sped interest began to flag, smothered under the
weight of figures and the placid eloquence of the Attorney-
General. On these last days, when successive cases in
the multifarious indictment have been closed, the evening
papers have made gallant attempts to revive public
spirit by the issue of gigantic posters, proclaiming the
verdict and sentence. Success has been but momentary.
Jabez Balfour disappears from the scene without the
poor pleasure of knowing that his exit has been watched
with breathless attention.

The reason is not far to seek. His appearance in the dock on a criminal charge was a sort of anti-climax following on the dramatic incidents of his flight, his capture in Argentina, and his home-bringing. The slow unfolding of his case led up to no surprises. The public knew pretty well what he had done, and were not disposed to follow Sir Richard Webster through the dreary round of his detailed narrative.

Not the least remarkable episode in a notable career did not come out in the course of the trial before Mr. Justice Bruce and a special jury. As the evidence brought to light in court shows, in the year 1886 the fabric of desperate speculation and reckless finance, not stopping short of fraud, which Balfour had built, was tottering to a fall. In January of that year, Gladstone was forming his third Administration, and among the most persistent claimants for office was the Member for Burnley. He proudly presented, through the proper channel, the record of his public life and the claims he had established on the Liberal Prime Minister. He won Tamworth in 1889, and held the seat for five years. He fought Croydon and Newington at considerable expense, his lot ungilded by success. Then he brought back Burnley to the Liberal fold, whence it had been led astray by Peter Rylands. In addition to these specific claims on a Liberal Ministry, Jabez was able (though here embarrassed by feelings of modesty) to hint at the widespread national benefit that had followed upon his efforts, through the Liberator and kindred societies, to inculcate principles of thrift among the working-classes. Under pressure of similar claims those of the Member for Burnley, duly considered, were postponed, a decision for which subsequent events must have given Gladstone occasion for profound gratitude. During the last six years the Liberal party has suffered some hard kicks at the foot of fortune. To have had the founder of the Liberator Society included within its ministerial ranks would have been the most damaging blow of all.

I do not remember having heard Jabez take part in parliamentary debate during his membership for Burnley. There were at this epoch increasingly pressing calls upon his time and attention which handicapped him in his patriotic desire to devote his energies to the public service. He generally put in an appearance about question time, picking up the voluminous correspondence awaiting him at the post office, and buzzing off to the library to deal with it. A short, stout man, of florid countenance, he looked much more like a country shop-keeper, or a farmer in a small way of business, than a great city financier, accustomed to deal lightly with commissions of £10,000 for handing over other people's money to needy borrowers.

Memories of the House of Commons must have crowded his mind when he took his stand in the dock. Whilst he was still Member for Burnley, the leading spirit of half a dozen colossal and apparently prosperous institutions, a justice of the peace for Surrey and Oxfordshire, member of the Devonshire and the National Liberal Clubs, with a town house at Marlborough Gate and a country residence at Abingdon, he had for colleagues in the House of Commons the judge who now towered over him from the Bench, the Attorney-General who slowly but irresistibly laid bare the story of his fraudulent career, and Sir Robert Reid, who appeared with Sir Richard Webster for the Crown. His own counsel, John O'Connor, affectionately known in the House of Commons as "Long John," sat on a bench close by his client through the Parliament of 1886-92, till such time as the Member for Burnley, finding the police uncomfortably close at his heels, bolted for sanctuary in Argentina.

December 3.

There still linger in Cumberland stories of the first Lord Lonsdale, affectionately remembered as "The Wicked Earl." In the autumn, staying in the house of a well-known Cumberland family, I heard several. Born in the middle of last century, he was made an Earl in 1807, and lived till 1844, making the round of the century within thirteen years. He was a Tory of the narrowest sect. Just after the Reform Bill my host's grandfather was returned in the Liberal interest as one of the Members for the county. A prominent and a popular man, he seemed peculiarly fitted for a seat on the county bench. But Lord Lonsdale, who held the Lord-Lieutenancy, would much more readily have bestowed the Queen's Commission upon his horse than have been the means of securing it for a Liberal.

When the object of his neighbourly detestation became a Member of Parliament for the county, he must needs be placed on the Commission of the Peace. Lord Lonsdale's spite was equal to the occasion. He carefully made out a list of obscure and not particularly reputable persons, placed the new Member's name at the end of it, and submitted the proposal to the Sovereign. The persons named were all placed on the Commission of the Peace. The M.P., treating the manœuvre with silent scorn, never qualified, nor in other manner recognised the distinction thus thrust upon him.

One time the Earl went to stay for a week with a friend, whose house was twenty miles distant from Lowther. On arriving his valet tremblingly told him he had omitted to put in a supply of clean shirts.

" Oh, no matter," said the Earl, with benevolent smile. " Take a horse, ride back to Lowther, and bring a shirt. But, mind, *bring only one.*"

The unhappy man rode off on his long journey, marvelling why his master, who he knew was going to stay for a full week, should want only one shirt. The secret was out next day, when the Earl ordered him off to Lowther to bring another shirt. So day by day, throughout the week, the wretched man had to ride forty miles through what chanced to be midsummer weather.

" He never forgot my shirts again," was the Earl's smiling commentary when he told the story.

December 4.

Since Lord Dufferin was sworn in Lord Warden of the Cinque Ports he has rarely been seen at Walmer Castle. This is contrary to usage, Walmer having been long accustomed to home the Lord Warden in permanent residence at the Castle. Lord Granville lived there for the larger half of the year. He was much attached to the place, spent thousands of pounds upon its improvement and embellishment, and through the summer months usually had a house party.

Poor W. H. Smith, Lord Dufferin's predecessor in the Wardenship, looked forward with keen anticipation to spending the closing years of his life under a roof that had homed Pitt, Wellington and Palmerston. He lived there just long enough to die in it. There was something pathetic in the sight of his yacht, the *Pandora*, lying at anchor in the Downs, waiting for the master who was never more to voyage afar in his beloved ship. Towards the end, when he could not walk from his bed, he was wheeled out on to the ramparts in a chair. A crane was erected, and chair and Lord Warden gently lowered on to the deck of the yacht. Then the *Pandora* slowly steamed down the Channel at a funereal pace, which too surely betokened the new Lord Warden's rapidly nearing destination.

Short as was his tenure, Mr. Smith succeeded in performing one good action that will ever keep his memory green. He collected from far and near the dispersed mementoes of the Duke of Wellington's tenancy of the Castle. When, on the death of the Duke, Lord Palmerston became Lord Warden, he, with characteristic freedom from sentimentality, did not think it worth while to buy in the personal effects of his illustrious predecessor. If not exactly sold by auction, they were picked up by miscellaneous curiosity hunters, and taken away.

W. H. Smith bought back all he could find, and endowed
the Castle with them.   Lord Salisbury will find them all
there when he takes up his residence at Walmer, together
with a modern telescope of the power of which Pitt never
dreamed when, nearly a hundred years ago, he walked
up and down the ramparts on the look-out for the fleet
which Bonaparte never succeeded in dispatching from
Boulogne.

December 5.

Prince Bismarck is employing the leisure of his old age
in preparing documents that will serve for his memoir.
He has them printed in a volume which he circulates
among some of his private friends.   One who lives in
London is the honoured recipient of the precious work.
The arrangement is somewhat higgledy-piggledy, letters,
memoranda, and extracts from diaries presenting themselves much as they might turn out of a waste-paper
basket.   There is a good deal about Bismarck's life in
Paris, where, thirty-four years ago, he resided as Ambassador of the King of Prussia to Napoleon III, from
whose hand—the same that signed the capitulation of
Metz—he received the Cross of the Legion of Honour.

One of the letters, dated 1862, gives an account of his
first dinner at the Tuileries.   He sat next to the Empress
Eugenie, whom he describes as lively in manner, talking
wittily, and apparently without restraint.   Horses, toilets,
home and foreign politics, the Crimea, and recent attacks
on the Emperor's life were all chatted about in a fashion
that seems to have enchanted the Prussian Minister, then
in the prime of his manhood.

" The worst of it was," he writes, " that I felt I should
not eat more than Her Majesty did, which, unfortunately,
was very little."

The Emperor, little dreaming of what would come to
pass before eight years were sped, was most gracious in
his bearing towards the Prussian Minister.   After dinner
he sat down with him in a retired corner, and talked at

large. Bismarck's discriminating eye assured him that the Empress was a much better friend of England than was the Emperor. In other quarters, as is mentioned in a later letter, he found much distrust amongst the French people of their neighbours across the Channel. He quotes with evident approval a picturesque proverb, " *L'Anglais est mauvais coucheur. Il tire toute la couverture à lui.*" This estimate, which does such injustice to our unaggressive national disposition, is, as we have recently had occasion to learn, widely spread among the nations of the earth. In South Africa, Siam, and Venezuela, Germans, French, and Americans all join in the refrain, " The Englishman is a bad bedfellow. He pulls all the clothes over himself."

From Archibald Forbes

1, Clarence Terrace, Regent's Park, N.W.
December 26, 1895.

My dear Lucy,

I am reading with great interest and entertainment your diary of the Salisbury Parliament. The humour, the light, graceful badinage, the intuitive characterisation, which are so delightful, flow in an unbroken, sparkling stream.

You, writing in 1890, speak of Disraeli's Manchester speech at which he got drunk (I had understood on port wine) [1] as having occurred "more than twenty years ago." This is an error; it was in 1873. I remember, because at the beginning of the agricultural labourers' strike in that year I was at Wellesbourne, inventing Joseph Arch, and describing the situation of the clods. I had boarded myself with a labourer's widow, to ascertain what in truth were the rations of a labourer's family, and had written of the experience. Toward the close of Dizzy's speech he, maundering *de omnibus rebus et quibusdam aliis*, spoke of me as "devouring the substance of the widow and the fatherless." He was not himself, else he would not have

---

[1] In his " Life of Benjamin Disraeli," Mr. Buckle says the beverage was "two bottles of white brandy, which he drunk in doses of ever-increasing strength till he had consumed the whole ! "

added, as he did, " I can speak for at least the agricultural
labourer of Bucks as being in a very comfortable and
prosperous state."

I read the speech on the following morning on my
way from Warwickshire to attend a meeting of Cam-
bridgeshire labourers on strike.   Instead, I cut across
country to High Wycombe, and wrote an article on
" The Agricultural Labourer of Hughenden," which made
rather a stir.   The labouring folk about Hughenden I
found in a deplorable state.   Some years previously
Dizzy had pronounced an encomium at the agricultural
show on an ancient labourer who had spent his life on
one farm, handed him the money prize, and pinned
a rosette on his breast as if he were one of the show
bullocks ; predicting also that in course of time he would
die honoured and respected by all the community.   This
ancient worthy I found in the local workhouse ; he
produced the rosette, and his prayer was that for the
love of God I should give him a " bit of bacca."   You may
remember my article in the *D.N.*

Yours always,

ARCH. FORBES.

CHAPTER VI

May 13, 1896.

THE sudden death of Colonel North has removed a notable figure from various circles of English life. The Colonel was as well known on the turf as in the city. He had the inborn Yorkshire love of a horse, and was no mean judge of its points. Once or twice I caught a peep of him in the bustling life he lived at his office in Gracechurch Street, with convenient contiguity to the Woolpack restaurant. What struck me when I saw him there, drinking whisky and water with relays of fresh-comers before luncheon, was the apparent impossibility of his doing any work. But the Colonel's big, green-gooseberry eyes saw far, and with unvarying accuracy. He knew what he was about at all hours of the day. What he chiefly enjoyed was playing the rôle of the country squire down at Eltham.

Eight days before his sudden cutting off I went down to Eltham to luncheon. The Colonel took me all over the place, the garden, the stables, and the farmyard, where he had some massive bulls and prize shorthorns. He was dressed in what I fancy he regarded as the best style of a country gentleman—light trousers and coat, with white waistcoat and a flowered silk necktie. In further keeping with the character he carried an umbrella, though a cloudless sunlit sky hung over Avery Hill. On the night before he had banqueted three hundred and fifty railway servants, members of a provident association of which he was president. The feast was spread in the picture gallery, and the Colonel glanced with pleased satisfaction on the immense collection of empty champagne bottles, testifying to the rare enjoyment of his guests. He

6

was specially proud of the fact that all the meats supplied at the feast had been bred, fed, and killed on the estate.

He did everything for himself, including the making of the electric light lavishly burned all over the house. £180,000 the place cost him in building. A well-known house furnisher contracted to do certain work for £3,000. " I didn't get him out of the house under £12,000," said the Colonel, not without a twinkle of satisfaction at having managed so cheaply. £120 a week was the aggregate of wages paid in this domestic establishment.

The Colonel's taste in pictures, which lined all the walls of a really fine gallery, would not satisfy some standards. The best thing in the way of decoration was a sideboard in the dining-room, containing, under glass, trophies of the Colonel's success on the racecourse, whether with horses or greyhounds. He also had a rare, perhaps unique, collection of relics dug out of the nitrate fields of Chili. On his last visit to South America he brought home with him two ghastly trophies in the shape of blackened mummies. Buried a thousand years ago in the nitrate grounds, they still preserved a ghastly semblance to humanity.

It is pleasant to find in the obituary notices that crowd the newspapers how universal is the tribute to the Colonel's goodness of heart and uprightness of dealing. His manners had not that repose which stamps the caste of Vere de Vere. But they were the rugged covering of a kind heart. His prosperity did not spoil the born simplicity of his character. He was on visiting terms with the King of the Belgians and the Prince of Wales, but was not therefore puffed up. He was hail-fellow-well-met with cabman or costermonger, and never turned a deaf ear to a story of genuine distress.

A couple of months ago I chanced to sit next to North at a dinner given by Sir John Pender in connection with his cable works. It turned out to be the costliest meal I ever ate. In the course of conversation the Nitrate

King spoke of a new business he had on hand in Chili. He had purchased a hitherto unworked tract of nitrate ground which promised to exceed former acquisitions that made him a semi-millionaire, and gave him the genuine pleasure of enriching his friends, some of them ranking in highest estate. The affair had not yet gone beyond the stage of the syndicate. A favoured group had been permitted to subscribe a limited number of £10 shares, the aggregate providing funds for preliminary expenses, including a deposit on purchase money of the land. In due course the property would be offered to the public at an adequate price, the proceeds being divided among the members of the syndicate. The company was happily named in advance Buena Ventura. What the city thought of the venture appeared from the circumstance that the market price of the original £10 shares divided among the syndicate was not less than £230 each.

North intimated that I would do well to possess myself of some of this treasure-trove. I told him that my money was hardly earned by the exercise of my pen, and that I could not afford to dabble in speculation. " You are quite right," he said. " But I should like to do you a good turn. If you care to buy some of these syndicate shares, I will take them off your hands at the price you pay if at any time you do not care to hold them."

This was good enough for the least venturesome. If the thing went well I should make a few hundred pounds. If it failed I should lose nothing. Accordingly, I bought five £10 shares for which I paid £1,150, with an additional £11, the brokers' charges. Weeks passed and I heard nothing of the development of my Buena Ventura. North had more than once invited me to pay him a visit at his country house at Eltham. Growing a little uneasy about my £1,161—a sum that represented a good many special articles in newspapers and magazines—I bethought

me I would run down one Sunday to have a chat with
the Colonel.

This was the visit referred to above. My definite
intention was to ask North to set down in writing the
generous terms of his personal undertaking which
induced me to buy the nitrate shares. I have no doubt
that had I done so, he would have complied with the
request. But he was so heartily genial in his welcome,
so sanguine of ultimate success of the venture, that I
felt it would be unworthy of a guest to hint at distrust
by asking for a formal pledge of indemnity. So I said
nothing about it.

This was on a Sunday. On opening the paper on the
morning of the Tuesday week following I read that on the
preceding day Colonel North, smitten by a fatal stroke,
had died. I bore him no resentment and cherish none
for his memory. I am certain that in this transaction he
had no other desire or intention than that of benefiting
me. All the same, my sole possession in the phantom
nitrate field of the Buena Ventura (somewhere in Chili)
is a document certifying that I am holder of five £10 shares
in the syndicate of that name, for which I paid £1,161.

May 20.

There is a tradition in London Society of the existence
of a Servants' Club, where high life downstairs meets
at regular intervals, and apes the airs of Boodles and
of Whites. It is all quite true, for I—*moi qui parle*—
have been privileged to sit for awhile within the charmed
circle. How I was inducted is a secret not wholly
mine. The visit was arranged under the most favourable
circumstances, and I was the object of much polite
attention, under the impression, somehow conveyed,
that I was a member of the establishment of an eminent
turf personage, and that I knew a good deal about the
probabilities of the St. Leger. This led to my being
talked to by the Duke, and even smoking a cigar at his
expense. In private life the Duke is the butler of an

illustrious personage.   At our Club, in common with other
representatives of the nobility, he is simply " the Duke,"
as others are the Marquis, Lord This, and Lord That.

The Duke did not speak to everybody in the room,
which made the more pleasing the attention paid to
me. " Have a smoke ? " he said.   " Thank you," I
replied, having a pleasing anticipation of sampling one
of the ducal special brand.   But, whatever may be
the domestic custom in this respect, at our Club we
don't produce our (so-called) masters' cigars, but pay
for our own.   Calling up the obsequious attendant, the
Duke ordered a cigar.   " A threepenny ? " asked the man.
The Duke frowned.   " You know," he said, in
tones wherein indignation was smothered in reproach,
" that I always smoke a fourpenny."

So I had a fourpenny and a tankard of beer.   Beer
was the principal drink.   Champagne, Château Lafitte,
Steinberg, and such like, we could get at home on nights
of frequent dinner parties.   They are liquors apt to pall
on the fastidious taste.   Accordingly we had beer,
even 'arf and 'arf.   We were a merry company, noisily
appreciative of each other's jokes, always with an eye on
the Duke to see how he was taking the fun.

I confess that the fine bloom of the wit and humour
displayed disappears on reflection, leaving only the husks
of personal pointless chaff.

June 11.

Grand Night at the Inner Temple.   In addition to
judges and eminent Q.C.'s belonging to other Inns,
there were among the guests men of such diverse careers
as the Archbishop of York, Lord Cranbrook, long known
in the Commons as Gathorne Hardy, Sir Henry Fowler,
and Alma Tadema.   I have not seen Lord Cranbrook
at close quarters for some time, and was struck with
his marvellous vitality.   According to authorised records,
he was born in the year before Waterloo, and two years
ago passed the border line of fourscore, after which

a man's strength is but labour and sorrow. To all appearance his age might be guessed at sixty. Immediately opposite him at dinner sat Frederick Bramwell, a youth four years his junior. He also is a marvellous man for his years. His face, more particularly the lines about his mouth, bear a strong resemblance to that older and nobler Roman than them all—Mr. Gladstone. But his years are clearly written upon his face, crowned as it is with a wealth of snow-white hair. Lord Cranbrook is just unobtrusively grey-haired.

A judge next to whom I sat at dinner, a chicken of seventy, confessed he was "old enough to remember how young Gathorne Hardy used to be talked of as a coming man in political life." That was probably half a century ago, some time before he took his seat as Member for Leominster. The promise was abundantly fulfilled, the young Yorkshireman pressing forward through various stages of a ministerial career till he reached the Cabinet and a Peerage. He was, in his time, the most popular and the most thoroughly trusted spokesman of the Conservative party in the House of Commons. What the country gentleman thought Gathorne Hardy said, with a fluency and a breathless vigour that gratified the country gentleman with conviction of his own debating force.

Happily, there is no speechmaking on Grand Nights at the Inns of Court. Formerly the dinner was held at six o'clock, an hour to this day observed in the case of the students. Under strong pressure, the conservatism of the Bench was moved to the extent of postponing the hour till seven. The Benchers and their guests assemble in an ante-room of the dining-hall. When dinner is announced they are told off two and two, as if they were entering the ark—a Bencher and a guest. At the door stands the butler, whom, and whose predecessors through the ages since the Inn was established, Providence gifts with stentorian voice. This he uplifts in announcing the successive Bencher and guest as they emerge from the ante-room. Meanwhile the students and the barristers, dining at the tables below the daïs where the Benchers sit at meat, remain standing to greet the procession. After dinner Benchers and guests retire to a room upstairs, where is spread a mahogany table upon whose glossy surface is reflected, as in a mirror, the decanters, glasses, and dishes with which it is covered. There is only one toast—"The Queen." It is loyally drunk upstanding. After dessert another move is made to the Library, a stately labyrinth of bookshelves, where coffee and cigars are served.

The Inner Temple Hall, where dinners are spread, is a handsome structure, but does not date further back than 1870. The Old Hall, on whose site it stands, was built in the time of James I. There took place the last revel of the Inns of Court. Of the ancient style there is still preserved the silver that graced the table in Stuart days. One of the Benchers told me that a little more than fifty years ago, when he was a student, it was the custom on Grand Nights to send round the loving-cup filled with sack. Having gone the round of the Benchers' table it was passed, in custody of the butler, down to the tables flanking the wall on the right where the students sit. According to immemorial usage, each student was restricted to "a sip" of the delectable contents of the cup. A sip is, of course, not a quantity recognised in imperial standards of measure. Thus it came to pass that on one Grand Night, there being less than seventy students present, thirty-six quarts of sack were disposed of!

July 22.

"I am delighted with Charles's precocity," Charles Dickens wrote when his eldest boy was five years old. "He takes arter his father, 'e does." Dying yesterday in his fifty-ninth year, it must be admitted that Charles

Dickens the younger used up in the precocity of his childhood all his stock of the qualities that go to make a successful career.

Of the great novelist's considerable family, born and nurtured under advantageous circumstances far remote from his own pitiful boyhood, there are only two who have done anything to establish the principle of the heredity of genius. In both cases its development was wide apart from that which blazed in the case of their illustrious father. Dickens's daughter, Mrs. Perugini, is a clever and successful artist. A younger son, Henry Fielding Dickens, is on his way to achieve a foremost position at the Bar.

As for the eldest son, Charles, he struggled through life with the cheery hopefulness, and not much fuller measure of the success, of Wilkins Micawber. The last time I heard from him was a letter he addressed to me in his capacity as so-called literary adviser, really secretary, of George Alexander. A humble position for one who signed the name at foot of the note.

July 24.

Yesterday Henry Irving's son was married to Miss Baird, who made her fame on the stage by creating the part of *Trilby* in the play dramatised from Du Maurier's novel. Delighted to read in one of the morning papers giving an account of the ceremony how the officiating clergyman "addressed the congregation at considerable length." "At the conclusion of the address," notes the unconscious humorist who supplies the account, "the beautiful and stirring ' Now thank we all our God ! ' was sung."

That seems a little hard on the well-meaning parson ; but it was a very hot day.

July 30

During the last two years Queen Victoria, for more than half a century a marvel of sustained health, has greatly altered in appearance. With the aid of a stick she walks with difficulty, and, when the Prince of Wales is at hand, gratefully accepts his proffered arm. Wherever her residence may temporarily be fixed a lift becomes a necessity, it being practically impossible for her to mount a staircase. It is this infirmity which finally made it impossible for Her Majesty to open Parliament in person when the whirligig of time again brought round the advent of a Conservative Ministry. It has been a main source of the personal happiness and prosperity of the Queen's long reign that she has never (or hardly ever) displayed political predilection. But she has a right to control her personal action in minor matters, and if since 1876, when Disraeli was firmly established in power, she intermitted her long absence from the parliamentary scene, and reserved repetition of her visit for Conservative auspices, no one has the right to complain. But she cannot now manage the few stairs that lead on to the level of the Throne Room, and will never more be seen in the Chamber of the Lords.

Happily, this failing, and the general appearance of decrepitude it lends to the Queen's coming and going, is due to local weakness. She suffers from rheumatism, which attacks her in the knees and makes walking a burden. Otherwise, she is in a condition of good health almost miraculous for her age. Lord Rowton tells me that having occasion for a long interview on her return from the Riviera, he was amazed at her vigour, both physical and mental.

"As far as I can judge," he said, "there is no reason why the Queen should not fulfil all the functions of her high position for another dozen years."

As this would bring her age up to eighty-nine, the forecast seems sanguine. It is made deliberately by one having the fullest opportunities of observation and the most direct of information.

Whilst such a career would beat the record of crowned

heads, it creates a quite unique position for the Prince of Wales. There is no parallel in English history to the case where the Heir Apparent has been so long kept out of his heritage. That is not a matter upon which H.R.H. is to be effusively condoled. In the position he has so long adorned he has had all the advantages of Royalty without its attendant cares and responsibilities.

August 5.

Just before Li Hung Chang, Viceroy of China and Special Emissary to this country, left London on a tour through the big provincial towns, I met him at a small luncheon party at the Mansion House. I had the good fortune to be seated immediately opposite him at table, a position favourable for observing his face and manners. During the meal, not a moment being lost by him in animated conversation and in keen observation of matters brought under his notice, I did not hear him laugh or see him smile. But I should judge from his countenance that he has a keen sense of humour. His gold-rimmed spectacles lent to his face a benevolent aspect, which some of the rebels whom, he told the Duke of Devonshire seated at his right hand, he shot in place of grouse, had reason to discover was not an indication of permanent mood. His interpreter, Lo Fing Loh, who spoke admirable English, differed from his master in this respect, since he was always ready to break into a merry laugh.

The Viceroy did not eat any of the rich foods provided, nor drink any of the costly wines, save a little claret. He was attended by his own cooks, who in some back premises prepared his mid-day meal. I do not know what the dishes consisted of. They were almost interminable in number, looked nice, smelt savoury, and gave His Excellency undisguised satisfaction. Once he had four dishes before him at the same moment, all smoking hot. Holding his ivory-topped, silver-handled chopsticks lightly in his right hand, he fished about indiscriminately among them, fetching out all manner of delicacies.

For a European they would, perhaps, not have been appetising. What made the mouth water were the dainty little China basins in which the food was served. When the Viceroy had made final choice of a dish, he held it under his chin with his left hand, and with great dexterity pitchforked the contents into his mouth with the chopsticks. This method of feeding himself made it convenient for him to eye with curious intentness a plate of large French asparagus just served to his neighbour. I don't know whether the attraction was one merely of curiosity, or of desire. But the Viceroy, placidly feeding himself, could not take his eyes off the asparagus. I expected every moment he would, in accordance with invariable practice when anyone was presented to him, ask how old they were. In my case he added the further inquiry, " How much a year do you earn ? "

Lunch was served at the unusual hour of noon, in order to meet the convenience of the Viceroy, departing elsewhere by a special train timed to leave at ten minutes past one. When the hour struck, and the guests were seated, Li Hung Chang was nowhere to be found. After anxious search he was discovered fast asleep in one of the retiring-rooms. His arrival at the table thus delayed, subsequent proceedings were somewhat hurried. Nothing less than an earthquake could hasten the movements of this interesting old gentleman. Lo Fing Loh was in a state of considerable uneasiness as the hour arrived for the departure of the train. He was the proud possessor of a turnip-shaped watch of an area somewhat less than the Island of Korea. It was to be got out of his pocket only by a process of hauling and tugging that would have sufficed to tow a barge. Li, quietly continuing to stoke himself with the assistance of the chopsticks, turned his oval eyes in the direction of his struggling interpreter, who finally succeeded in hauling out the watch. His serenity was not disturbed in the slightest degree. He meant to finish his meal, whether the line were blocked for his special train or whether it were not. His health being proposed, he rose and genially drank it with the rest of us. He stood up when the Queen's health was proposed, but declined to fall in with the example set by the host and others of standing whilst the band played the National Anthem. To do him justice, he followed exactly the same course when the health of his Imperial master was proposed.

When he had finished luncheon one of his servants approached from behind, took away his serviette, dived into one of his pockets, and produced Li's cap, which he placed on the old gentleman's head. The host was getting restless. There were signs on the part of Lo Fing Loh of intent to haul out the warming-pan watch again. So, with a sigh, the Viceroy rose, and bowing to the company, who stood up to bid him farewell, he turned and toddled after the host. The last thing I saw of him was a back view of his white and red-booted legs dangling below the chair which four pallid, perspiring commissionaires carried.

Much has been written in contemporary reports of the Viceroy's habit of continuous smoking. The process, observed preliminary to the meal and the doze, was a remarkable one, a ceremony to be performed only by a man of large leisure, the master of many servants. The pipe itself was a contrivance the like of which most of those present had never before seen on sea or land. Apparently made of metal, it had a stem about half the length of the ordinary British " churchwarden." The Viceroy being seated dictating some telegrams, made a sign with his right hand. Straightway a fat-faced Chinaman stepped from behind, and placed the mouth-piece of the pipe between Li's lips. The servitor held

the pipe with one hand, and with the other applied a
lighted taper to a tube about an inch and a half long,
projecting from where, with an English pipe, would
be found the bowl. The Viceroy puffed three whiffs
in his supremely leisurely fashion. The fat-faced man
withdrew the pipe from his master's lips, took out the
funnel, and blew through the stem, a wreath of smoke
issuing. Then from where the bowl of the pipe should
have been he took a pinch of tobacco, filled up the tube,
replaced it in the pipe, and approached the pipe towards
his master's mouth. The lips slowly opened, closed over
the pipe, three more whiffs, and the process of refilling
was gone through as before. A few steps beyond the
fat-faced man was another Chinese, not quite so fat in the
face, who held a supply of tapers. These were in themselves a curiosity. The flame died out when the pipe
was lit. When the attendant, puffing out the fatness
of his cheeks an inch or two more than their abnormal
condition, blew on the taper, the light burst forth again.

On his return from his trip to Provincial centres of
population and prosperity, where I fancy few useful
points escaped observation, I had the good fortune to
meet the Viceroy again. It was at a luncheon given
in his honour at the works of a great electric cable manu-
factory at the East-end of London. The happy thought
occurred to the chairman of the company to invite
the illustrious guest to use their cables for dispatch
of a message home. Li Hung Chang accepted the
offer with alacrity. Seating himself at a table he dictated to the inseparable Lo Fing Loh a dispatch which,
translated and paid for at the current charges of the
company, would have cost at least £50. It was pretty
to watch the countenance of the chairman as what was
expected to be a brief greeting lengthened out on this
scale. But the heathen Chinee does not habitually get
his cable messages sent gratuitously, and Li Hung Chang
was not the man to miss a chance opportunity.

August 15.

There has been something pathetic in the dumb tragedy long fought out by the bedside of Sir John Millais. The case was, from the first, hopeless. No one understood this more fully than the patient himself. Often in his written communications with his old friends and colleagues who called to see him he expressed the " wish that they would let me die." It was, of course, the duty of the doctors to keep alight as long as possible the feeble spark of life. They were kind only to be cruel. The single gleam of comfort in the case is that he suffered little pain. But it has been a sad, slow ending, and those who loved him most may secretly have wished that the thread had been snapped on the night, now some months past, when there was performed the surgical operation that left him such an unconscionable time dying.

When the surgeon was called in at the crisis, it was so nearly over with the President of the R.A. that delay of five minutes would have been fatal. It was one o'clock in the morning when he was called, and found the house, save in the sick-room, lapped in sleep and darkness. There was not time to use chloroform, or even to obtain proper light. The delicate operation of tracheotomy was successfully performed by the glimmer of an oil lamp, held in the trembling hand of the nurse. In such circumstances Millais was snatched back from the very jaws of death into a state of semi-existence, from which death has long been looked for as a happy respite.

He has much altered in appearance since his enforced retirement from public view. His beard is quite white, and so is his scanty hair, the falling away of which reveals in fuller view the extreme shapeliness of the head. He continues to take a keen interest in all that relates to the art world, and likes to hear from the lips of old friends what is passing behind the scenes. His share of the conversation is carried on by means of paper and pencil. Always a lovable man, he was prime favourite through his long career with fellow-workers. His patience through long suffering, with the shadow of death hovering darkly over him, endears him still more. Those who have recently seen and talked with him speak of him with faltering voice and eyes dimmed by tears.

August 18.

Back in town, having been over the seas to Skye. Had the good fortune to be included among Sir Donald Currie's guests in the first cruise of the new Castle liner. Amongst many interesting episodes of the too short voyage, what I liked best was the visit to Dunvegan Castle, the ancient pile from which the new ship borrows her name. The Castle has been the home of the McLeods for centuries. Rory More McLeod, a famous knight in the retinue of James VI of Scotland, added something to the ancient pile commenced in the ninth century. In the dining-room there is a portrait of him, a disappointingly inoffensive person, with nothing aggressive about him save the colours of his tartan.

There still stands on the mantelpiece Rory More's drinking-cup, a cow's horn warranted to hold three quarts. When a new chief came of age this was filled with claret, and the heir to the chieftainship had to attest his manhood by drinking it right off. This and kindred habits probably account for the melancholy fact that at the time of our visit we found that the McLeod of these degenerate days—the twenty-fifth chief in lineal descent—had let his castle "for the summer season," and was living in a lodge on the far-reaching estate.

In his tour through the Hebrides, Dr. Johnson visited Skye, and stayed for a week a guest at Dunvegan Castle. Boswell was of course with him, and tells all about it in his journal of a tour in the Hebrides. "I was elated," writes Boswell, "at the thought of being able to entice such a man to this remote part of the world. In London, Reynolds, Beauclerk, and all of them are contending who shall enjoy Dr. Johnson's conversation. We are feasting upon it undisturbed at Dunvegan." To this day Dr. Johnson's portrait looks down from the mantelpiece of the dining-room at Dunvegan, and a letter from him to his host is religiously preserved.

Among Sir Donald Currie's guests on the *Dunvegan Castle* was Lord Kelvin. Born seventy-two years ago, at work in Glasgow University at the age of eleven, he still does a well-ordered day's task with a zest and energy not excelled by Gladstone. He should be particularly at home on board a big steamer, since, wherever he turns in connection with the finest mechanism in use, he will find his name emblazoned. On the ship's binnacle his more familiar style, Sir William Thompson, is printed large, and underneath, in brackets, Lord Kelvin.

At the moment I came across him he was standing with the captain and first officer right astern, watching the operation of his contrivance for ascertaining the depth of water whilst the steamer is proceeding at full speed. Before this remarkable invention was evolved out of his fertile brain, it was necessary, preliminary to heaving the lead, to stop the steamer, a process which, often repeated, as is necessary in approaching land, appreciably added to the length of a voyage. With Lord Kelvin's new depth-finder—a simple-looking portable apparatus—the exact position of the ship in respect of depth of water can be ascertained with unerring accuracy whilst a ship is going (as we were at this particular juncture) sixteen knots or more. Since he invented the instrument Lord Kelvin has introduced many improvements. Even now, as with keen eyes and gravely kind face he looked on whilst the wire to which the depth-finder was attached rapidly paid out, he discerned something fresh, of which those who go down to the sea in ships may presently hear.

CHAPTER VII

IRISH members belonging to the old parliamentary guard marshalled under the captaincy of Parnell and the lieutenancy of Mr. Biggar, are naturally chary of assumption of knowledge of the secrets of the Fenian brotherhood. I find, however, common to one or two with whom I have spoken, a conviction that Tynan is not the terrible " No. 1 " who loomed grimly over the tragedy of the Phœnix Park murders. They believe that Tynan's connection with the murder and the general conspiracy that led up to it was nothing more important than that of letter-carrier. His business as commercial traveller made it easy for him to pass from place to place without exciting suspicion in the breast of the watchful police, and he was thus used to maintain communications between the various sections of the gang. " No. 1," these authorities say, was not an individual, but a title, assumed in succession by various leaders of the confederation. Moreover, they affirm that Scotland Yard is not deceived on this point, as it has known all along precisely what part Tynan played in the business, and has held him cheaply accordingly.

This assertion of accurate information of everything connected with the Phœnix Park murder possessed by the police authorities is confirmed by a remarkable statement made to me by a high authority when, three years ago, I was staying at the Viceregal Lodge, Dublin. He told me that before noon on the day following the murder, whilst the world was dumbfounded by the total disappearance of the men who had done to death Lord

Frederick Cavendish and Mr. Burke, the heads of the Dublin police knew the name of every man engaged in the crime, and had already begun to weave the net that finally brought into the dock Joe Brady, Curley, Fagan, Kelly, Councillor Kearley, and the rest.

October 6.

Since I have enjoyed the privilege of a seat at the *Punch* dinner-table — now alack ! fifteen years — death has been busy among the small band that gather every Wednesday night round what Thackeray called the "mahogany tree." At fullest muster, as shown in Linley Sambourne's sketch of the dinner-table published in the Jubilee number, we are but fourteen. Out of that number, within the time I speak of, five have passed into the Silent Land ; for them " all winds are quiet as the sun, all water as the shore." Even since we banqueted on Jubilee Day, 1891, there are three empty chairs.

The first to go was the Professor, the name by which the old man was so habitually addressed and spoken of that we almost forgot he was known elsewhere as Percival Leigh. He was one of the earliest of the literary staff of *Punch*, his " Mr. Pipp's Diary " having appeared in 1849. It was he who introduced John Leech to *Mr. Punch*. The Professor died in the autumn of 1889, and less than two years after was followed by Charles Keene. Then dear, gentle Gil. A'Beckett died. William Bradbury went next, and now a big gap is made at the familiar board by the cutting off of Du Maurier.

At the table each man has his ordered place, and through the revolving years sits in it whenever he attends the dinner, taking an identical position even when, as sometimes happens, *Mr. Punch* carries his young men off to dine up the river or in the country. It is a gruesome reflection that, in prowling round the table, Death has persistently poked his skinny finger round my chair. For years Charles Keene sat next to me on the right, and next to him the Professor, whilst Gil. A'Beckett was my companion on the left. Now only their shades and their memories keep us company.

When I first joined the table Du Maurier was one of the most constant attendants at the Wednesday dinner. As he then, and within two years of his death, lived at Hampstead Heath, the pleasure of the occasion was rather heavily paid for. As the *Punch* dinner is served at seven o'clock, it is not necessarily or usually a late hour when the company breaks up. But it is a far cry to Hampstead, and cabmen engaged in Fleet Street, anxious for a two-shilling short fare, do not care to face the long drive. When Du Maurier came to live in Oxford Square, it was with the avowed intention of more frequently joining the dinner. Unfortunately for us, he never carried out the design. Soon after he settled down in his new home came the *Trilby* boom, which, I strongly suspect, had something to do with shortening his life. Before he flashed like a rocket across the literary horizon, he plodded steadily along, doing his weekly work for *Punch*, at one time supplying a monthly picture for *Harper's*, and occasionally illustrating books. *Trilby* brought a whirlwind into his life at a time when he was past its full vigour.

Success such as comes to perhaps only one man in a generation had not the slightest effect in the direction of turning his head. When both the New World and the Old were ringing with praise of *Trilby*, whilst the Haymarket was blocked with a crowd patiently waiting for chance to gain admission to the theatre where it had been placed on the stage, the author was, in his relations with his family and friends, precisely the same simple-mannered, delightful companion as before (as he said) he "struck ile." Nevertheless, there was a palpable change in him, possibly the result of fading health. He felt that success had come too late, and was apt to fall into unwonted moods of depression. He was, he said, "Soured by Success," and was so charmed with the phrase that he laughingly undertook to write a novel up to the title. There was in truth no sourness in his sunny nature. But he was growing very tired.

I never heard him complain of the effects of a lecturing tour he was induced to undertake some three or four years ago. It was a hard grind, coming on top of his other work. He permitted himself no luxuries, travelling, he told me, third-class, and putting up at second-rate hotels. For many years he earned a handsome income. But he was a family man, and his position in the social and artistic world necessitated the keeping up of an establishment that involved considerable outlay. *Trilby* put that all right, making him rich beyond the dreams of an artist in black and white.

" Too late, too late," he murmured. The first news of his serious illness appeared in the newspapers contemporaneously with bold announcement in the advertisement columns that so great had been the rush for the number of *Harper's* containing the opening chapters of his new novel (*The Martian*), that on the day after publication a second edition was made necessary. Du Maurier did not think much of *Trilby*. To his mind, his first book, *Peter Ibbetson*, was a greater work. Greater still in his estimation was *The Martian*. He felt he must work up to the point of expectation created by the enormous success of *Trilby*. He set himself to the work conscientiously, laboriously, and died believing he had succeeded.

His method of composition was peculiar, being necessitated by the state of his eyesight. He wrote with pencil, on paper held on his knee, wrote rapidly without attempt to follow with dim sight the formation of words or sentences. Afterwards his wife or one of his daughters copied out for the press the blurred manuscript. One of his vain regrets was that he had hit upon what he was inclined to regard as his real calling too late to use up the abundance of plots and fancies with which his mind was stored. Early in the year, when he was approaching the completion of *The Martian*, he told me he had in his mind the plot of a fourth novel.

October 8.

Du Maurier's friends still lament his death. But sorrow is to some extent soothed by thought of what he would have suffered had he lived to witness the reception of his last novel. He often talked to me about *The Martian* whilst it was yet in unfinished state, and did not conceal his conviction that it was by far the best thing he had ever done, eclipsing *Peter Ibbetson*, and dimming the glory of *Trilby*. Critics have dealt gently with it. But no one can conceal or mitigate the totality of its failure to interest. It is fortunate for the publishers that they had receipts on *Trilby* to average against their takings for *The Martian*. Contemplation of the situation is, from their point of view, made the more saddening from consideration of the fact that whilst they bought *Trilby* for £1,000, they gave £10,000 for *The Martian*.

October 9.

Reference in a magazine article recording a conversation with Gladstone, in which he spoke of Cromwell with almost vehement dislike, brought a shrewd and striking commentary from Lord Rathmore. Writing from The Oaks, Wimbledon, he says: " Your tale about the G.O.M. and Cromwell is characteristic of the constant conflict in the mind of the former between the Toryism which to the last, I think, he really *loved*, and the Liberalism which his reason and his interests dictated to him."

October 10.

For many sessions there was no figure more familiar in the Lobby of the House of Commons than that of Lord Kensington. In Opposition through the Parliament of 1874, in office from 1880 to 1885, he acted as Whip. His first chief was Mr. Adam, his second Lord Richard

Grosvenor. But for the fact that he lost his seat at the General Election of 1885 he would certainly have been Chief Whip in 1886, when Grosvenor severed himself from the Liberal party on the question of Home Rule. Born to an Irish peerage, Gladstone made him a Baron of the United Kingdom. Having for many years acted with Richard Grosvenor in " telling " the Liberals in the House of Commons, he in the House of Lords nullified by his vote the action of his old colleague, now Lord Stalbridge.

Kensington was not exactly popular as a Whip. In his eyes, for a Member to be absent unpaired was an unpardonable sin. At the approach of the dinner-hour, and after Members had returned from their meal, he was always found on guard by the door giving exit from the Lobby. In the long sittings which marked the 1880–1885 Parliament he, towards midnight, assumed an attitude of repose on the comfortless bench assigned at the doorway to the use of the Whips. If any supporter of the Government thought he might, by taking pains, add an hour or two to his night's repose by passing the Whip unobserved, he was speedily undeceived. At the very moment when, walking softly, he approached the door, and in another moment would have passed the portal, Kensington, waking out of what seemed profound sleep, was on his feet, with his hand on the deserter's shoulder, prepared, if need were, to drag him back by the collar.

Physical force was in these circumstances never necessary. The glare of Kensington's eyes, his opening remarks, were sufficient. " Where are you going ? " roared the farmer, with a thick whip in his hand, coming upon a small boy who had crawled half-way through the hedge into his orchard. " I am going bak agen," said the boy, rapidly suiting the action to the word. Members thinking of the comforts of home as compared with the House of Commons at midnight, and setting forth to enjoy them, always went " bak agen " if caught at the doorway by Lord Kensington.

October 17.

Lord Rosebery's letter addressed to the Liberal Whip announcing his retirement from leadership of the party, has created profound sensation. Talking to me at the time of the fall of the Ministry last year, he said : " There are two supreme pleasures in life. One is ideal, the other real. The ideal is when a man receives the seals of office from the hands of his Sovereign. The real pleasure comes when he hands them back." It is probable that there are few happier men in Great Britain to-day than Lord Rosebery, freed at last from a position in which he had not even the consolation of what are called the sweets of office. The position he has filled with in- creasing prominence during the past few months has been that of an effigy elevated at convenient height for passers-by to shy stones at. He is still a young man, and his years of ministerial life—beginning, oddly enough, as subaltern to Sir William Harcourt at the Home Office— do not go further back than fifteen years. Yet in that time he has learned how much sharper than a serpent's tooth is political ingratitude.

Before he accepted the Premiership there was no man, not even Gladstone, of wider popularity amongst Liberals. When in 1886 the Thanes fled from the veteran statesman, Lord Rosebery stood faithful by his side. His acceptance of the Foreign Secretaryship in January 1886 was at the time regarded as a matter of the primest importance as affecting the cause of Home Rule and the fortunes of Gladstone's Ministry. He was at the time ill in health and indisposed to take upon himself the burden of office. But he saw his old Leader deserted by former colleagues. He watched the Liberal party staggering under a blow that threatened—and presently fulfilled the promise— to efface it. Setting aside all personal predilections he stepped forward to share the falling fortunes of the Liberal party and their dauntless Leader.

When in 1892 Gladstone came back with his frail

majority of forty, it again became the question of the day whether Lord Rosebery would accept office. He was at the time suffering from the affliction of insomnia, one of the deadliest ills to which human flesh is heir. He would have preferred to stay outside the Cabinet circle, and try to get some sleep. Again he sacrificed his convenience and personal desires to a sense of public duty. His return to the Foreign Office was greeted with acclaim, in which the Conservatives joined with even suspicious enthusiasm. All this inevitably led to the Premiership, and with it began the first troubles of a hitherto prosperous public life.

The new Premier was beset by two misfortunes entirely beyond his control, a combination that inevitably proved fatal. In the first place, he was promoted over the head of a veteran general of the Liberal army, who was not constitutionally prone to acquiesce in effacement ; secondly, he was born a peer, and in the eyes of the militant section of the party that is a disqualification for the Premiership not to be overlooked even in the case of so genuine a Liberal, so able a Minister, so supreme a Parliament man, as Archibald Philip Primrose.

A third misfortune, minor in its character, was not without influence on the result. Labouchere convinced himself that it was the personal interposition of Lord Rosebery that prevented his being invited to serve in Gladstone's last Administration. There is not the slightest shade of foundation for this phantasy. Lord Rosebery never lifted a finger to prevent the fulfilment of Labouchere's desire. I believe that, so far as he expressed any opinion on the subject, he was favourable to the recognition of active services performed in opposition. He certainly, in no fashion, openly or covertly, played the part Labouchere's suspicious fancy attributed to him. The ban placed upon the fulfilment of Gladstone's friendly intention came from a more august authority.

Labouchere thought he knew better, and from the

commencement attacked the new Premier with a personal
rancour that would have defeated its own purpose save for
the ground skilfully chosen whence to direct the attack.
What Labouchere avowedly objected to was vesting the
premiership of the Liberal party in the hands of a Member
of the House of Lords. At a time when curtailment
of the power of veto of the Lords was a main plank
in the Liberal programme, it certainly was illogical
that a Member of the obnoxious body should be Leader
of the Liberal party. Encouraged by the knowledge
that he was supported by strong prejudice on the subject
in Radical quarters, Labouchere kept up the fusilade
weekly. Undoubtedly this continuous dropping of water
from the well of *Truth* had something to do with the
wearing away of the stone.

Lord Rosebery's action is a serious blow to the fortunes
of the Liberal party. It reveals under fiercest light
that lack of cohesion that has ever been its bane.
He will, by this time, have discovered that what he
describes as " a considerable mass of the Liberal party
who differ with him on the Eastern question " is
actually ludicrously small in point of numbers. But
it has been noisy, and the great mass of the party,
not realising the effect upon a sensitive mind of daily
peppering with venomous darts, have been too quiet.
" Scarcely from any quarter," Lord Rosebery writes,
" do I receive explicit support." It would have been
forthcoming with overwhelming force had there been
even suspicion of the probable effect on his mind of the
twittering of a comparatively insignificant few.

December 12.

The auctioneer has this week been in possession
of the Amphitryon Club, and has disposed of all " its
useful furniture and a small stock of excellent wine."
There is something pathetic about the smallness of the
stock of wine. Time is not far distant when the

Amphitryon was one of the marvels of London, the very cream of clubs. It was started under the highest auspices by a famous chef. The subscription was not particularly high, but the prices for wine, meat, and cigars made up the average. Champagne was not to be had under a sovereign a bottle, and vintage wines were much more. A spoonful of brandy, served in a liqueur glass, cost a shilling. Cigars ranged from that modest figure up to seven shillings and sixpence. The dining-room on the ground floor was studiously plain in its arrangements, more like a grill-room or even a kitchen than the dining-room of the wealthy *gourmets* of London. Upstairs was another room decorated so that it might live up to its name—the Louis Seize room.

I dined there one night early in the past season, one of an interesting party of ten. The host was Mr. Chaplin, one of the most familiar customers of the club, alike at luncheon or dinner. He had bestowed upon this feast more loving care than he had given even to the ministerial bill of which he was in charge in the House of Commons. Not approving the hock in the "small stock of excellent wine" which on Tuesday vanished amid the last glories of the Amphitryon, he sent some from his own cellar, also a bottle of cognac of the 1820 vintage. Apart from these contributions, I fancy, from what I have heard of charges in the room below, his dinner bill would amount to between £70 and £80, a touching proof of the prevalence of agricultural depression. That was cheap compared with the famous dinner given at this same club to Lord Randolph Churchill on the eve of his departure for South Africa, when for a much larger company the charge per cover was £10.

It seems strange that with these prices current, and a distinguished clientele, the Amphitryon could not be kept going. There were two reasons against its success as a commercial enterprise. In the first place, its opportunities were strictly limited by what is known as the London season. During its recess there was no call for luncheons, dinners or suppers. Meanwhile the rent ran on and the establishment had to be kept up, if not at its normal height. Another even more serious drawback was the difficulty on the part of the proprietor in obtaining payment from his noble customers. The Amphitryon, like all other clubs, was ostensibly founded on the ready-money principle. But amongst its members was a large proportion of bucks, old and young, who ordered and consumed the best of everything, and when they had finished walked out, nodding genially to the proprietor, with promise to pay him another day.

In other ranks of life that method of obtaining a meal is occasionally practised at coffee-houses and cheap restaurants, with the result of conducting the diner-out to the police court. But the hapless proprietor of the Amphitryon felt he could not afford to cross his noble patrons with strict rules about money down. So at the end of last season the Amphitryon closed its doors, and the passer-by has seen announcement of the now accomplished sale of its useful furniture and its small stock of excellent wine.

CHAPTER VIII

LORD ROSEBERY'S revenues from the racing field are swelled from a surer source than the betting ring. He owns the Paddock at Epsom—a much better thing than being owner of Ladas. The Paddock is an indispensable accessory to the racecourse. At Epsom there is no ground available except that pertaining to the Durdans estate. So for this little patch of ground Lord Rosebery draws a rental of £2,000 a year. He told me on the day after his triumph that his most miserable moments were spent whilst, preparatory to the race, his horse stood in the Paddock. In the stable, or at morning gallops, it was possible to protect a valuable life against deliberate and designed hurt. In the Paddock, with a crowd pressing almost to the heels of the horse, there would be no difficulty in a resolute villain, whose interests it might serve, furtively inflicting damage on the favourite, which, if it did not permanently render it worthless, would spoil its chances in the pending race.

March 12.

One minor personal effect of the inquiry into the Jameson Raid has been to bring about a reconciliation between Chamberlain and Labouchere. In his earlier parliamentary career Labouchere was one of Chamberlain's most intimate political friends, most valued of allies. During the Parliament of 1880-85 the Member for Birmingham, enjoying the confidences of Cabinet rank, kept touch with the Radical section of the party through confabulations with the Member for Northampton. When Gladstone's unfolding of the Home Rule flag led to

cataclysm in the Liberal party, Labouchere, promptly
breaking ancient bonds of friendship, turned and rent
his former companion. Week after week he devoted
pages of his animated journal to denouncing and, as
he put it, exposing the recreant course of the trans-
mogrified Radical. For years the parted friends never
spoke, ignoring each other's presence if they chanced
to be confronted in the Lobby of the House of Commons
or other semi-public resort.

Reconciliation commenced during the preliminaries
of the appointment of the South Africa Committee.
The proposal that Labby should be appointed, in a
judicial capacity, to deal with a case he had notoriously
prejudged was warmly opposed. Chamberlain, seeing
his opportunity of hooding a dangerous falcon, insisted
that if he wished to join the Committee he should have
a seat at its board. That settled the matter, and was
the beginning of the end of a bitter feud. Readers of
Truth will now look in vain for those venomous passages
about " Joe " which once seared its pages. It used to
be said that whilst unpaid magistrates took their turn
week by week in the pillory of *Truth*, Chamberlain always
stood in it. He has now descended from the eminence.
As a statesman and a politician he may be no worse
than he was, nor any better. Anyhow, Labouchere
has withdrawn his knife.

March 28.

Lady Hayter's party last night was a brilliant affair.
Although the House of Commons was sitting in further
consideration of the important question of the financial
relations of Ireland and Great Britain, a large contingent
of Members brought their wives and daughters. Some
years ago Lady Hayter was one of the few *grandes dames*
of the Liberal party. Two or three times in the parliamentary session her house in Grosvenor Square was
thrown open to a host of political guests. The Whips
on either side have the fullest confidence in the efficacy,

for party purposes, of such hospitality, and the Liberal team was grateful to one of the comparatively few London ladies who were able and willing to entertain. Lady Hayter's enthusiasm for the Liberal cause was justly chilled by the curious neglect with which her husband's claims to recognition were treated. When colonial governorships and even peerages were being given away to Liberal partisans, Sir Arthur Hayter was consistently overlooked.

In one particular case, arising in the last year of the Rosebery Administration, a colonial governorship for which Sir Arthur did not disguise his hankering was not only withheld, but was bestowed upon a Liberal-Unionist. Since then, up to this week, Lady Hayter has not been " at Home " at the corner house in Grosvenor Square. With last night's party it seemed as if she were about to resume her brilliant social campaign. But the festivity was a mere incident. Sir Arthur and Lady Hayter will return on Monday to the East of Europe to carry on their good work among the suffering Armenians.

March 30.

The Needlemakers' Company are not wealthy enough to dine together with the frequency that distinguishes some other city guilds. When, as last night, they make up their mind for a little festivity they do it exceedingly well. I do not speak of the excellence of the wines and viands, but of the company, which, numbering some of the best-known men in literature, art, and the drama, was distinguished far beyond the ordinary run of city dinners.

There was an unreported incident in connection with the Duke of Teck's chairmanship which hugely delighted the guests. It fell to the Duke's lot to propose the health of Her Majesty. He had prepared a little speech, almost devout in its loyalty, which he read with extreme unction. When he approached the last sentence he paused and drew breath, with intent to do it more justice in delivery. Unhappily, the company thought he had made an end of speaking, and broke into a cheer. That would have been remediable ; but the band in the gallery, taking the cue, boomed forth the strains of " God Save the Queen."

The almost reverential attitude of the Duke was changed in a moment to one of extremest rage. He shook his royal fist at the startled band, and shouted out, " Stop that ! " It was some moments before the bandmaster realised the mistake. When silence was restored the Duke delivered his final sentence. It was some time before his temper recovered its ordinary equanimity.

May 10.

Stage coaches and omnibuses, as seating congeries of humanity, ever had attraction for Gladstone. Dining last night with James Bryce he talked for ten minutes in charming reminiscence of London 'buses, of which he was one of the earliest patrons. The one he most frequently used travelled between Charing Cross and Hyde Park Corner. It was a two-horsed vehicle, moderate in speed, practically springless, and matted with wisps of straw.

" Whether you went part of the way or all the way," he added in that deep voice that marked profound emotion, " the fare was sixpence."

Here obtruded a touch of ineradicable nationality. Over a lapse of years, mountains in heights and oceans in depth of their interest, there lingered in his mind resentment of the enormity of this charge. As he spoke there crossed the mind vision of another Scotsman, with his immortal lament : " I had no been in London half an hour when bang went saxpence."

On one occasion, in the far-off time of his youth, Gladstone was perched on the box seat of a coach behind an old driver of bibulous appearance, with whom, to beguile the time, he began a conversation. The fare was young enough to be proud of a fine repeater carried in his fob. By way of interesting the driver, he showed it him, explaining its complicated mechanism. The driver took a more or less intelligent interest in the works. After a period of profound reflection he said :

"What I want to know is, how do you wind that watch when you're drunk ? "

May 15.

Lord Roberts among the booksellers was a pleasant sight to see. He dined with them last night at their annual dinner, and was made much of, as became a man whose book, " Forty-one Years in India," has reached its eighteenth edition. " Bobs " is prouder of this fact even than of his capture of Cabul or the relief of Kandahar. He was in the Lobby of the House of Commons at the end of last week, and I took the opportunity of congratulating him upon having run into a seventeenth edition with a book published at thirty-six shillings. " The eighteenth edition," he said, almost severely. The last time I had noticed it in the book lists it was in the sufficiently encouraging position of the seventeenth edition, and had, it seems, since moved one up.

Though naturally pleased with this success in a new field, Lord Roberts as an author is as modest as " Bobs " is unquestionably the greatest soldier of modern times. Anyone seeing Lord Wolseley in mufti would guess the soldier. To see Lord Roberts as he stood the other night in the crowded Lobby of the House of Commons— a little gentleman in plain black clothes, carefully self-provided with an umbrella—no one would imagine that he has twice received the thanks of both Houses of Parliament for his generalship ; that upon State occasions he wears on his breast the Mutiny medal, with clasps for Delhi, Relief of Lucknow, and the Siege ; the Indian frontier medal, with clasps for Umbeyla, Lushai, and Burma ; the Abyssinian medal, and the Afghan War medal, bearing the proud names Peiwar, Kotal, Charasia, Sherpur, and Kandahar.

He is on his way to the Continent, going to take the waters of Contrexville like any ordinary peaceful citizen temporarily troubled with liver, or in danger of being out-manœuvred by that arch-enemy gout.

June 15.

Passing down Park Lane this morning I observed Barney Barnato's new palace blossoming like a summer garden. Workmen were busy filling the windows and balconies with choice plants. Considering that the previous midnight had brought a telegram from Funchal announcing the suicide of the millionaire, homeward-bound from the Cape, there seemed a grim irony in this joyous decoration of the house he would never enter. It was all a simple matter of business. The master was expected home in a few days; the Jubilee was at hand; the costly mansion was just out of the hands of the builders. Nothing was more natural than to seize the opportunity to decorate it, after the bright fashion common to all West-end mansions in these summer days. The order was last week given to a florist. And here, on the very morning the town was stunned by news of the tragedy off Madeira, the gardeners, whistling at their task, were busy decorating the house of Death.

The first impulse on hearing news which some of the morning papers hesitated to publish was that things had gone queer with Barney, that the structure of his colossal fortune was akin to that of a house of cards, and that at a touch it would be shattered. On the Stock Exchange there was instant rush to clear out of the Barnato market. It was checked by the steadiness of people who are supposed to know. The final result of the first day's transaction showed a depreciation in the values of Barnato's stocks. It was comparatively unimportant.

8

The fact is that within a narrow, financially important circle the news caused no surprise. It was known that for a long time poor Barney had shown signs of mental and physical derangement arising from overwrought nerves. It was whispered that his sudden and successful dash from the deck of the *Scot* in search of rest and oblivion in the depths of the ocean, was not the first effort made during the week to cast off an unendurable coil.

I met Barney once, sitting next to him at a little dinner given in the House of Commons. He struck me as an attractive mixture of simplicity and shrewdness. His manners were quiet, but his speech betrayed his origin. With all his millions he had not been able to supply himself with h's sufficient to go through a brief dinner-hour. He was a marked specimen of the not unfamiliar amalgam of lavishness and penuriousness. An intimate friend said of him, "He lavished gold, but he would scramble to pick up a dropped penny."

June 23.

Save for the affectionate homage personally paid by the mob to the Queen on her journey from Buckingham Palace to Westminster to prorogue Parliament, the colonial troopers and the imperial service troops from India carried off the honours of the day. By an arrangement which some, jealous for the claims of the colonial troops, cavilled at, they were placed in the vanguard, apart from the Royal procession. This secured for them the advantage of coming upon the scene before eyes were weary watching its ever-varying length, or voices had grown hoarse with cheering. For the first time in the history of the Empire all its outlying, far-reaching sections were directly, personally represented. To watch the squadron of colonial troopers riding past, followed by the swarthy contingent of the Indian native forces, was for Londoners to recall the grouping of the multitude in another city on the day of Pentecost. Parthians and Medes and Elamites, the dwellers in Mesopotamia and Cappadocia, in Pontus and Asia, all seemed crowded into the retinue of Queen Victoria on her Diamond Jubilee day.

The colonial and Indian contingent was led by the bravest soldier, the most popular general, in the British Army, Lord Roberts. " Bobs," as the populace called him, rode the white Arab steed that has borne him unharmed in many glorious marches and triumphant fights. It is getting old now, but " Bobs " loves it as a comrade-in-arms, and insisted that it would never survive the neglect if it were left out of the business of to-day. The breast of the hero of Kandahar was ablaze with medals, a distinction he shared with other soldiers of his standing, notably Lord Wolseley. Only " Bobs's " charger wore a war medal round its neck—a distinction conferred upon it by the hand of the Queen herself.

June 25.

Whilst all the world wondered at the majesty and might of what was a mere section of the British fleet anchored at Spithead in Jubilee week, there flashed along the water a strange craft. It is the latest development of marine construction, from its arrangement of motive power called the *Turbinia*. Without going into technical details, it will suffice to say that this little vessel, revolutionising modern appliances of steam-power, rushed about the crowded fleet at the rate of thirty-one knots an hour. I happened to be in the company of Lord Charles Beresford as this strange apparition flashed past the *Teutonic*.

" If that thing ' does,' [1] " said this experienced seaman, who has closer knowledge of all that relates to battleships

---

[1] The thing " did " so well that to-day all battleships of modern construction and all new passenger ships are fitted with turbine engines. This flashing round of the little *Turbinia*, with her constructor Charles Parsons aboard, was the first public demonstration of an invention that has revolutionised ocean steaming.

than most men, " we shall just have to begin again and rebuild our fleet."

The *Turbinia* is as yet in the experimental form of development. So were steamboats in the days when the frigate was still the most perfect realisation of the speed and strength of the British fleet. The *Turbinia* may eventually prove impracticable or impossible in the adaptation of its system to big ships. But with the hundreds of millions invested in our Navy it is a little startling to have a practical man coolly talking about having to begin all over again.

July 1.

Mrs. Chamberlain's party of last night was specially designed for those favoured with invitations " to have the honour of meeting their Royal Highnesses the Prince and Princess of Wales." All the world of London and of some adjacent parts were present. But they did not have the honour of meeting the Prince and Princess of Wales. The fact is that their Royal Highnesses, having made several attempts to approach the entrance of 103 Piccadilly, finally gave up the attempt, and quietly, perhaps gratefully, went off home. Chamberlain, whose ideas in these later times are all on an imperial scale, incurred vast expense in hiring for the occasion the big house in Piccadilly where the late Julian Goldsmith lived. It did not prove nearly large enough for the company that thronged its hall, its staircase, and its rooms. The night was oppressively hot. The thunderstorm that had in the afternoon chased Lord Onslow's guests from Clandon Park to the station, still loured sullen and unbroken over London. The first impulse of guests on entering the rooms was to get out again. Egress was impossible in face of the crowd streaming up the staircase, and there are few even of the biggest houses in London that have a double staircase leading into the front hall.

The Duchess of Devonshire, whose enterprise and

perseverance nothing can withstand, made early escape by a back stairway. Later, this proved a means of deliverance to some hundreds who might otherwise have been suffocated. It led to the kitchen, and *grandes dames* hurrying down were brushed against by servants carrying up supper. Some having reached the basement munched stray sandwiches, and even more gratefully accepted other refreshment from the waiters bustling by with bottles and jugs. It was a remarkable scene, testifying afresh to the arduousness of the life of London Society, more especially in Jubilee time. In the enforced absence of the Prince and Princess of Wales, Chamberlain led into supper the Duchess of York, the Duke of York escorting Mrs. Chamberlain. Arthur Balfour, who vastly enjoyed the scene, laughed his way through the crowd in charge of Lady Londonderry.

July 2.

The Queen has done a gracious thing in her effort to make amends for the banality of the officials at Buckingham Palace, when the Commons gathered to present to Her Majesty their congratulations on the sixtieth anniversary of her long reign. Amid all the incidents of the Jubilee, this was looked forward to in advance as the most interesting. According to an ancient statute, read at the opening of successive sessions, the Commons claim the right of free access to the Sovereign. The claim asserted, the privilege is left in abeyance. On Wednesday, upon the Queen's initiative, the Commons repaired to Buckingham Palace, and, with the exception of a score or so of Privy Councillors, distinguished in the eyes of flunkeys by their gold-lace dress, they found the doors shut in their faces.

As Her Majesty has been careful to make clear, she knew nothing of the incident, and of the consequent heart-burning, till she read her morning paper. It is safe to surmise that whosoever was responsible for the bungling business received severe wigging. The Queen, though she must be weary with a succession of festivities that have overweighted much younger people taking part in them, gives up to-morrow afternoon at Windsor to play the hostess, not only to the Commons, but to their wives.

It is an ill wind that blows no one any good. The wives of Members are able to bear with fuller measure of Christian resignation the indignity put upon their spouses last week, since it has resulted in an unexpected, unexampled, invitation to Windsor.

July 3.

When two years ago the Unionist Ministry was formed, and Chamberlain had his choice of posts, there was much marvel that he should have selected the Colonial Office. Up to that date, whilst usually filled by a Minister of Cabinet rank, the place had not attracted stars of the first magnitude. The Marquis of Ripon, Lord Knutsford, Lord Kimberley, and the Earl of Carnarvon were successive Colonial Ministers, who unmistakably stamp the former status of the post. The fact that, with one or two exceptions, the Colonial Secretaryship has been allotted to a peer is of itself significant. Even under the most aristocratic auspices Peers are not chosen, *per se*, for posts the administration of which calls for the highest qualities of statesmanship. Chamberlain is as long-sighted as he is keen-eyed. In taking so important a step as choosing the part he would play in an exceptionally strong Ministry, it is certain he did not decide without due deliberation.

Consequent on the sudden march of events in South Africa, it has come to pass that since the Ministry was formed the Colonial Office has had centred upon it the attention of the Empire and of the universe. Chamberlain did not, of course, two years ago foresee the Raid and all that it has led to. But it is clear from Blue Books that have seen the light, he was early in his new career prepared to front President Kruger with a resolute attitude hitherto unknown at the Colonial Office. This appears in his correspondence on the subject known as " the Drifts."

It now appears probable that what he had in mind when he made the choice of office that perplexed politicians was this Jubilee week and all it made possible to a statesman of imperial instincts. As far as London is concerned the pageantry of the Jubilee is past. The lights are fled, the garlands dead, and a host of the foreign visitors have departed. But there remains, and will, I believe, permanently live, the strengthening of the bonds of the Empire following on the drawing together of its threads from the uttermost parts of the earth.

The idea of inviting the representatives of the colonies and some of the leading personages of the British Empire in the East to come to London on the sixtieth anniversary of the Queen's reign, and take prominent part in the ceremonial, was undoubtedly Chamberlain's. Its communication to the House of Commons was received with acclaim, echoed throughout the country. Thus encouraged, the Colonial Secretary has carried out the scheme with a largeness of scope and a minuteness of detail that has left no colony, no province, of the Eastern Empire overlooked.

This gathering of the clans of the Empire is, from a political point of view, twice blessed. It brings the colonies and the Mother Country within actual handgrasp. The spectacle it presents, unique in the history of the world, impossible to any other nation, creates a surging feeling of pride that warms towards one another the hearts of mother and children. Beyond that, it is an object-lesson to whom it may concern outside the boundaries of the Empire. The advance guard of the mighty procession last week was formed of troopers and foot-soldiers from the colonies. Later, forming part of the Sovereign's escort, came some splendid Indian troops. These together represent land forces excelling in number anything any military monarch of the Continent could put in the field. The British fleet has long stood alone in a position of supremacy. The parade on Jubilee Day showed the possibility of an innumerable British Army.

July 15.

The officer to whose lot it fell to recover the body of Sir Henry Havelock-Allan is just now in London on leave. He tells me an interesting incident in connection with the tragedy, which did not appear in the published accounts. At the time of his killing Sir Henry wore his father's watch, a precious heirloom from which he never parted day or night. When the body was recovered the watch was gone. Efforts to recover it have hitherto been unsuccessful. Publicly to offer a reward would have defeated the object in view. Such a proclamation would have been construed by the Afridis as putting a price on the head of the thief, who would probably have sought immunity by destroying the watch.

Havelock-Allan's appearance on the scene gave an infinitude of trouble and anxiety to the military authorities. They felt responsible for his safety, and with full knowledge of his constitutional recklessness, knew they had their hands full. The strange part of the story is that at the time he met his fate it was reckoned that danger was past. He and his escort had safely traversed the Khyber Pass, and emerged upon comparatively open country.

Sir Henry left behind him in England his most faithful and cherished companion, his Arab horse. The relations between the two were curiously intimate. The horse seemed to understand every word or sign addressed to it by its master. If Sir Henry, dismounting, told the horse to remain where he left it, neither force, coaxing, nor strategy would induce it to move a step till its master returned.

July 16.

No authentic news is yet to hand of the fate of Herr Andree, who with his two gallant companions a fortnight ago vanished into space from Spitzbergen. The myth about the carrier pigeons was speedily disposed of. There is more probability in the story of the Dutch captain who saw in the White Sea what he believes was the wrecked balloon. I have not met anyone who from the first entertained expectation that the project would prove successful. Still there were few who looked for the safe return of Nansen. That intrepid Arctic explorer is naturally taking a keen interest in the adventure. In one respect there is a close parallel with his own case. One of Herr Andree's companions was married only a short time before he set out skywards in search of the North Pole. Nansen had been married a little more than a year when he embarked on a voyage only less perilous.

When he came back he told me a pathetic little story. His child was born a few weeks before he set out. He was passionately attached to it, and sorely hungered for some close memento to carry with him. The happy thought struck him that if he could get the little one to crow into a phonograph, he might carry the precious cylinder with him, and nightly, before seeking his rest amid Arctic seas, might turn on the sweet " Good-night." Obstacles prevented the carrying out of the plan, and the cry of the child never broke the silence of the Arctic night. After long interval Nansen spoke with tender regret of the disappointment that befell him.

CHAPTER IX

THERE was some talk of following up the Devonshire
House Jubilee fancy dress ball by display before a large
audience. It was proposed to hire the Albert Hall,
or some other big place, wherein the Duchess of Devonshire's guests might disport themselves in the interests
of charity. It was reckoned that thousands of people
would pay their half-guinea, or even a guinea, to see
so fair a sight. Some ladies and gentlemen approached
on the subject were as willing as was the habit of
Mr. Barkis. Others, including some of the grandest
of the dames, objected to making a show of themselves,
even in the name of charity. So the project was abandoned.

A pretty story is told (perhaps invented) about Lady
Burton, wife of the head of the great brewery house.
She made up her mind to go to the Devonshire House
ball dressed as the Queen of Sheba.

" But," she complained to a friend, " there are in
pictures so many Shebas. I don't know which to select."

" You should go as Beer-Sheba," said the friend,
who, it need scarcely be added, was not of the male sex.

July 26.

The Queen has promised, on her return from Scotland,
to pay an afternoon visit to Hatfield. This is not the
first time the early home of Queen Elizabeth has been
so honoured. More than fifty years ago Her Majesty,
then a young wife and happy mother, visited Hatfield,
escorted by the Prince Consort. They stayed several
days, the Long Gallery being one night lit up for a

State ball, in which the Queen trod a measure with her host, father of the present Prime Minister. At the time of the Queen's visit our Lord Salisbury was a slim youth of sixteen.

There is a tradition at Hatfield that the young Queen displayed the keenest interest in everything linked with the memory of Queen Elizabeth. There are not less than five portraits of that mighty monarch. In one she is presented under a massive jewelled headdress. On her shoulders are a pair of gigantic wings, ethereal to transparency. She is gowned in a yellow dress that Sargent would love to paint, though he probably would not have added, as the earilier artist did, embroidery of human mouths, eyes and ears, not to mention the serpent on the sleeve. The Queen holds a rainbow in her hand, on which may be read the modest motto, *Non sine sole Iris.*

When, in 1846, Queen Victoria left Hatfield, she carried away an acorn from the oak tree under which, according to ancient testimony, the Princess Elizabeth was seated when news was brought that her sweet sister Mary was dead, and she was Queen of England. The acorn is now a lusty oak tree at Windsor. "Queen Elizabeth's oak," in the avenue of Hatfield Park, has never grown another. Having paid tribute to the far-off successor to Queen Elizabeth, it peacefully completed the long, slow process of dying.

July 27.

To-day Colonel John Hay, the American Ambassador, lunched with us at Ashley Gardens. Speaking about Clark Russell, he told me that when *The Wreck of the Grosvenor* came out he recommended it to Mr. Fox, Secretary to the Navy, the man who began to give the United States a navy. Fox, meeting him some time afterwards, said, "*The Wreck of the Grosvenor* is a great book, not a rope's-end mislaid." With intent to cheer up Russell I wrote and told him. He replied in the following letter, which throws sad light on his daily sufferings :

BATH,
July 31.

MY DEAR LUCY,

Best thanks for your letter and for your friendly thought to forward me so high a compliment. The book never deserved the praise it received. If I survive by a line it will be in *The Convict Ship*.

I am utterly run down in nerves, and am obstinately putting down my pen for six months. I shut up this house on Monday next and shall crawl to the summit of Combe Down, where the air is fresh and reviving, and there I shall stick till I feel better.

I gather from your brisk note that you are well, and am thankful to hear it. Our kindest regards to Mrs. Lucy.

Yours sincerely,

W. CLARK RUSSELL.

August 7.

The Marquis of Lorne tells me that it was at Cliveden, during one of his many visits, that Gladstone met the Duke of Argyll, and in conference with his friend decided on the momentous step of moving the Resolutions upon which were founded the Bill for the Disestablishment of the Irish Church. At that time the friendship between Gladstone and the Duke was as that of an elder and younger brother. They had many kindred tastes, not the least being the ecclesiastical turn of mind which to this day marks the lives, the writing, and the speeches of both. When, shortly after this memorable meeting, the general election of 1868 placed Gladstone in supreme power, the Duke of Argyll joined the Cabinet as Secretary of State for India. In 1880 he again became Gladstone's colleague, but the chasm which has since hopelessly widened had already begun to show itself. Gladstone as he grew older became more Liberal in his politics. The Duke of Argyll followed the common human tendency of growing incrusted with Toryism. The breaking of this ancient friendship, marked on the Duke's side by bitter attacks on his former chief, was among the sorest of Gladstone's many kindred sorrows.

The Duke's main characteristics were shrewdly summed up in a remark by an Oban innkeeper, who had occasionally opportunities of studying his Grace. " The Duke of Argyll," he observed, " is in a verra deeficult poseetion whatever. His pride of intellect will no let him associate with men of his ain birth, and his pride of birth will no let him associate with men of his ain intellect."

September 18.

London lost one of its most cherished sights consequent on the death of Lord Redesdale, for many years Chairman of Committees in the House of Lords. In addition to dressing himself in the fashion current when William IV was King, he, throughout the session, drove down daily to the House of Lords in a big yellow coach, with a footman standing behind. Fifty years ago it was, I am told, the fashion for carriage people in London to go about with a footman hanging on behind. Since Lord Redesdale's death the only personages who observe the custom are the Lord Mayor and Sheriffs on State occasions. The nearest approach to the old fashion is reached by Lord Rosebery, who may sometimes be seen driving a cabriolet, with a minute tiger in tights and top-boots perilously slung behind.

September 20.

The portrait of Billy, the Speaker's famous bulldog, is now finished, and Mr. Gully is its proud possessor. I fancy the artist congratulates himself that the task is safely accomplished. Like most bulldogs, Billy is, in ordinary circumstances, of almost angelic temper. Of course, if there were work to do, he might be counted upon to seize it and never let go. But among friends he is even indolently harmless. There are, however, as the artist discovered, bounds to his patience. For the purpose of securing a good pose, Billy was induced to stand with his forepaws resting on a low stool. This

bored him excessively, and it was only by lavish treatment in the way of tit-bits that he endured the position.
At a particular stage of the work the artist, wanting to
catch Billy's sharp attention, snapped his thumb and
forefinger. Billy pricked up his ears. The signal was
renewed. An ominous light gleamed in his eyes. At
a third repetition of the snapping Billy sprang over
the stool, knocked the alarmed artist on the flat of his
back, and stood guard over him.

From Lord Roberts.

September 30, 1897.

DEAR MR. LUCY,

I am concerned to see from the cartoon in this
week's number that *Punch* questions the wisdom of
what is called the " Forward Policy " in regard to the
north-west frontier of India.

Believe me, the present troubles are not caused
by any " Forward Policy," but by our having no fixed
policy in our dealings with the border tribes, and of
our being weak and timid in our action towards the
Ameer of Afghanistan. The question is a very difficult
one, no doubt, but I believe, if the causes which have
influenced those who, like myself, are accused of encouraging a " Forward Policy " were clearly explained
to the public, we should have the majority with us,
and any Government that decided to adopt a fixed
and firm policy would be supported. In no other way
can future tribal troubles be avoided, or any satisfactory
scheme for the defence of the north-west frontier be
carried out.

I hope that, ere long, I may have an opportunity of
putting my views before the public. Meanwhile I should
much like to talk them over with you or with the Editor
of *Punch*, if he would kindly allow me to do so.

I shall probably be in London towards the end of
next month.

Believe me,

Yours very truly,

ROBERTS.

In accordance with the suggestion thrown out in this letter Lord Roberts lunched with me *tête à tête* at Ashley Gardens. In a lengthy conversation he set forth his views on a question at the time viewed with anxiety by the Government. I found him convinced of the inevitableness of a conflict in the Far East between Russia and Great Britain. Where is it best for England that it shall take place ? On the banks of the Oxus or in Afghanistan ?

"We must meet Russia at Cabul," said "Bobs," the light of battle gleaming in his eyes.

Believing that we should do well to await the shock of battle on the north-western frontier of India, he was emphatic in expression of the opinion that we must possess the roads leading into Afghanistan, and must, as he put it, "have these fellows with us"—meaning the frontier tribes. This last declaration seems to go to the root of the matter, suggesting the whole question at issue in public controversy of the day, as to whether the course taken by Lord Salisbury's Government, beginning with the reversion of Liberal policy in respect to the occupation of Chitral, was best designed for securing an object Lord Roberts insisted was indispensable. He, however, was not disposed to trace the matter back to that breach of faith with the Swatis, wherein many found the germ of the frontier outbreak.

His explanation was at least precise. For fifteen years the Khyber Pass had been kept open on the Indian frontier by the Khyber Rifles, under the command of Colonel Warburton. When that officer retired on account of age, he was succeeded by Colonel Barton of the Guides, who, accompanied by his wife, took up his position at Lundi Kotal. When signs of disturbance in the neighbourhood made themselves seen and felt, Colonel Barton rode over to Peshawar to obtain reinforcements. These were refused, and the garrison at Lundi Kotal, attacked by the insurgent tribe, found themselves left in the lurch.

The defenders who escaped with their lives became centres of disaffection among the Afridis, each being in his own person a witness to the weakness of the creed of British faith and invincibility upon which the Afridis had relied.

To this political blunder, as he described it, Lord Roberts traced the beginning of the trouble. Had Lundi Kotal been promptly and effectually reinforced the Afridis would have relapsed into their long-established condition of friendly service to the British. As it was, the mullahs (priests) saw their opportunity. In the Swat country the growing prosperity of the people consequent upon the security of British rule had the concurrent effect of weakening their influence. The Swatis, waxing fat, were kicking against priestly authority. Now was the time to fan the flame of revolt burning at the mouth of the Khyber Pass.

The desertion of the Khyber Rifles was, Lord Roberts repeated, the first and fatal blunder of the operations of the previous year. It may be objected that the argument stops short of the beginning, inasmuch as it does not explain the condition of things which led to the threatening signs that induced Colonel Barton to demand the rein-forcements. Lord Roberts admits that for some time previous to the threatened attack on Lundi Kotal there had been a movement of unrest among the frontier tribes. As history testifies, the territory has never been a pasture of smiling peace. Heretofore outbreak has been made for a special reason by a particular tribe, other tribes in adjacent zones remaining quiescent. Prior to the present outbreak there were, Lord Roberts conceded, signs of a combination among the tribes unknown in his earlier long and close experience. Of course, there was the occupation of Chitral in breach of the solemn undertaking given to the Swatis on behalf of the Indian Government, that if British troops were permitted to pass through their country, they would, after doing necessary punitive work at Chitral, peaceably and finally retire.   Lord Roberts would have none of that explanation.

First of all, he insisted, trouble was due to the mullahs, fighting with the craft, vigour, and determination with which, in the Far East as in the West, priestly establishments resent incursions on their power and position. Next it is the Ameer.   It is true His Highness, appealed to by the insurgent Afridis for countenance and help, sternly repulsed them, telling them, in modification of the English phrase, that they had made their bed and must lie on it.   Lord Roberts shrewdly pointed to the date of that rebuke.   On July 27 the Malakand and Chukdara positions were attacked.   Less than a fortnight later Shubkudhr was assailed.   On August 18 the Afridis and the Orakzais took the field, and on August 23 came to blows with the British forces in the Khyber Pass.   All this time the Ameer said never a word.   It was only when he found a British force, thirty thousand strong, advancing on the frontier that he deemed it expedient to disavow the Afridi delegates.   His scholastic method of treating them roused suspicion in the mind of a man who has not spent forty-one years in India for nothing.

" The Ameer," said Lord Roberts, " is absolute master of Afghanistan.   No one, even of the frontier tribes, dare lift hand or voice against his known wishes.   If he had been altogether in earnest about the Khyber Pass affair he would not have lectured the Afridi emissaries.   He would have hanged them on the nearest tree."

So much for the past.   As for the future, Lord Roberts has no anxiety if only a definite policy be adopted.   First of all, Great Britain must have the right of marching along and holding the roads to Cabul.   That can be done only with the co-operation of the frontier tribes, above all the Afridis.   He believed that the permanent gain of such allegiance was not difficult, far less impossible. He was convinced that the tribesmen would gratefully accept a state of things wherein to the manœuvring of

9

the mullahs, fearful of their occupation being gone, or to the wiles of emissaries of the Ameer, they might reply that they were bound by definite bargain to serve England —must obey their masters and none other.

"Pay them some little subsidy," said Lord Roberts. "It will be far cheaper in the end than military expeditions."

While putting his trust in the power of money the veteran soldier was steadfastly inclined to keep his powder dry. He would have backed up the sweet influence of monthly or quarterly wage with the manifest presence of determination on the part of England to hold her own on the frontier of India. In the main he was in favour of Sir Robert Lowe's contention, that for the series of small posts over which the British flag has hitherto waved on the north-western frontier there should be substituted large military positions, with garrisons in sufficient strength to take the offensive in case of sudden emergency, and in most imaginable cases to hold the fort till the arrival of reinforcements. He was further in favour—a conviction not for the first time expressed —of arrangements whereby the frontier districts should be withdrawn from the charge of the Lieutenant-Governor and placed under a Chief Commissioner. In brief, he desired to see established on the north-west frontier the policy that has made the once turbulent Beloochistan at least as quiescent as our own Borough Road.

"Sir Robert Sandeman," said he, "did all that was needed in Beloochistan. Let us do the same from Dirbund, on the right bank of the Indus, to the northern flank of the road from Kohat to Thull, and we shall hear nothing more of risings of the tribes."

March 13, 1898.

Nansen's book is still holding its own at the libraries, and, what is better still for publisher and author, with the booksellers. Quite apart from its special interest as a record of adventure, it has high literary merit. I was

talking of this the other day with H. M. Stanley, who
fully admitted the fact, and made an interesting
commentary thereupon. He pointed out the vast difference existing between the circumstances under which
Nansen performed his literary task and those which
encumber a land explorer. The Arctic voyager has his
full share of discomfort, and sups daily of danger. But
at least he has the shelter, quiet, and comparative warmth
of his sleeping berth and the dining-hut. Through the
long winter night he has nothing to do, and is even
grateful for the call to take up his pen and write up his
diary.

With a man on the track of Livingstone, for example,
or of Emin Pacha, the case is quite different. Through
the hot day he is on the march, probably with insufficient
supply of food and water, with potential enemies lurking
in a too-evident jungle, with recalcitrant followers always
on the look-out, if not for opportunity to bolt, at least
for chance to shirk their work. By the time the traveller's
tent is pitched, and his evening meal cooked and eaten,
he is so worn out both in body and mind that he is much
more disposed to fling himself down on the ground and
go to sleep than to sit up polishing sentences.

CHAPTER X

May 20, 1898.

In Mr. Gladstone's long and noble life there has been nothing finer than his passing away. It might all have been so different, a great career marred by months or years of fretful senility. To speak of infinitely lesser men, we know how much better it had been for the fame of Lord Brougham and Lord John Russell had they died some years earlier than the stroke befell. Up to the last, like some noble oak which falls in the night before its prime is past, Gladstone was at his best, only in physical strength falling short of the majesty of his normal height. The patience with which he bore extreme suffering was fresh testimony to the nobility of his character. To him it was a new experience to suffer pain, to have an habitual condition of bounding health hampered by physical infirmity. That made the visitation harder to bear, more heroic the patience with which it was suffered. In his paroxysms of pain his prevailing thought was of those watching by his bedside; above all, for the faithful companion of his toilsome, often stormy career.

"Don't say anything to Mrs. Gladstone," was his whispered entreaty to the doctors and nurses when smitten with exceeding anguish.

Save for the local affection that undermined his strength, there was, apparently, no reason why he should not have lived on for another ten years. His marvellous powers of recuperation were proved in this test struggle with death. More than once during the week it had seemed that the end was within touch of the enfeebled hands lying on the coverlet, if indeed the end had not come. After a while he rallied.

Next to the death-bed scene within the room at Hawarden Castle, there is nothing more beautifully pathetic than the multitude outside watching and waiting for news. The throng included the peoples of the civilised world. It is no exaggeration to say that within the last century no man has done more for his fellow-men than the statesman now lying in everlasting rest. It is fitting that mankind should stand with hushed voice and tear-dimmed eyes round his death-ded. Through a long period of his public life Gladstone was the object of the bitterest personal animosity. At home he has had his windows broken. At his club threat was made to throw him out of the window. In the House of Commons he has stood with silent dignity, watching a mob of English gentlemen howling at him behind the closed glass doors of the division lobby. When he lay dying all animus passed away. Amid a nation's mourning he joined in the eternal rest of Westminster Abbey, Peel, Disraeli, and other statesmen whose names are linked with his in the history of England.

> Here lapped in hallowed slumber Saon lies
> Asleep, not dead ; a good man never dies.

August 3.

Major Stuart Wortley, who is going out to Khartoum with Kitchener, tells me something I was proud to hear of the ever-lamented friend whose acquaintance, prelude to a long and affectionate intimacy, I, oddly enough, made in a balloon. The Major says that but for Fred Burnaby the column attacked at Abu Klea would have been overwhelmed and destroyed, even as was the ill-fated army of Hicks Pacha. Burnaby rode with the column without being in any position of command. He was on his way to join headquarters. Soon after the start his military instinct and keen eye discerned fatal weakness in the formation of the troop. By his advice this was altered, with the consequence that when the attack of the Mahdi's horde became imminent, the British and Egyptian troops readily fell into the formation of the square, and were able, after prolonged and desperate struggle, to beat off the assailants.

It was out of an opening in the corner of the square that Burnaby rode to the help of a wounded private, " sitting his horse as quietly," Major Stuart Wortley says, " as if he were riding on to parade."

September 8.

Colonel John Hay has just had time to make himself at home in London when comes the American President with the, for us, abhorred summons of withdrawal to nominally a higher, actually a less well-paid, post. It is noteworthy, when we come to recall recent appointments, that the United States should have such an apparently illimitable and only slightly varied collection of delightful personages to send to represent her at the Court of St. James's. We all remember Lowell, whom it seemed impossible to replace. Yet after him came Mr. Phelps, a man of quite distinct character and associations, not one whit less successful in the personal aspects of his mission. Perhaps it may be admitted that Mr. Lincoln, who succeeded, did not do anything to add to his father's renown as a companion and conversationalist. Mr. Bayard was attractive in many ways, including his personal looks.

Handicapped by deafness, he sometimes succeeded in carrying the infirmity off only too well. There is a story told, probably invented, about him at a country house which is at least characteristic of his manner. At the dinner-table someone told a tale that vastly amused the company, to all appearances none more than the American Minister, whose handsome face beamed with laughter.

" Capital ! " he said ; " that reminds me of a story, perhaps not so good, certainly "—this with a gracious bend of his head to the raconteur—" not so well told, but perhaps you will allow me to repeat it."

Forthwith he started, and to the consternation of the company he began to recite the very story they had just applauded. Seated at the other end of the table, he had not caught the drift of the first man's narrative. Happily it was a polite, well-bred audience, and it was not till His Excellency had finished that the laughter that choked them was allowed to burst forth. Bayard probably thought he had never before told that particular story to so appreciative an audience.

Colonel Hay has the national gift for telling a good story, and indulges in the accomplishment without the drawback that unhappily attended the efforts of his predecessor. He is also equal to the fame of his nationality as an after-dinner speaker. As a conversationalist in the ordinary give-and-take of a bright dinner party he is delightful. For his years—well, he is only sixty— he is a marvellously young-looking man, alert, with the bloom of thirty on his cheek and ready laughter in his eyes.

" I am more sorry to leave England than you can imagine," he wrote to me on the eve of his departure. " There were so many interesting things to do, so many charming people I wanted to see more of. I would like to leave an astral body here, cavorting about in agreeable irresponsibility, while the earthly frame went definitely home to work. I have not seen enough of you. But for what I have seen I am thankful, and should be sorry to think we should not meet again.

" I am,
" Always faithfully yours,
" JOHN HAY."

October 15.

Lord Edward Cecil, just home from the Nile, is full of praises of the Sirdar. He served on his staff as aide-de-camp, rode in his suite when he entered Omdurman, and accompanied him on the expedition to Fashoda. He describes the personal labour and endurance of

Kitchener through the campaign as something marvellous. He overlooked everything, seemed to be ubiquitous, and was simply tireless.   On the night before the battle of Omdurman he got only three hours' sleep, taking it wrapped in his cloak on the desert sand, having previously dined and supped on bread and water.   He was the first man to enter Omdurman, riding forward regardless of the sniping going on from every corner and many huts.   Remonstrated with by his staff for needlessly incurring this danger, he answered, " Well, well ; they are very bad shots."   What the Sirdar is prouder of even than his complete victory is the fact that he has achieved it at an expenditure less by £300,000 than the War Office estimate.   That is the result of careful planning and of patient personal supervision of details. The campaign will cost a trifle over a million sterling, which the Sirdar's staff complacently compare with the eight millions spent on Lord Wolseley's campaign.

Lord Edward's description of the discovery of Major Marchand at Fashoda is particularly interesting.   He confirms all that has been said of the hopeless condition of the French force.   Marchand was encamped on a swampy bank, lacking food and clothes.   He seems to have made a most favourable impression upon the Sirdar and his staff.   Lord Edward describes him as a man of charming manners, with a cool intrepidity that made light of his perilous position.

The only difficulty met with was the action of one of Marchand's officers, who, in spite of long privation, had succeeded in preserving constitutional plumpness. " The fat Frenchman," as Lord Edward describes him, was so overcome with joy at the sight of the deliverers that, in the effusion of gratitude, he insisted upon embracing the Sirdar, with intent to kiss him on both cheeks in French fashion.   Beaten off in that quarter, he turned upon Lord Edward, who with the greatest difficulty evaded his attentions.

It is evident from the testimony of this eye-witness that if the Sirdar had delayed by forty-eight hours his appearance on the scene, there would have been no Fashoda question. The Dervishes, slowly closing in on the hapless and helpless little force under the command of Major Marchand, would have crushed them out of existence.

October 28.

The widespread lamentation when news of the sudden death of the Duchess of Teck was flashed upon London, testifies far more than usual, in analagous circumstances, to the goodness of the woman rather than to the fallen estate of the Royal Princess. Few members of the Royal family were more popular than the smiling, buxom, motherly-looking lady, whose unheroic life has been rounded off with a touch of something like tragedy. The Duchess had her part in the Royal procession on the last Jubilee day. But her great occasion was on the marriage of her daughter to the heir to the Crown of England. On the former occasion she sat amongst ordinary princes and princesses in the cortège. On the wedding-day she sat in a glass coach facing the Queen, and with a heartiness that amused Her Majesty only less than it delighted the crowd, she took to herself and beamingly acknowledged the thunderous acclaim that greeted and followed the Royal coach. It was a bright summer day of the kind not too often seen in London. Nowhere in the wedding procession or among the multitude looking on did the sun find brighter reflection than on the irradiated countenance of the happy mother and bride.

Whilst the Duchess was on terms of *cameraderie* with the man and the woman in the street, she was most loved by those who lived nearest to her. During her life the pathway to and from White Lodge, Richmond, was not always of primrose dalliance. For awhile,

as is well known, the household found it convenient
to retire to more economical quarters on the Continent
till a temporary storm of vulgar impecuniosity blew
over. Of late years, time and circumstance mellowed
under the sun of York, the Duchess lived happily in
her park-girt home, chiefly occupying herself in doing
good. I have chanced to see her in many circumstances
amid public and private surroundings. Never was she
more estimable or more admirable than when bustling
round among the bales of miscellaneous tributes gathered
in by her on behalf of the London Needlework Guild.
This is an institution, wisely designed and admirably
administered, for the distribution of articles of clothing
among the class in straitened circumstances who prefer
to suffer the pangs of poverty rather than to clamour
for charity. The Duchess of Teck was the life and soul
of the Guild, giving up to it through the year as much
personal attention and actual work as, devoted to wage-
earning, would have comfortably maintained her.

Members and associates of the Guild undertook to
prepare annually, or to purchase for presentation, two
articles of useful clothing, which, being forwarded to
a centre of administration, were carefully distributed
amid deserving cases personally known to agents of
the Guild. I remember the amused astonishment with
which, before leaving White Lodge on my first visit,
I found myself enrolled as an associate of the Needlework
Guild, pledged to send a yearly tribute. I am ashamed
to say that this year the engagement slipped my memory.
Nothing, in whatever minute detail, escaped the notice
of the President of the Guild. Last week I received the
following notification : " Will you kindly send your
work and that of your associates to Her Royal Highness
Princess Mary, Duchess of Teck, White Lodge, Richmond
Park, Surrey, not later than October 27th." Before
day broke on the morning of the 27th Princess Mary,
Duchess of Teck, had finally changed her residence.

November 19.

According to the terms of his will, the personal presents received by Mr. Gladstone were distributed among his family. With the possible exception of Prince Bismarck, there was no man upon whom the public showered more tokens of personal affection and admiration. He rarely visited any centre of manufacture without the workpeople combining to give him some specimen of their craft. Not only from home quarters, but from the remotest parts of the world came tributes of popular esteem. Naturally, his passion for woodcutting brought him the tribute of innumerable axes. The first thing that struck a visitor to Hawarden whilst Gladstone was still in residence were the axes that stood in the hall. On the occasion of the golden wedding miniature axes wrought in gold largely figured. Of earlier date is a pencil case in silver, which used to be on Gladstone's desk, reserved for his labours in literature. Shaped as an axe, it served as a pencil-case, on the blade being engraved the legend, " For axeing questions."

On his golden wedding the Prince of Wales, always a faithful friend whether in sunshine or storm, sent him a double inkstand in solid gold. The Shah was another contributor to this personal treasure-trove. Other things one remembers seeing lying about the tables were an album, handsomely bound, containing the names of more or less obscure Italian students grateful for his labours on behalf of Italy, and a large silver cylinder, containing tapestry, the gift of natives of India, to whom his name and personality were something sacred.

November 21.

In spite of his vanity and self-confidence, which habitually reach the pitch of patronising the Deity, the German Emperor is said to be a slave to superstitious fears. There is one tradition about the house of Hohenzollern which particularly disturbs the Imperial mind.

It is that three Emperors of the House would reign
in a single year ; that the third would have six sons, and
would encompass not only the destruction of his dynasty,
but the ruin of the Empire.   What on the face of it is
the most audacious prediction—three Emperors in
succession within the limits of twelve months—has already
been fulfilled.   The latest came to the throne in the year
his grandfather died and his father reigned.   At the
present time the Kaiser's family includes five sons.   No
one can say what a year may bring forth, and if the
Imperial family were blessed by a sixth son, the coincidence would be stranger than fiction.   For the rest,
apart from prophecy, the Kaiser is just the man to bring
about the fulfilment of the third prediction.[1]   If his
meddlesomeness abroad does not result in foreign war,
his tyranny at home is well calculated to arm the so-
cialism against which he wars.   Anyhow, the dark saying
is extremely curious, especially since it has just claims
to remote antiquity.

November 30.

A movement, set on foot in parliamentary circles, to
raise funds in order to place a bust of Gladstone in his
old college at Eton, threatens to prove a fiasco.   The
proposal was that Members of either House who had
been at Eton should subscribe a guinea in order to
commission a sculptor to do the bust.   As not more than
£150 was required for this purpose, and as there are in
both Houses of Parliament between four and five hundred
old Etonians, it seemed, to begin with, that the only
trouble the committee would have would be an embarrassment of riches.   The duty of secretary and
treasurer was gracefully undertaken by Mr. Ian Malcolm,
a young Conservative Member.   After more than two
months' hard labour, Mr. Malcolm tells me he has not
succeeded in raising more than £80, little more than one-
half the necessary funds.

[1] He has done so.

The hopelessness of the situation, as viewed by him, is indicated by the fact that he has retired from pursuit of the coy guineas, and the running has now been taken up by some of the masters at Eton. It was a happy thought to perpetuate in the school-house the memory of Eton's most famous and most brilliant boy. It is not easy to account for the failure, which can scarcely be due to any lingering feeling of political animosity. Possibly it is all due to agricultural depression and the decay of rent.

A parallel movement to do honour to another famous Parliamentarian has been more successful. Contemporaneously with the floating of the subscription to place a bust of Gladstone in Eton College, there was started a scheme for adding one of Lord Randolph Churchill to the possessions of the House of Commons. The area of subscription was limited to men who, whether in the House of Commons to-day or not, had at some time the privilege of sitting in the same Parliament with him. The invitation was responded to with encouraging spirit and unanimity. Amongst the subscribers are Mr. Asquith, Mr. Arthur Balfour, Sir William Harcourt, Sir M. H. Beach, Sir Henry Drummond Wolff, and Sir John Gorst. Even Lord Cross, whom Lord Randolph in his impatient way couldn't abear, has come forward with his forgiving guinea. Mr. Storey, who has just finished a life-sized statue of Lord Randolph designed for Blenheim, will do the bust, for which a position has been assigned in the passage leading out of the Central Lobby. Lord Randolph will have for close companion a bust of W. H. Smith, upon whom he, out of his infinite scorn, once conferred a partnership in the drapery firm of Marshall & Snelgrove.

CHAPTER XI

THE death of Lady Ridley, the latest victim to the plague of influenza, has saddened London Society. She was one of the sweetest-natured, prettiest-mannered of the ladies who adorn it. In every way the most richly endowed hostess in London, she, from the opening of the present season, looked forward to excelling herself. A day or two before she was stricken down she sent out cards for an unusually prolonged series of festivities. "Lady Ridley at home," the invitation runs, "Saturdays, February 18 and 25, and Saturdays in March."

To-morrow is the third Saturday in March, and truly Lady Ridley is "at home." But there is only one guest.

> The day is fixed that there shall come to me
>   A strange, mysterious guest ;
> The time I do not know ; he keeps the date ;
> So all I have to do is work and wait,
>   And keep me at my best,
> And do my common duties patiently.
>   .
> So we pass out, my royal guest and I,
>   As noiseless as he came ;
> For naught will do but I must go with him,
> And leave the house I've lived in closed and dim.
>   It only bears my name ;
> I've known I should not need it by-and-by.

The profoundest sympathy is felt with the Home Secretary. Those privileged to know Lady Ridley as a friend most nearly, but only vaguely, feel the immeasurable, irreparable loss to the closest companion of a long and happy married life.

45, MECKLENBURGH SQUARE, BLOOMSBURY.
April 5, 1899.

MY DEAR LUCY,

It is very good of you and Mrs. Lucy to show such friendly interest in the success of my book [*Number 5 John Street*]. I must say that though I had hopes at the beginning, I ended with fears on the eve of publication, and that the result was as great a surprise to me as it has been a delight to my friends. The papers have been more than kind ; the publisher has now ordered his seventh thousand. What more can I desire than that the public may continue in the same laudable frame of mind long enough to give me my place among the writers of the day ?

Yes, there is still something left to wish for, and that is an equally favourable verdict from America, where the Century Company has purchased the copyright. Good luck all along the line may have precious results for me.

With kindest regards to *chère* Mrs. Lucy,

Very sincerely yours,

RICHD. WHITEING.

April 14.

The funeral services in connection with the death of the late Liberal Whip, Tom Ellis, testified, alike at Bala and at Westminster, to the sterling worth of the man. His career was one that did honour to himself and credit to the system of public life that made it possible. In an ordinary way the post of Parliamentary Whip is one of the appanages of the Peerage. On both sides it has been the custom to promote to vacancies either the younger sons and brothers of peers, or scions of great territorial houses still ranking with the commonalty. Tom Ellis was the son of a tenant-farmer. When invited to contest the county of Merioneth, he frankly said he had invested his patrimony in his education, that he was willing to give his services if they were called for, but someone else must find the money.

On those terms he was elected, and in surprisingly short time made his way to a position in which he became the confidant of Cabinet Ministers, the trusted agent of a great party.   His death at the age of forty is a calamity to his friends, an irreparable loss to the Liberals.   Not so for him.   After all, there is some recompense in dying before you have had time to make a mistake or be met by adversity.

As one of his colleagues finely said by the graveside among the Welsh hills, " Tom Ellis died in France last week.   He will never die in Wales."

April 20.

At the inauguration of the Great Central Railway at Marylebone Station to-day I came across John Hollings-head.   After a life of varied labour and experience equalled by few, he might pass in a crowd for a man just turned fifty.   He recollects quite well how, sixty years ago, he made his first railway journey.   He travelled as a third-class passenger, and having taken his ticket, was shown the way into an open truck, which, when not in use for passenger traffic, carried coals, cattle, or anything going its way.   For the convenience of the passengers one side of the wagon was let down, making a gangway by which they entered the van.   When the train was about to start the side was lifted up, more or less securely hooked, and, to the amazement of mankind, the train rumbled off at fully twenty miles an hour, third-class passengers jolting on springless wheels.

If it snowed, or rained, or blew the stout north-easter that Kingsley (comfortably writing in his study) greatly loved, they had just to put up with it to their journey's end.   There were no means of shelter.   Sitting in one of the sumptuously appointed third-class carriages of the Great Central Railway, hearing a man recall these early experiences, brought more vividly to the senses the enormous strides made by railway enterprise during the last half-century than would the study of innumerable tomes of history.

May 2.

Henry Fawcett, who, in spite of his blindness, lived to be Postmaster-General, from time to time amazed and interested the House by *tours de force* in the way of speechmaking. He could, with apparent ease, speak for an hour—of course, without the assistance of notes—on the most abstruse subject. Since he disappeared from the scene nothing so marvellous has been achieved till Courtney spoke to-night on the Budget. All is not absolutely dark to him, as it was to Fawcett. He can walk about unaided, and recognises his friends and acquaintances. But he cannot see to read or write, and is unable to count upon the assistance of notes in making a speech. To a practised debater that, on ordinary occasions, would not greatly matter. When it comes to dealing with the Budget statement notes were indispensable even to Gladstone.

To-night Courtney met the difficulty in a fashion that adds to the marvel of his success. He brought his speech fairly written out in the handwriting of his wife. He handed the manuscript to Hobhouse, who sat next to him below the gangway. As he spoke Hobhouse followed the manuscript, prepared to prompt him if necessary. For an hour and twenty minutes Courtney went on, dealing with a mass of figures and conducting an elaborate argument. Only once, and that after an hour had sped, did he hesitate and turn to his prompter to get his cue.

As a feat of memory this is even more remarkable than Fawcett's everyday doings. He studied his subject; then, out of the sometimes fatal fullness of his vocabulary, he made his speech. Courtney dictated his speech in his study, probably had it once read over to him, and recited it with an accuracy only once at fault.

May 4.

Last night met the Duke of Cambridge at a private dinner given by the high sheriffs of Surrey in the storied hall of one of the city companies. The Duke is now in his eightieth year, and would perhaps be better quietly dining at home. But he shrinks from the prospect of absolute retirement. So he goes out dining still, a pathetic figure with his bowed back, his blue ribbon of the Order of the Garter, and his mechanical method of walking round a room when he enters it, and shaking hands with people he thinks he knows.

He made a speech in response to a friendly toast, a kindly loyal speech, telling us all to be true to the interest of the Empire. There was danger of his breaking down when he referred to the Army and his being no longer responsible for its command. But he brisked up again when he went on to affirm, what it is pleasant to know he fully and firmly believes, that the present efficiency of the Army is entirely due to his personal initiative and exertions, and that his successor can scarcely be expected to maintain it.

May 17.

Leaving the House of Commons at close of sitting to-day, I came upon a pathetic sight. In Palace Yard, in front of the entrance to Westminster Hall, stood a wagon to which were harnessed two heedless horses. On the cart lay a great mass covered by a white cloth, showing the outline of a gigantic human figure lying helpless on its back. It was, the policeman told me, the statue of Gladstone on its way to the pedestal in the central lobby, where to-morrow it will be unveiled.

I thought of the many times I had seen him walking with springing step past the place where the great dumb figure lay prone on the cart. Almost exactly a year ago I stood there among the bareheaded crowd watching the coffin borne out of Westminster Hall to be carried to its last resting-place in the Abbey. Already a year has gone! And in the meanwhile the world has plodded on pretty much as it did.

May 19.

Arthur Balfour is just now the hero of a little story which no one enjoys more than himself. He makes a habit, broken through only for imperative State reasons, of spending Saturday to Monday with friends in the country. Last Sunday he was one of a house party at a well-known place where the park encloses golf-links. A game was proposed in the afternoon. He demurred, on the ground that, whilst he saw no harm in the exercise, it might give public offence if news went abroad of how he spent his Sunday afternoon. Assured that he might enjoy the exercise without fear of being observed, he joined in the game.

Presently there appeared on the scene a group of villagers exercising their immemorial right of passing through the park. Balfour was much annoyed, lamenting the hard case of a public man who ever paid the penalty of his position by forfeiting the rights of privacy common to the humblest citizen. If he were plain Mr. Balfour, of the city or the suburbs, he might take a little desirable exercise on a Sunday afternoon, and no one would be the wiser or the sadder. The case was different with the First Lord of the Treasury, Leader of the House of Commons, one of the most prominent men in public life.

He was consoled by a fellow-guest who, standing near the group of onlookers, overheard the conversation.

" Who's 'e ? " one asked, pointing to the future Premier.

" Don't know," replied the other. " Anyway, he's a duffer at golf."

May 31.

Looking up Mr. Chamberlain's record in that indispensable volume, *Who's Who*, I find it stated that he is a member of the Reform Club. Many years ago he resigned his membership in circumstances that make the incident memorable. When his brother Richard was elected Member for West Islington, standing as a good Liberal.

he was, as a matter of course, put up as a candidate at the Reform Club. The animosity towards " Joe," which that strong personality has in all the varied circumstance of public life succeeded in evoking, found expression in more than sufficient black balls to keep the new M.P. out.

Chamberlain, incensed at this rebuff, forthwith resigned his membership, and has never since entered the stately hall of the Reform. It was said at the time that this incident, rankling in his mind, had something to do with his secession from the Liberal party, which followed within the space of a few months. One sometimes sees his son Austen at the Reform. That is a chance visit, paid on the occasion when the Devonshire is undergoing its annual cleaning, and its members are temporarily housed at the Reform.

June 7.

Last night Dr. Wallace, Member for East Edinburgh, died almost in presence of the House of Commons. The tragedy is infinitely deepened by attendant circumstances. Occasionally there appear in the reports of coroners' inquests accounts showing how the police have been hopelessly in doubt on the question whether a man picked up in the street was drunk or dying. Poor Wallace, stubbornly struggling in the grip of death, was for some moments regarded by the House with the angry impatience reserved for one who has too freely dined. He had long established himself as a prime favourite in debate. His style and humour were entirely his own, a sarcasm made more mordant by his stolid attitude, his deep, rolling voice, and his grave countenance. When, towards half-past eleven, he rose, the House, worn out with long debate and eager for the division, immediately assumed an attitude of pleased expectation. There was sure to be some fun with Wallace on his feet.

As usual, he had prepared notes of his good things, and at the outset got on well enough. At the end of five minutes his voice broke. Members, looking up to see what was the matter, observed him groping in futile search of his eye-glasses. His body swayed to and fro. He seemed as if he would fall over the bench by which he stood. Indubitably drunk was the general conclusion. Members sitting near attempted to assist him to resume his seat. One hastily handed him a glass of water, spilling it in passing over the shoulders of Harcourt, seated on the Front Opposition Bench, who was naturally exceedingly angry that the vagaries of a diner-out should incidentally subject him to this annoyance.

In other parts of the House resentment was felt and expressed only in less open manner. It was all very well, by no means an unfamiliar thing, that at this time of night, especially in sultry weather, after-dinner effects should manifest themselves in debate. But, really, for a man to get up, catch the Speaker's eye, begin a speech, and then become incoherent, even tottering, was too much. Meanwhile, amid angry cries of " Order! Order! " Wallace sank back on the seat a huddled heap, to be carried out, practically a dead man, in the arms of stalwart John Burns.

It was a pitiful ending to the tragedy of a lifetime. There are few men in the House of Commons who could compete with Wallace in pungency of debating power, fewer still in depth and scope of scholarship. He might have won his way to the highest position. Having filled more than one of high renown, he sank to the level of the applicant for a coronership.

His nearest parallel in intellectual capacity to be found in modern times is Robert Lowe, whom in his parliamentary gifts and attitude Wallace much resembled.

From Sir John Lubbock.

June 29, 1899.

My dear Lucy,
Many thanks for your note. It is as you say. When I found that the contest on municipal trading was likely to turn in part on the telephone, I sold my shares.

I was rather sorry to do so, as I have always felt some pride in having taken a part in introducing the telephone and the electric light into this country. I hesitated, as I thought no one could suppose that the trifling difference which the Bill might or might not make on a few shares could influence one's judgment.

However, on the whole it seemed better to sell, and I need not say that I am now very glad I did so.

Yours very sincerely,
JOHN LUBBOCK.

July 1.

Mr. Chamberlain, I have good reason to know, scouts the idea of war with the Boers, holding unshaken the belief that President Kruger will see the hopelessness of the attempt to confront the power of England with his little army of burghers, stout and plucky though they be. Cecil Rhodes is, or was, of the same opinion. Talking to me at the time arrangements were being made for the Bloemfontein Conference, he expressed the opinion, since verified, that the meeting would come to nothing.

" Kruger," he said, " when he comes in contact with our people, always plays the game of bluff. If Milner is armed with authority to let him know that if he doesn't give way he will be forced to, he'll come round. Failing that, he'll show himself as stubborn as a mule, and will threaten to be as vicious."

CHAPTER XII

October 14, 1899.

LOOKED in at the burial vaults below St. George's Chapel, Windsor, now being overhauled and rearranged. Hear some interesting particulars. In these vaults lie what is left of George III, George IV, William IV, and other members of the Royal family, the latest comer being the kindly hearted Duchess of Teck. For more than a century some of these coffins have rested on a centre table in the vault.

A figure in English history more attractive than any personality of the Hanoverian Royal family sleeps in this vault. Two years before Waterloo the Duchess of Brunswick, mother of the then Princess of Wales, was here buried. In the course of preparation for the interment, the workmen came upon a nameless coffin, which, on being opened, was found to contain the body of Charles I.

There was no mistake about it. On removing the pall there was revealed a plain leaden coffin bearing the inscription, " King Charles, 1648." An opening being cut in the upper lid, there was found a wooden coffin much decayed, with the body carefully wrapped in a serecloth. This unrolled, there leaped forth from the dead centuries the face of King Charles, in a marvellous state of preservation. The oval shape of the face was plainly discernible. The hair on the head was still thick, save on the back near the neck, where it had been cut short as part of the business of the executioner. The loosened head was lifted up and shown to the assembled company, which included that estimable gentleman, the Prince Regent. Identity being established, the head was replaced, the coffin soldered down, and the vault closed.

So it remained for three-quarters of a century, when there befell the curious proceedings alluded to. One day in the winter of 1888 Edward Prince of Wales, accompanied by the Dean of Windsor and two members of his suite, privately visited the vault. The coffin of Charles I was reopened, something was placed inside, the coffin re-soldered, and the much-disturbed King left in his solitude. What happened was that " certain relics " of the hapless King, removed from the coffin during the investigation presided over by the Prince Regent, having come into the possession of the Prince of Wales, were reverentially replaced.

The explanation of the mystery is not less curious than the story itself. When the coffin was opened in 1813 the head, being lifted out, fell to the ground, and there parted from it a portion of the vertebra. It was picked up by Sir Henry Halford, a great physician of the day, who begged the Prince Regent to allow him to keep it. Anybody else's vertebra was of small account to that prince of sons and best of husbands. Permission lightly given, the physician added the treasure to his collection, and it remained in the family till about a dozen years ago, when the grandson of Sir Henry presented it to the Prince of Wales. His Royal Highness, with natural delicacy of feeling, felt that its proper place was in the coffin of his far-off kinsman, and thither it was returned.

October 30.

The unfeigned regret expressed upon Davitt's announcement of his retirement from parliamentary life is creditable alike to him and to the House of Commons. He makes no secret of the fact—rather he glories in it—that he is a born rebel. The reason he publicly assigned for the step determined upon is his conviction that no just cause can ever find support in the House of Commons unless it be backed up by force. If such force were at his command he would gladly lead it against imperial power. Nevertheless, with full knowledge of his treasonable proclivities, the House respects him as an honest man, absolutely free from motives of self-interest.

The downfall of Parnell was, alike on personal and public grounds, a sore discouragement to him. He wrote to me at the time:

4, CECIL STREET,
January 2, 1891.

DEAR MR. LUCY,

It is almost too late to thank you for the kind note you sent me on the 19th of December, and which reached me during the fight in North Kilkenny, but it is not "too early" to wish you a Happy New Year and many more, each happier than the other.

It was very good of you to say such kind things of me just then. I know they were said sincerely, and that is why I appreciated your opinion so much. Parnell's fall has all the elements of tragedy in it—the *Times* (and to some extent the Government) failing a short time ago to do what he has himself accomplished! Had you seen and heard him during the contest in Kilkenny you would have stood amazed. As Jerry Jordon put it in Biblical language, he was "possessed of a Devil"—especially near the end of the fight, when he saw he was being licked. He turned in his mad wrath upon me and lied like a Trojan in nearly everything he uttered about me.

However, he is played out. He has destroyed what promised at one time to have been a unique and brilliant career, and went within an ace of doing what the ancient victim of the other Delilah did in his madness.

But "Thank God the cause is saved," anyhow. Again wishing you all the happiness of the season.

Yours very truly,
MICHAEL DAVITT.

November 5.

There is something deeply moving in Redvers Buller's letter to a humble war comrade, in which he bursts into lament for his son, who died in India this year, and who otherwise might have shared the danger and the glory of the campaign in South Africa. It happened that a year ago this very week I was a shipmate of young Howard's. Though Sir Redvers speaks of him as "my son," and evidently loved him as such, he actually stood to him in the relation of a stepfather. He was off to India to join his regiment. I was going no further on the same ship than Marseilles, on the way to Tunis. Redvers Buller and Lady Audrey came to see him off. Sir Redvers made us acquainted, and asked me to "cheer the boy up" as long as we voyaged together. I saw nothing of him for a day or two, he keeping his cabin during a boisterous passage in the Bay of Biscay. When he came on deck I found no signs of the depression at leaving home fondly fancied by anxious parents. On the contrary he was full of life and eager anticipation of a career in India. He landed at Bombay just before Christmas. In July he was asleep in a grave far from home.

November 12.

This morning the Queen, lately returned to Windsor Castle from her residence in Scotland, inspected the Household Cavalry about to leave for South Africa. There will probably flash across Her Majesty's mind memories of a day, dating forty-five years back, when she reviewed the Guards under orders for the Crimea. On that occasion she stood on the balcony in front of Buckingham Palace side by side with the Prince Consort. It is the same crack regiment, the same Sovereign ; but in its ranks there does not march one of the gallant fellows who, nearly half a century ago, stepped forth to the lively strains of the band, with Alma and Balaklava in the unseen distance. To-day the Queen sits alone to watch their successors go forth to a war which, in respect of the sorrow it has already spread through British households, finds its parallel only in the Crimea.

There is a pretty, but, I fear, apocryphal, story told
about the scene of forty-five years ago. It is said that, as
the last company trooped by, the Queen, stooping down,
took off one of her shoes and threw it amongst the men
" for good luck."

The late Lord Malmesbury used to tell another story
which in its day passed for gospel truth. When relics of
the troops came back from the Crimea they were reviewed
by the Queen, and some of the veterans decorated. After
the ceremony, Mrs. Norton, meeting Lord Panmure, the
War Minister of the day, asked : " Was the Queen
touched ? "

" Bless my soul, no ! " said Lord Panmure, shocked at
the mere suggestion of such indiscretion. " She had a
brass railing before her and no one could touch
her."

" I mean, was she moved ? " said Mrs. Norton.

" Moved ! " cried Lord Panmure, staring in growing
bewilderment. " She had no occasion to move."

Here Mrs. Norton dropped the subject.

November 17.

Talk of alliance between Japan and China, directed
against the common enemy, Russia. Another sign of
the times is the sudden flight from London of Mr. Morrison, the famous Pekin correspondent of the *Times*. He
arrived in England only a fortnight ago with the intention of spending a well-earned holiday in this country.
He had not been here many days when he received instruc-
tions to return to his post of observation, and is already on
his way back to Pekin. In a conversation I had on the
eve of his departure with this high authority on affairs in
the Far East, I gathered the impression that he believes
in the reality of the reported *rapprochement* between
Japan and China, and looks for some important developments in the spring.

Morrison is a young man to have achieved his record,

culminating in world-wide renown for his journalistic feat achieved in Pekin. " That terrible Pekin correspondent," Sir William Harcourt used to call him when confronting a belated Under-Secretary of Foreign Affairs with important news (such as the concession to Russia of Wei-hai-wei) of which the Foreign Office were still ignorant, and with respect to which they were inclined to be incredulous. A quiet-looking man of modest manner, he is not the kind of person one would instinctively recognise as having explored New Guinea, walked across Australia from sea to sea, and made his way on foot through China, from Chin-Kiang to Bhamo.

Of his journey across the Australian continent he told me some interesting things. He was alone, had not even a donkey as Stevenson had when he trudged over the Cevennes, and had to carry both food and bed. The latter was something in the nature of a sack, in which he found much wholesome sleep. The former was dried salt beef and flour. Of this last he made bread as need arose. He stumbled on many discoveries in his tramp through an unknown country. I fancy none gave him greater joy, nor does any dwell in his mind with sweeter satisfaction, than the result of an experiment which certified the fact that in the unavoidable absence of yeast a judicious mixture of fruit salt with flour makes admirable bread.

From Lord Wolseley

November 16, 1899.

DEAR MR. LUCY,

If the ignorant people in and out of the House who have lately induced our Cabinet to put the clock back had had their way, we should have had no army to mobilise. The Army owes a deep debt of gratitude to Lord Cardwell, and my one regret is that he did not live to see how thoroughly his reforms are now appreciated, even by the extensively misinformed men who opposed all reform because it was a change.

I had a very pleasant dinner at the Authors' Club, and hope you may be equally fortunate.

Believe me to be,

Very truly yours,

WOLSELEY.

November 24.

Sir Henry Colvile, who has assumed command of the Guards Brigade north of the Orange River, is an interesting personality. In appearance and in gentleness of manner he suggests rather the West-end drawing-room than the tented field. Yet few men of his age have more frequently fronted death. I made his acquaintance fifteen years ago on my way home from Japan. He joined the ship at Suez, having concluded a long and lonely ride along the valley of the Euphrates. He was one of the earliest practitioners with the Kodak, just then invented, a primitive form at which later developments would contemptuously snap. I have a lot of photographs, their surface little larger than a postage stamp, given to me as a souvenir of his journey.

His most prominent service was in connection with Uganda, where he served as Commissioner, a post in which he has just been succeeded by Sir Harry Johnston. He nearly died there, being at the end of two years' residence carried down to Zanzibar almost literally a skeleton. Though he looks a man of delicate fibre he has a splendid constitution, and rapidly pulled up.

December 10.

It is said that at a dinner-table where Millais was seated, conversation arose on the question of the maximum earnings in several professions. Among the guests was a Royal Prince, who inherits the curiosity about other people's private affairs which marked his illustrious forbear, George III. Having pumped a great doctor and a successful lawyer, who were happily able to pitch the note of income pretty high, H.R.H. turned to Millais, and

asked how much a successful painter might earn in a
year. "£35,000" was the reply. Incredulity being
politely hinted, Millais added that in the previous year he
had cleared £40,000, and could have made more if he
had not unduly lingered on a Scotch holiday.

December 16.

Lord Salisbury has returned to work, finding in
its abstraction some surcease from abiding sorrow.[1]
He has been deeply touched by the manifestations of
national sympathy in his bereavement, a demonstration
made without reference to political or social distinction.
He is agreeably surprised to find how wide and deep is
his personal popularity. The guerdon is the more pleasing
since it was never sought. Beyond all public men, not
excluding the Duke of Devonshire, whom in this respect
he resembles, Lord Salisbury has never courted the favour
of the masses. On the contrary, he has, upon occasion,
sometimes perhaps without occasion, gone out of his way
to flout them. It is impossible that a statesman of his
clear judgment and long experience should really regard the
House of Commons as an inconsiderable body compared
with the House of Lords. Nevertheless, he with great
success systematically affects that conviction.

It is one of his distinctions among his peers that he
never condescends to visit the House of Commons. Herein
he differs from the Duke of Devonshire, who is generally
seen yawning in the front row of the Peers' Gallery on
nights when it is crowded in anticipation of a big debate.
I cannot call to mind any occasion when Lord Salisbury
has been seen looking down on the assembly in which,
first as Lord Robert Cecil, then as Lord Cranborne, he
earned his spurs in the political lists. Behind this aloofness and scornful mien he only partially conceals a kind
heart and a highly sensitive nature, both just now profoundly touched by a nation's sympathy in a domestic
sorrow.

[1] The death of Lady Salisbury.

CHAPTER XIII

From the Duchess of Sutherland

"LILLESHALL, NEWPORT, SALOP.
December 18, 1899.

DEAR MR. LUCY,

Sincerest thanks for your kind and discriminating notice of my book.[1]

Under encouragement I thrive, and am full of ambition for the future.

But alas! What is ambition? One never attains the ideal!

It's a bore to be a Duchess. However, the thorniest obstacles demand the boldest leaps (I write in the hunting season) so, "Hark, halloa, forrard——"

With apologies for this flippancy, and earnest congratulations that you are able to leave the gloom of that appalling London for a time.

I remain,

Very truly yours,

MILLICENT SUTHERLAND.

January 26, 1900.

The late Lord Coleridge, whilst holding the office of Lord Chief Justice of England, enjoyed, amongst other personal distinctions, the unique one of possessing two gold chains of office. When the Queen opens Parliament in person, the Lord Chancellor, who in these later times reads Her Majesty's speech, wears over his robes a great gold chain. It is also visible on other occasions of supreme ceremony. "The collar of S.S." is its official name, though why they call it so the Little Peterkins of the Bar never could make out.

I submitted the case to Lord Moulton, who replied :

[1] *One Hour and the Next.*

57, ONSLOW SQUARE, S.W.
July 11, 1900.

DEAR LUCY,

S.S. means Sanctus Spiritus—though how the
L.C.J.'s office became connected with the Order of the
Saint Esprit, I do not know.

Each Chief used to have a chain—though a
different one. That of the Chief Justice of the Common
Pleas is in the family of Lord Coleridge, who was the
last of the line. It dated from Henry VII.

I don't know how old that of the present L.C.J. is,
but the chain of the chief Barons of the Exchequer
was, I believe, broken up by Pollock, who divided it,
giving a link to each of his twenty-two children !

Yours in haste,
S. FLETCHER MOULTON.

There were two such collars, one worn by the Lord
Chief Justice (said to come down in direct descent from
the possession of Sir Thomas More), the other the appan-
age of the Chief Justice of the Common Pleas. When
Lord Coleridge was appointed Lord Chief Justice of
England, he passed from the Bench of Chief Justice
of the Common Pleas. No successor being appointed,
he retained the chain, and thus had two.

On his death-bed he personally committed the chain of
the Lord Chief Justice to the charge of Lady Coleridge,
and bade her convey it to the great lawyer who was then
Sir Charles Russell, who to-day wears it as his successor
on the highest seat of the Judicial Bench.

What became of the other chain is, like the birth
of Jeames, "wropt in myst'ry." The Junior Bar,
who know everything, say it went to Lord Coleridge's
son and heir, with other paternal goods and chattels.

It seems questionable whether such an historic heirloom
could be regarded as private property.

February 10.

The fact that of the many leaders of the Irish parliamentary party John Redmond, captain of the smallest

contingent, should have been unanimously elected
to the chief command, puzzles many people. The wire-
puller in the business was Tim Healy. He has worked
in this direction, not because he loved John Redmond
more, but because he liked John Dillon less. Early
in last session he made a communication to me indicating
that negotiations were going forward that would in
a very short time result in the reunion of the Nationalist
party. His hope was defeated, closer confabulation
appearing to show the impossibility of the project.
But Tim is not a man to be lightly put off from any
purpose on which he deliberately sets his heart. He
has not in any public way shown himself in the matter,
but as the scheme was due to his initiation, so its accomplishment is chiefly the work of his hands.

It cannot be said that the amiable peacemaker, by
his attitude in the House of Commons, contributes
to realise the idea that millenium now reigns in the ranks
of the Nationalist party. He sits on the same bench
below the gangway with John Dillon. Frequently the
movement of Members leaves him with Dillon as his
immediate neighbour. Before the pact of peace, when
he and Dillon were accustomed to attack each other
on the platform and in the press, Tim, fixing himself
in his corner seat, aggressively turned his back on his
compatriot. Under altered circumstances he has not
varied this genial habit.

February 17.

A colleague of Lord Salisbury's, intimately connected
in ministerial affairs with him, tells me the Premier is
the hardest worked man in England. His daily task begins immediately after breakfast, and does not close till
one o'clock next morning. Most men (unless indeed they
live in the House of Commons), after working incessantly
through the day, draw a line of demarcation at the evening meal. With their morning clothes they put off the
day's work. Lord Salisbury, whether in Arlington

Street or Hatfield, retires to his study immediately after dinner, and sets to work as if he were beginning a new day.

Even in ordinary times the mass of correspondence that daily reaches the Foreign Office is overwhelming. The usual procedure on the part of the Minister is, after having read the shorter communications, to glance over the lengthier dispatches, awaiting full study until they shall have been printed. But every day brings up its arrears. Lord Curzon, when he was Under-Secretary at the Foreign Office, estimated that five hours of every day was required for the reading of printed matter alone. Lord Salisbury shirks no part of his task. It can be accomplished only by the hours added to the computation of an ordinary day's work gained by shutting himself up after dinner and slaving till one o'clock in the morning.

March 10.

The fat is in the fire at the Reform Club. When, fourteen years ago, the Liberal party was broken up on the Home Rule question, the club was brought to the verge of extinction by systematic blackballing. Whenever Unionist members proposed a candidate the Home Rulers pelted him with blackballs, the Unionists taking their turn at the game when opportunity presented itself. The consequence was that for more than a year no new blood was introduced, whilst the drain occasioned by death and other forms of removal kept its normal rate. In the end a truce was called. Wholesale blackballing ceased, and, save for personal reasons, all candidates put up were elected.

Last week the Duke of Devonshire nominated a gentleman who is a paid official of the Unionist political organisation. This was resented by Liberal members of the club as going a step too far. The Duke was privately communicated with, suggestion being made that, to avoid unpleasantness, his candidate should be withdrawn. The Duke declined to take the hint. His man went to the ballot, and was heavily pilled.

It was said that the Duke, following the example of Mr. Chamberlain when two of his brothers put up as candidates were pilled, would resign his membership. He has not yet made any movement in that direction ; but the Unionist members openly announce their intention of taking revenge, indiscriminately blackballing candidates put forward by Liberals.

Another shadow that has fallen on the historic club in Pall Mall arises in connection with the death of " Chicago Smith." This is the gentleman whom Hicks-Beach in his Budget speech, acknowledging payment of £900,000 death duty for his estate, described as living on fifteen shillings a day. There was a vague idea that Mr. Smith, who for many years made the club his home, would in some fashion or other remember it in his will, an expectation chiefly based on the fact that a year or two ago he endowed it with a lift. Possibly there were one or two members who dreamed that the munificence of the millionaire might take a personal direction. With quaint humour the old gentleman left his watch, chain, breast-pin and rings to a member of the club, forgetting all the rest.

The disappointment, though it exists, is not nearly so keen as was marked in another case. There was a member of the club, reputed to be fabulously wealthy, who wantonly and deliberately excited hopeful visions in the breasts of several old cronies. In moments of touching confidence he not obscurely hinted that when he departed this life the natural grief of his friends would find substantial consolation.

There were at least five men in the club who had reason to believe that, if not left sole heir to the estate, they would largely benefit by its distribution on the death of the benevolent owner. Death befell just four years

ago, when discovery was made that the old gentleman's accumulated property did not do more than
pay his debts and provide for decent interment. To
this day it is regarded as an unclubable thing to
mention his name in the hearing of any of the five
expectant legatees.

From Mr. Speaker Gully.

SEAFORD, SUSSEX.
April 12, 1900.

MY DEAR LUCY,

I do not wonder that Lord Peel's attention was
attracted to the debate last Friday. Nothing could
be more audacious and unveracious than Harcourt's
statement that the rule which prevented Courtney
(as he, Courtney, admitted) from discussing the terms
of peace originated in a single *obita dictum* of Peel's.

When you are next in town turn to *Hansard* of
the 24th November, 1882, the first case under the new
S.O. as to motions for adjournment, and you will see
that Brand then expressly ruled—the point having
been argued by Randolph Churchill and Drummond
Wolff—that a " bogus " notice of motion in the order
book prevented discussion of a *bona fide* motion for adjournment to raise the same subject. And there are
many instances of the application of the rule by Denison,
Brand, and Peel.

But the Press—and notably the *Daily News* (save
and except H.W.L.)—accepts Harcourt's fabrication as
gospel truth. That method of assuming, without knowledge or examination, that the only reliable history is
history as told by an advocate on your own side in a
party speech, destroys the value of Press comments. I
wrote to Peel on the subject yesterday.

Yours very truly,

W. C. GULLY.

April 21.

Considering that he was something of an amateur
journalist, Lord Glenesk, engaging Mr. Winston Churchill

as a special war correspondent for the *Morning Post*,
made a pretty bold bid. He offered him a four months'
engagement, at a salary of £1,000, with all expenses
paid. It is, by the way, significant of the spirit in
which the war was entered upon that at the time this
interview took place, an experienced man of affairs
calculated that four months would see the thing through.
The term having lapsed, the special correspondent's
engagement has been renewed on even more favourable
terms. His letters certainly have been one of the journalistic triumphs of a campaign in which the war correspondent has been sorely hampered.

April 28.

Mark Twain, ostensibly on his way home to Connec-
ticut, still lingers in London. He has many friends
here, and he and his charming wife spend a good deal
of time dining and lunching out. Considering the great
cloud that suddenly closed over him at a time of life
when he might reasonably have looked forward to resting
upon his laurels and living on the fruit of his labour,
Mark is pretty spry. Like Walter Scott in a curiously
analogous case, he has by incessant hard work cleared off
the liabilities imposed upon him in connection with the
New York publishing house, whose failure involved him
in heavy losses.

He is full of good stories. One not yet, I believe, in
print, relates to his return home after his last visit to
London.

"Did you go to Westminster Abbey?" someone
in New York asked him.

"No," said Mark, "I went to the Langham"—an
hotel still frequented by the Americans.

June 2.

A lady well known in London Society, bound on a long
course of country visits in the west of England, went down
to Southampton, *en route* accompanying friends going to

join their regiments in South Africa. Affecting farewells were taken, the lady waving her last with fluttering handkerchief as the Castle liner put out to sea. On going back to the station to pursue her journey, she could not find her abundant luggage, stocked with things necessary for country visits. After agonised search, the conviction was forced upon her that her baggage, whipped up by some active porter, had been carried on the steamship, and was now well on its way to the Cape. Her apprehensions proved only too well founded.

June 10.

Little has been heard of late years of Arabi Pacha, who once loomed large on the horizon of Europe. Now, it is said, he has declined overtures for his return to Egypt, preferring to die, as he has long lived, in exile. This is a change from his mood and his tireless hope when I, on my way home from Japan, visited him. That, alack! was sixteen years ago. I found his home of exile some three miles out of Colombo, reached by a long dusty road sometimes skirting the Indian Ocean. There was no difficulty in approaching him. He had neither jailer nor guard, being free to do what he pleased within the limits of the island. I well remember him seated in the stoep fronting his house, dressed in loose light-brown overcoat, white duck trousers and waistcoat, only the fez justifying in the matter of dress his proud signature " Ahmed Arabi the Egyptian." He was hard at work learning English, and showed, with childlike pride, the laboriously developed letters by which he had spelt out " By and by," " A time will come," and other simple sentences from his exercise book.

Arabi, who spoke English much more freely than he wrote it, was very bitter against Tewfik, the newly established Khedive. " Ismail," he said, " is a clever man, but a rogue. Tewfik is not clever enough to be a rogue; he is simply foolish. I will never go back to

Egypt so long as it is enslaved by Tewfik. I have no desire to see Egypt whilst it is a land of slaves. Once it was a country that smelled sweet to the nostrils. Now it stinks. Its wells are covered with earth. There is no refreshment in it." Tewfik has long passed away. Arabi, now getting on in years, a gentle-mannered, kindly faced man, still vegetates in Ceylon, and seems content to die there.

June 16.

The story about Sir William Harcourt's pending retirement from political life is denied, but there was every probability of its truth. An episode that seemed to have considerable effect upon his position in public life was the marriage of his son. The relations between "Loulu" and his father were pathetically close. The son over and over again refused tempting offers to enter the House of Commons, content to devote his life exclusively to the performance of secretarial work for his father. When he happily married, other and more imperative calls were made upon him. Without the constant companionship of his secretary, the duties of public life have become irksome to Sir William, and immediately after the marriage he practically retired from active participation in them. This session he has confined his attendance at the House of Commons almost exclusively to debates on the Budget. The Budget Bill passed, he went off to Italy, and though he is now at Malwood, he is not likely to be seen in frequent attendance at the House.

Sir William is not the kind of man to hide the mortification which followed on the reconstruction of a Ministry on the retirement of Gladstone. Rather is he disposed to nurse his wrath to keep it warm. The Liberal party have long been the butt of mischance. Of all the accidental misfortunes that befell it in recent years none has been so far reaching as the displacement of Harcourt in 1894. He had every right—by age, by position, and by accomplished work—to look for the reversion of the Premiership. To see the prize pass into the hands of one who some time earlier had served as his junior at the Home Office was more than could be meekly stood by a man of more equable temper than Harcourt claims to possess. Lord Rosebery was young and might have waited his turn later on. It was, as time has shown, the veteran statesman's last chance.

It does not make a thing more pleasant to contemplate from the point of view of the interests of the Liberal party to know that the ill-fated muddle arose out of purely personal prejudices and considerations. Harcourt is exceptionally gifted in many forms; but his endowments do not include an angelic temper. If he had shared the sweet serenity of Lord Granville's temperament he would have been Premier in succession to Gladstone, and the subsequent history of the party would have been delightfully different. When in the mood he can be a charming companion. When he isn't he recalls the reflection of the Scottish mother who heard that her soldier son, taken captive in flight, was chained to another. " I am sorry," she said, " for the man that's tied up with my Jock." Harcourt, sitting in a Cabinet presided over by a young colleague who, according to his view, had supplanted him in the leadership, would not be an absolutely sweet-tempered companion.

This explains much in the otherwise bewildering turn of events which, following on the retirement of Gladstone, prepared the way for fresh disaster to the Liberal party.

June 20.

The ceremony of the funeral of Mrs. Gladstone was appropriately simple in its character, genuine in its evidences of personal sorrow. Gathered within the Abbey were most of the people privileged, through varying length of years, to know something of the home life of the couple finally reunited. In the political arena men, and women too, wrangle with ferocity around Mr. Gladstone. The sweetness and simplicity of his home life commanded universal admiration, and had much to do with the establishment of his marvellous popularity with the multitude. There was something pathetic about Mrs. Gladstone's devotion to her husband. It was more akin to the watchfulness of a mother over a babe than the ordinary relations of wife and husband.

I remember one afternoon at Dalmeny, during one of the Midlothian campaigns, a deputation from Edinburgh waited upon Mr. Gladstone, who, after luncheon, repaired to the library, where they were assembled. Mrs. Gladstone hurried after him with a plaid shawl, somewhat the worse for wear, and as he, with his dignified bearing, walked up the floor of the library to greet the upstanding deputation, she, without saying a word, wrapped it round his shoulders.

It was not a particularly cold day, but the change from the dining-room to the library might perhaps be fraught with peril.

The last time I saw Mrs. Gladstone she stood framed in the doorway of the *Tantallon Castle*, a quaint, almost weird, figure. It was the last morning of the historic trip to the opening of the Kiel Canal. Breakfast was just over, and in another hour the guests would part. An address to our host, Sir Donald Currie, had been drawn up, acknowledging his munificent hospitality. At the last moment Mr. Gladstone undertook to present it, which he did in a gracious speech. Mrs. Gladstone was dressing in her cabin when news came that Mr. G. was making a speech. Hastily throwing on a dressing-gown, she hurried off to hear it. It was one of a succession of thousands—a mere ceremonial. But the faithful wife would not miss it for the world. So there she stood in the doorway, with dishevelled hair and unlovely dressing-gown, eagerly drinking in every word.

July 1.

Some time ago, writing in one of the magazines, I asked what had become of " the boy Jones," who more than once in the first year of the Queen's married life made his way into Buckingham Palace, and was hauled forth from beneath sofas and four-posters. A resident in Perth, West Australia, writes to me that the boy Jones being, after his last escapade, placed on one of Her Majesty's ships, was landed in the then infant colony of West Australia. Settling down in Perth, he rose to the high estate of town crier.

Unfortunately, his fame had preceded him. When he went forth, bell in hand, to perform his important functions, the naughty boys of Perth were accustomed to gather round him and make pointed inquiries as to the approaches to Buckingham Palace, the health of the Queen, and the appearance of the baby who is to-day Dowager Empress of Germany. The man Jones, angered beyond self-restraint, occasionally made dashes at the enemy, committing assaults which made his appearance in the police court familiar. He died about four years ago.

July 7.

Mr. George Smith was " at Home " last night, and invited a small party to meet the editors and contributors to the *National Dictionary of Biography*. It was a notable gathering, not marked, as is the wont of Park Lane parties, by gay dresses and flashing jewels, though the stately hostess lived up to the highest standard in this respect. The guests were mostly of the kind never seen at an evening party. Whilst their faces are unfamiliar in such circles, their names are known wherever English literature spreads.

Mr. Smith's beautiful house is full of mementoes of the connection of the publishing house of Smith, Elder with great men and women of the past. There is a portrait of Thackeray, taken late in life, more fully than any I have seen justifying his assumption in the pages of *Punch* of the *nom de plume*, " Our Fat Contributor." Another, even more striking, likeness is one of Charlotte Brontë. Browning is represented not only by his portrait, but by the manuscript of *The Ring and the Book*, preserved under a glass case, and reverently regarded by his worshippers. The handwriting is much plainer than is the meaning of many of the printed lines of his poems. Another treasure is a statuette of Carlyle—an infinitely sad face, looking out on a world of which he seems to bear all the sorrows.

It is characteristic of George Smith's princely dealing in the business of literature that from the first he has been uncheered by prospect of return of his expenditure on a work which fitly appears as a crowning glory of a memorable century. He has expended upon the enterprise close upon £150,000. It will take much time and steady flow of sales to make up this expenditure of capital. Meanwhile, compound interest will be accruing, with its proverbial magical results.

July 21.

The Prince of Wales has made his first journey in a motor-car. The vehicle that carried Cæsar and his fortunes is the property of Mr. Scott Montagu,* M.P., one of the earliest, now rated amongst the most skilful, drivers of motor-cars. The Member for the New Forest was this week staying at a country house, the party including H.R.H. According to his habit, he arrived in his motorcar, in which the Prince took the liveliest interest. An early opportunity was found for an experimental drive, which proved highly successful. It is quite on the cards that very shortly H.R.H. will have his own motor-car, a circumstance that will give a great impulse to a rising industry.

* Now Lord Montagu of Beaulieu.

August 4.

When Archibald Forbes was at the height of his fame, and Hubert Herkomer was struggling into his, the artist painted a portrait of the war correspondent. It was one of the successes of the year in the Royal Academy, and has since hung in the dining-room at Forbes's house near Regent's Park. It was left with his other property to Mrs. Forbes, who tells me she intends to bequeath it to Aberdeen University.

That was Forbes's Alma Mater. He did not leave behind him any brilliant record of scholarship. In later years, when he had made a world-wide fame, his old University reclaimed him by bestowing upon him the degree of LL.D.

August 6.

Among well-known Members of Parliament who will " return to Lochaber no more," is Henry Stanley. That long indomitable man has at length been forced to own himself dompted. During his last visit to Africa he contracted an illness that still pursues him. From time to time he is prostrated by an attack which lasts for weeks, during which he is unable to take solid food. Early in this year he was at brief intervals four times smitten by his mysterious visitant, and straightway made up his mind that he would not offer himself for re-election. He has been very little in the House this session, and has not joined in any of the debates. Last year he purchased a snug little property not far distant from London, and has taken with zest to the life of an English country gentleman.

His withdrawal from the political arena (for which he had no aptitude) makes the House of Commons poorer by the loss of a delightfully unconventional personage. No one present one night shortly after Stanley had taken his seat will forget his reply to a Member sitting close by, who had interrupted with a correction. In a painfully long pause in his speech, Stanley looked his hon. friend up and down as if he were mentally calculating whether it were worth while, or indeed possible, to lift him up, carry him outside and punch his head. He decided in the negative. But the ominous manner in which, fixing a glittering eye on the offender, he warned him to be cautious in the future, hugely delighted a crowded House.

CHAPTER XIV

NEWS comes from Cape Town that after long suffering in the grip of heart disease, Cecil Rhodes died yesterday in the little village of Muizenberg, whither he had retreated out of the hurly-burly. I made his acquaintance at a breakfast party given in the parliamentary session of 1892 by Munro-Ferguson, not yet G.C.M.S. or dreaming of occupying the important post of Governor-General of the Commonwealth of Australia. The guest of the morning arrived late, and chanced to drop into an empty chair by which I was seated. This happy accident was the opportunity of establishing a friendship which, with increasing warmth, lasted to the day of his too early death. Two years later my wife and I paid a visit to the Cape. On arrival of the steamer we were greeted by the aide-de-camp of Sir Henry Loch, Governor of Cape Colony, bearer of a letter of warm welcome and of invitation to lunch on the following day at His Excellency's country quarters a short distance out of Cape Town. Among the guests was Cecil Rhodes. Again favoured by fortune, I found myself seated on one side of him, my wife on the other. In the course of conversation he told us that his country residence, Groote Schuur, was in course of renovation, adding that if we did not mind the discomfort of the presence of workmen about the premises, he hoped we would be his guests during our stay at the Cape.

We were doubly grateful for the proffered hospitality. Primarily it offered opportunity of closer intimacy with a fascinating personality. In the second place, it delivered us from the depressing circumstances of hotel life in sun-baked Cape Town. On our voyage out, consulting residents as to the best hotel in the town, we selected the one most strongly recommended. It was a doleful place after the fresh air, the state cabin, the roomy accommodation on deck and below, enjoyed on our sea voyage. If this was the best hotel in Cape Town, jaded fancy shrank from picturing what the worst, or even the second-rate, might be. The hostess, a cheery but not over tidily apparelled Irishwoman, paid the delicate attention of providing us with a table apart from the main one at which the general company, a mixed collection of Boers and British, sat at meat. Our isolation was only apparent. We sat down to our meal in company with at least two hundred other guests who, unbidden and non-paying, insisted on sharing what was on our plates, in our cups and glasses. They were flies which, attracted by the unswept, undusted, condition of rooms and tables, swarmed in the hotel.

The next morning Rhodes called for us with his Cape cart, and carried us off bag and baggage to Groote Schuur. He had been fortunate in finding within a mile or two of Cape Town an old Dutch house set at the foot of Table Mountain in the lovely suburb of Rondebosch. Originally, as its name (Dutch for the " Great Barn ") implies, it had been a granary. It was plainly and strongly built, the architect, under Rhodes's personal supervision, greatly improving it by raising it in height a story, and extending its base by the addition of a new wing. Rhodes's ambition was to furnish the old mansion in a style suitable to its age. He was ever on the look-out for old furniture, whether to be found in Dutch homesteads in South Africa or in salerooms in London. I have a pleasant recollection of a wardrobe in the bedroom where we slept, a massive structure in black oak, severely simple in design, a silver lock and silver hinges glistening on its dark surface. As we had been forewarned, the builders were in possession, and the living-rooms were limited to a couple of bedrooms, a dining-room, and the library. Our host slept in a hut in the garden at the back of the house, giving up the only bedrooms to his guests. Among the passengers on the Castle liner was Horace Plunkett, an Irish Member, Unionist in politics, patriotic by instinct and practice. I spoke of him to Rhodes, who forthwith called upon him, and insisted on his joining us at Groote Schuur. Not more loth to leave his hotel than we had been, he by his company added greatly to the pleasure of the house party.

Two years after our visit Groote Schuur was destroyed by fire, and with it many of its garnered treasures. The calamity wounded Cecil Rhodes only less sorely than the disasters that followed fast on Jameson's footsteps when he raided the Transvaal. There were particular reasons that endeared the place to him. It was a home of his own making, upon which, amid pressing business of imperial scope, he had lavished much money, infinite thought, and personal trouble. He was not, however, a man idly to lament an irreparable misfortune. He rebuilt the place on its original lines, and with sublime prophetic faith in the country's destiny, bequeathed it on his death for the use of the Premier of South Africa. Dr. Jameson occupied Groote Schuur after Rhodes's death until General Botha, first Prime Minister of the Union of South Africa (the fulfilment of Rhodes's vision) entered it as his official residence in 1910.

Another matter Rhodes found time to deal with during a flying visit to London was a project to do honour to the gallant Britons who died with Major Wilson (December 5, 1893,) when Lobengula turned at bay at the Shangani River, and fought his pursuers. The bodies were found where they had fallen, rifle in hand. By direction of Rhodes, the remains were collected and carried a distance of two hundred miles, to be buried at " World's View," in the Matopo Hills, in the neighbourhood of one of the prehistoric ruins that are among the marvels of South Africa. His desire was that these gallant fellows should

have a memorial worthy of their deeds. He conceived
the idea of building round their common grave a stout
wall, setting within it medallions in *basso-relievo* containing portraits of the heroes, each with his name
inscribed below. He commissioned an eminent London
sculptor to work out this unique memorial, which was in
due time set up in its appointed place.

When the great Matabele king died, after his flight
from Buluwayo, his three boys were left without provision
and with few friends. It speaks volumes for the reputation Cecil Rhodes established with the savage tribe he
vanquished, that the first thought of the orphaned
children's guardians turned to the great white chief at
Cape Town. Escorted by two or three of the old king's
men, Lobengula's children made their way to Cape Town,
and presented themselves in Rhodes's doorway. He immediately took them in, gave them rooms, and undertook
to provide for them. He had an idea, the realisation of
which would, he believed, be attended by perfect happiness
for the lads. He was at the time having a portion of the
far-reaching land round Groote Schuur laid out for speci-
mens of the wild animals to be found in Africa. He told
me he would have the boys trained up to take charge of
these Zoological Gardens, work for which both their
instincts and their aptitude promised to qualify them. I
never heard how the project fared, but it is certain Rhodes
would make permanent provision for the orphans of his
ancient foeman.

He was even prouder of his library than of his old
furniture or the blue hydrangeas that glorified his garden,
and gave him special pleasure. He was always buying
books. Amid the pressure of his vast business, political
and commercial, he found time for reading only by sitting
up late at night, a habit which did not prevent his taking
an hour's ride at six o'clock in the morning. His favourite
study was the life and works of the Roman emperors.
He bought every book he could hear of bearing on this

12

wide subject. He had a rare collection of their portraits on coins or engravings, and many manuscripts specially copied from the Vatican and other libraries of Rome. The fascination " Imperial Cæsar dead and turned to clay " had for the founder of Rhodesia was complete, perhaps significant.

When I returned to London after visiting the Cape, people who heard I had been the guest of the financial magnate said, not without suspicion of envy, " You must have got some good tips." As a matter of fact, neither gold-fields nor diamond mines were mentioned in our many intimate conversations. Yes, there was an exception. Rhodes occasionally referred to the reputed site of Solomon's mines, whence he brought a handful of particles of gold, displayed on a plate in his library. But it was the regal state of King Solomon that interested him, not his possession of gold-mines, which, compared with the Consolidated Gold Fields of South Africa Rhodes established and controlled, were insignificant. In general society, gathered in a London house to do him honour, he was frigidly taciturn. Seated after dinner on the stoep at Groote Schuur, with the moon shining in a blue sky almost as brightly as the sun over London town, he talked by the hour about Ancient Rome and its warrior emperors.

One other subject he discussed—attractive as being imperial in its interests—was preferential tariffs between the Mother Country and the colonies, and between the colonies themselves. Speaking at Grahamstown in 1903, Jameson stated that the fiscal policy recommended by Chamberlain (at the time a subject of rancorous political controversy) was fifteen years earlier proposed by Cecil Rhodes. I am not aware of any general scheme of tariffs promulgated by him. He certainly did contemplate something of the kind as applicable to Cape Colony. He showed me correspondence in progress with the Canadian Premier, having in view the establishment of a bargain between the two colonies designed

for mutual profit. Canada was to admit Cape wine on
a preferential tariff, Cape Colony importing Canadian
wood at an exceptionally low tariff.

The Cape and Canadian Premiers made a tryst in
London for the following spring, at which the matter
was to be discussed. Delay interposed, consequent
on the illness of Sir Wilfred Laurier. Then came the raid
and all it led to, including the retirement of Rhodes
from a ministerial career. Had he lived through more
peaceful times he would certainly have developed, in
the direction of Australasia, a long-cherished idea.

Rhodes had a dinner party every night of our stay
at Groote Schuur, giving us opportunity of making
the acquaintance of the principal personages in public
life at the Cape. On one occasion came Jameson,
fresh from Matabeleland, where there had been trouble
with Lobengula. At the time, unconscious of a destiny
that would bring him a Privy Councillorship, a C.B., and
a baronetcy, he was known to his friends and the public
—the terms were identical—as " Doctor Jim." In the
course of conversation at dinner he privily told me how
much he suffered from the constriction of a starched shirt-
collar, worn after months of sartorial freedom on the veld.

When in the autumn of the same year (1894) Jameson
accompanied Rhodes on a visit to England, he came to
luncheon with us. The arrangement was characteristic
of the greater man. Abundant in his own hospitality,
he avoided London Society, hated going out, either to
luncheon or to dinner. Invited to Ashley Gardens, he
telegraphed (his private correspondence was largely conducted by telegraph) : " Don't ask anybody else and
I'll bring Jameson." So it was arranged, and we had a
delightful two hours listening to the talk of these two
Empire-makers in the freedom of unfettered conversation.
Then, as at our first meeting, I was struck by the innate
simplicity of Jameson, his amazing unconsciousness
of merit or distinction above the average man. An

affectionate confidence existed between him and his comrade in the battle for life in South Africa. To the hour of his own death, Doctor Jim silently mourned the too early cutting off of Cecil Rhodes. It is pleasant to think that they sleep together in everlasting rest on the lofty height of the Matopos, which looks far over the veld of Rhodesia. Loyal to each other during life, in death they are not divided.

I noticed with some surprise that when Rhodes was making up his lists for a dinner party at Groote Schuur (we were never more than eight or ten all told), the name of Sir Henry Loch did not seem to occur to him. The fact is, the two men, though socially on friendly terms, were not altogether at one politically. Rhodes wanted too much, and was impatient of restraint, gently but firmly applied by the hand of the Governor. Loch was at that time in a most delicate and difficult position, mastered with native tact and finesse. He found himself between the devil and the deep sea, represented by the crafty Kruger and the overmastering Englishman, bent on realising his dream of a line of British territory running from the Cape to Cairo.

He was one of the few Colonial Governors of my acquaintance who managed to retain his popularity. It was the same wherever he served, whether in the Isle of Man, Victoria, or the Cape. To this popularity his wife, most charming and tactful of women, largely contributed. Lady Loch ever cherished friendly recollections of her sojourn in Victoria. In the Governor's garden at Wynberg (near Cape Town), she had plants and trees carefully transplanted from her Australian home, tenderly cherished in memory of earlier days.

Except for a painful illness, which terminated fatally, there was no reason why Lord Loch should not have lived for another ten years. Last time I saw him, a week or two before he took to his bed, he had his usual bright, almost ruddy, look, and bore himself with customary upright carriage. It was impossible, looking at him and hearing him tell the story, to realise that forty-two years ago he was bound hand and foot in a Chinese prison, his jailers, with fiendish ferocity, several times a day making ostentatious preparations for his execution. His vigour and activity were shown a couple of years before his death. Driving down to the House of Lords in a hansom, the horse bolted in Parliament Street. Whilst galloping at full speed the septuagenarian fare lightly stepped out, retaining his foothold unhurt.

Rhodes told me he never trod the streets of London in his recurring visits without thinking of the time when he drove through them to take ship for the Cape. He was sent out to South Africa as the last resource against the advances of consumption. On one occasion he called on the London doctor in whose charge he had been. The astonished man, regarding the sturdy figure, ruddy countenance, and bright eyes of the Premier of Cape Colony, turned over his old books, and showed him an entry in which Cecil Rhodes was written down with circumstance as a hopeless case of consumption. The Cape and the whole of South Africa owe much to the energy and the ability of Cecil Rhodes. *Per contra*, to their splendid climate was due the lengthening of his life.

With all his hard exterior to the world at large, his imperious manner, and his habitual standoffishness to Society magnates, he had a heart tender as a woman's. I remember one morning at breakfast at Groote Schuur finding him in painfully depressed mood. I thought something serious had happened in State affairs concerning the Cape Government, or that there was bad news from Matabeleland, where, at the moment, Lobengula was in flight. After a while he told me that his butler had had a very bad night, with blood-spitting and other evidences of consumption. This was premonition of failure of cherished hopes. The young man was the son of an old parishioner of Rhodes's father.

He had found his way to the Cape, as many go thither, in an advanced stage of consumption. Rhodes, who knew nothing about him except that he came from his own home, took charge of him, sent him up country to the health-restoring veld, kept him there till he had made a cure, took him into his service, and finally advanced him to a position of high trust in his household. Now he threatened to break down, and tears stood in his master's eyes as he told the story and made careful preparations for his revisiting the veld.

Rhodes would have been pleased had he recalled the fact that in this matter he was imitating the action of Pliny, whose solicitude for his servants when they fell ill is incidentally recorded in his letters. One he sent to Egypt for change of air. Later he begged a friend on the Riviera to receive the same servant, "having frequently heard you mention the exceeding fine air and milk of your farm as very good in disorders of this nature." Rhodes was familiar with these classical records of life in Rome in the reign of Trajan, and possibly recalled this passage.

The year 1896 opened briskly with one of the most dramatic surprises of the century. That eventually there would be trouble in the Transvaal had been a certainty for the previous four years, recognised with increasing force by persons intimately acquainted with South African politics. The British public had begun to wake up to the existence of emergency. But no one was prepared on opening his morning paper on New Year's Day to read that Dr. Jameson, with a troop of armed men, had crossed the border and was making for Johannesburg.

This was a sudden, swift irrevocable action, more characteristic of the Middle Ages than of the end of the nineteenth century. What made the adventure the more portentous was a glimpse caught of the massive figure behind the adventurous Doctor. One of the commentators on the situation wrote: "Mr. Rhodes

is a clever man, but on this occasion Dr. Jameson seem
to have outwitted him." People who knew anything of
the personal relations between the two smiled as they
read this sapient remark.

Jameson, as was abundantly proved during his march
on Lobengula's capital and his subsequent administration
of the territory, was an exceedingly able man. He was
more like one of the maréchals of the French Empire
whom Napoleon trained in Italy and on German battle-
fields, than a country doctor. Behind them, overshadow-
ing them, inspiring and directing them, was Napoleon.
So behind Jameson stood Cecil Rhodes. In an official
communication to the Press, Chamberlain, Colonial
Secretary at the time, reported that Rhodes assured
him that Jameson acted without his authority, and
that when he heard of the projected raid he " at
once endeavoured to stop him, but found the wire cut."
Chamberlain makes no commentary on this picture
of the situation. But righteously angry as he was at
the dangerous embarrassment in which this joyful fili-
bustering involved the Imperial Government, it must
have been difficult for him to repress a smile when it
was presented to him.

Cecil Rhodes and Jameson visited London together
just a year before the raid. They stayed at the Bur-
lington Hotel, of which costly hostelry Rhodes, in his
imperial fashion, engaged a whole wing, with private
entrance. If he cared to reflect on the topic, he might
have consoled himself with the conviction that he was
the only denizen of a London hotel whose dinner was
served on silver plate. That was a detail due rather to
a sense of propriety on the part of the landlord than
to Rhodes's personal requirement. A man of the simplest
tastes, wanting little here below at dinner-time, he
wanted that little good and well cooked, with a moderate
allowance of the best wine, for which he had a delicate
palate. Overwhelmed with invitations to dinners, big

and little, he declined all, dining every night in his own rooms, always with Jameson, Rochfort Maguire (present on most nights), and two, at most four, friends to make up the small party. For Jameson Rhodes privately expressed boundless confidence and an esteem that bordered on affection. The only time they were separated during their stay in London was from a Friday to a Monday, when Jameson went down to Sandringham, the guest of the Prince of Wales.

The early acquaintance of the two men was formed whilst Jameson was still carrying on the duties of a family doctor. Perceiving in him capacities for quite other things, Rhodes provided him with opportunities which, vigorously and ably dealt with, brought him to the position of administrator of a territory larger than some kingdoms of Europe.

There was a delightful touch of comedy in Rhodes' explanation of his failure at the last moment to countermand his lieutenant's foray. I remember well the twinkle in his eye when one day, at Groote Schuur, conversation turned upon the different course events might have taken in Matabeleland if a particular message from Sir Henry Loch had duly reached Jameson. Lord Ripon, then at the Colonial Office, urged by strong protest made by Labouchere and others in the House of Commons, cabled to the High Commissioner of South Africa an order forbidding the Chartered Company's expeditionary force to engage in armed conflict with Lobengula. Sir Henry Loch sent on the message. When at length it reached Jameson Lobengula's army had been defeated, and the king was already in flight. The delay was most regrettable. Somehow or other the telegraph wire had broken down, and before foot-messengers could reach the invading force, all was over.

The South African Committee appointed to inquire into the circumstances attendant on the Raid met in February 1897. The Prince of Wales, an early comer at the first sitting, had a unique experience. He was kept waiting three-quarters of an hour whilst the Committee debated in private on matters of procedure. He bore the ordeal with genial good-humour, resting his folded hands on his walking-stick, and occasionally chatting with his neighbours right and left. As he remarked to one, the last time he had been in that part of the hall was in attendance at the Tichborne trial. The Grand Committee Room in which the Committee sat is built on the site of the old Court of Queen's Bench, in which forty-five years ago opened the trial at bar of the Claimant.

There are certain points of resemblance between the story of Warren Hastings and the career of Cecil Rhodes. Coincidence is not lacking even in the detail that both were tried in Westminster Hall. As far as the scene was concerned, similarity failed. It was in the Great Hall of William Rufus that Hastings was arraigned, " the old grey walls hung with scarlet, the long galleries crowded by an audience such as rarely excited the fears or the emulation of an orator." A modern annex of Westminster Hall, the Grand Committee Room where Rhodes was practically on his trial, is approached by a mean staircase. The only decoration of its walls whilst the Committee conducted its inquiry was a colossal map of Africa—the map of which (spread out before him on smaller scale in his room at Groote Schuur) Cecil Rhodes, with a rapid sweep of his hand from the Cape to Cairo, said to me little more than two years earlier, " I mean to paint it red from here to here." That achievement was peremptorily stopped by the Boers lying in wait for Jameson on his way to Johannesburg. But Rhodesia stands out boldly, and Rhodes, awaiting the coming of his judges, might well glance proudly at the map on the wall, at the base of which sat the Prince of Wales.

Throughout the bad three-quarters of an hour's waiting, Rhodes sat bolt upright at the end of a bench immediately behind counsel. Never at the height of his prosperity had I seen him looking so well. He was slighter, both in figure and in face, the change bringing into greater prominence his massive head and lofty brow. He did not speak to any one, and for the most part looked straight ahead of him. Occasionally his eyes glanced round the crowd to his right, but ever returned to the big map on the wall to his left. When called to the witness chair, he found himself in a curiously awkward position. He was seated at a small table facing, not his interrogators, but the shorthand clerk. After a while he, in accordance with habit, took the direction of affairs in his own hand, turned his chair round, and so fronted the benevolent visage of Sir William Harcourt. At the outset he was undoubtedly nervous, reading his statement at a pace that made some passages unintelligible. Fortunately it was printed, and copies were in the hands of the Committee, who closely followed the reading. When it came to cross-examination, he went to the other extreme, his answers being so long in coming that Harcourt occasionally passed on to another question without receiving a reply to its predecessor.

After a day's experience of the procedure and its surroundings, Rhodes grew so much at home that at luncheontime he drank his bottled stout under the eyes of the envious Committee, munching a ham sandwich whilst he explained to them his policy in South Africa. The restless movements, the nervous tension of his face, the long pauses in his replies all disappeared. He became quite chatty, occasionally confidential. The honours of the cross-examination were unexpectedly won by Mr. Blake, formerly leader of a political party in Canada, then an Irish Member, who succeeded where Harcourt's more elaborate method failed. In his hands the witness made no further effort to conceal the fact that for months before Jameson started on his famous raid he, as Premier of the Cape, was preparing for what he describes by that blessed word " eventualities." He

was determined to upset the Boer Government, justifying
his resolve on the double ground of injustice to the Out-
landers, and a disposition on the part of Kruger to dislodge
British influence in South Africa in favour of Germany.
Both these motives commended themselves to popular
opinion in this country. Consideration of them began
to work a revulsion of feeling in favour of Rhodes, which
steadily grew throughout the proceedings.

During the progress of the inquiry the illustrated
papers were full of portraits of Cecil Rhodes strangely
differing in appearance. The fact is, an additional bond
of sympathy existed between him and Lord Rosebery.
Each had strong objection to sitting for his portrait
before either easel or camera. The best portrait of
Rhodes hangs with its face to the wall in the studio of
an English R.A. Yielding to the wishes of a friend, he
consented to sit, and the commission was given to Luke
Fildes. It happened to be a period of unusual storm
and stress, which, acting upon a temper not constitutionally placid, brought Rhodes to the studio day after
day in increasingly irascible mood. He addressed the
artist in tones and terms unfamiliar to a R.A. He
pettishly declined to follow directions as to where he
should sit, declaring that if Fildes could not paint him
as he pleased to station himself, he must leave it alone.
One day Fildes, at the end of the tether of his patience,
decided to accept this advice and leave it alone. He
quietly informed his imperious visitor that he would
decline to receive him any more. Rhodes, somewhat to
his astonishment, was politely conducted to the door
with assurance that it would not again be opened for
him. This was rather a costly reprisal on the part of
the artist, since it meant forfeiture of the exceptionally
handsome fee named in the commission, and the portrait
was so nearly finished that it would not have taken long
to complete.

During his visits to London before the raid Rhodes, in

his capacity of Premier of Cape Colony, received much
attention in high quarters. Queen Victoria commanded
him to lunch at Windsor Castle. It added to the interest
of the occasion that the Empress Eugénie was staying
at the Castle when he was a guest. South Africa has
an abiding interest for the mother of the Prince Imperial.
She would prize the opportunity of seeing and talking
with the man who had spent days and nights on the
veld.

London hostesses almost literally fought for Rhodes's
presence at their parties. On one occasion I met him at
a house in Portland Place. Among the circle of well-known
people was Henry Stanley, for whom the occasion must
have had a melancholy interest. Not many years had
passed since he was the lion of London, the drawing-
rooms of happy hostesses who had captured him for an
evening being crammed with worshippers. I have
vivid recollection of seeing him, just home from his
discovery of Emin Pacha, at a party given by Sir John
Pender in Horace Walpole's old house in Arlington Street.
The room was crowded by the best-known people in
London. Just before midnight the late King of the
Belgians, who was among the company, gave his arm to
Lady Pender to conduct her to the supper-room. Close
behind in the procession walked Stanley, his head almost
up to the shoulders of the King. It was upon him that
all eyes were fixed. There were many kings, but only
one Stanley. On this subsequent night Stanley moved
about the crowded room in Portland Place almost unnoticed, all eyes being bent on the modest figure and
bravely smiling face of the much-bored Cape Premier.

During his visit to London in the summer of 1899
Rhodes and Kitchener saw a good deal of each other,
renewing and strengthening earlier acquaintance. Both
had in ordinary social relations a great gift of reticence.
In each other's company they were voluble. A couple
of years earlier they foregathered at Cairo. An officer

at whose quarters they frequently met gave me a graphic
account of how they spent one night there, as he puts it,
"sprawling on the floor grabbing at Africa." Their host
was the happy possessor of one of Stanford's largest and
most nearly up-to-date maps of Africa. This was spread
on the floor, Kitchener and Rhodes going down on their
knees and tracing their several proposed routes, Kitchener
coming down from the Soudan, Rhodes advancing from
the south, till, meeting, they made the way clear from
Cape to Cairo. When the Sirdar captured Khartoum,
one of his earliest telegraphic messages was dispatched
to Rhodes, with inquiry, "How are you?"

Not given to rhapsodising about other emperors than
the Roman, Rhodes was much impressed by his interview
with the German Emperor at the close of the Boer War.
He recognised in the Kaiser one of the smartest
business men he ever had dealings with. Of course, in
anticipation of the interview, the Emperor was well
primed in all the bearings of the conflict. Rhodes knew
it even more thoroughly. But he admits that he found a
match in the young Emperor. His quickness at seeing
a point, and making the most of it to the advantage of
his own case, has been rarely surpassed in Rhodes's
experience.

Public interest in Cecil Rhodes, dormant since Jameson
"upset his apple-cart," revived by his sick-bed. People
were glad to know that King Edward, who never forgot
to do a kind thing, personally communicated by cable
with the sick and wearied Titan. It was curious to note
how fatalistic his relatives were on the subject. His
brother and sister were both certain he would come safely
out of the wrestling bout with death. Eight months
before he was beaten in the struggle I met Frank Rhodes
at a country house party. He was *en route* for Cairo,
where he had tryst with his brother. They were bound
for Khartoum, and Cecil intended to return to the Cape
by the eastern route, touching at Zanzibar. Colonel

Rhodes told me that when early in the autumn of 1901 his brother arrived from the Cape, there were symptoms of heart disease that gave great concern. A quiet stay in Scotland pulled him together, and when at the end of October he set out for a leisurely journey to Egypt, he was quite a new man.

" Cecil," Colonel Rhodes said, " doesn't mean to die till he has completed his project of connecting Cape Town with Cairo by railway and telegraph. When he has made up his mind to do a certain thing, he generally sees it through."

.   .   .   .   .

Nothing in the life of Cecil Rhodes more sharply struck the public than the provision in his will directing his entombment. The picture of the funeral procession making its way northward over the South African veld till it reached the mighty Rhodesian mountain he had selected for his mausoleum, created profound impression. An old friend and colleague of the South African magnate told me an interesting story in connection with this episode. Rhodes drew from the Bible the inspiration that found realisation in his magnificent burial-place. He was a constant reader of the Old Testament, particularly delighting in the Book of Job. He frequently, more especially when depressed by overwork or bowed down by extreme anxiety, quoted Job's lament that he had not died in infancy : " For now should I have lain down and been quiet ; I should have slept ; then had I been at rest with kings and councillors of the earth which built up waste places for themselves."

The varied quotation given in the margin of the Revised Version is " built solitary piles." This idea of the kings and councillors of the earth lying in majestic loneliness on hill-tops fascinated Rhodes. He carried out the idea with peculiar appropriateness, taking his last sleep on a hill-top commanding far-reaching views of the vast territory he had added to the Empire.

CHAPTER XV

THE death of Sir James Carmichael breaks another link
with the personal memory of Gladstone. Seventeen
years ago, when the veteran statesman was returned to
power by an enormous majority, an altitude from which
he took the fatal dive into the sullen depths of the Home
Rule pool, Sir James was his private secretary. He
remained at his post till the following year, when the
magnificent majority given by the general election of
1885 melted, and the Liberal party was shattered.

One of the most striking features in the memorable
scene in Westminster Abbey on Saturday morning,
May 15, 1898, was the group of the dead statesman's
private secretaries standing at the head of the coffin,
waiting to fall in with the funeral procession. They had
entered his service young men, unknown to fame. Of
the four Carmichael was the only one who had nothing to
show for his services. His baronetcy came to him by long
descent. He held no salaried post after leaving Downing
Street. Of the rest, Edward Hamilton, created K.C.B.,
passed out of Gladstone's service into the Treasury, and
has risen to the important and highly paid office of
Assistant Secretary. Algernon West, Privy Councillor
and K.C.B., was promoted to the chair of the Board of
Inland Revenue, where he was succeeded by Henry Primrose, also made Knight Commander of the Bath.

Carmichael, one of the most modest men in the world,
was scion of an illustrious Scotch family. I remember
one night, whilst he was still Member for one of the
divisions of Glasgow, allusion was made in debate to a

holder of three peerages content to sit in the House of
Commons. Few recognised in this reference the un-
obtrusive Scotch Member, lineal descendant and heir
of the dormant titles, Earl of Hyndford, Viscount Inglis-
berry and Nemphlar, Lord Carmichael.

May 20

The turnover of ready cash in connection with the
Coronation will be colossal. A good deal will be circu-
lated by foreign visitors. But the disbursement per head
of the loyal Britisher of all degrees will be considerable.
Trade, long suffering on account of war and periods of
mourning, will hold a carnival. Dressmakers', milliners',
and all the drapers' shops are already working at high
pressure. The hotels have their rooms engaged in
advance ; private lodgings are at a premium. In the
matter of seats to view the procession hundreds of thousands
of pounds will change hands. It is estimated that the
Peers alone will, on account of themselves and their
wives, spend half a million sterling in robes and frocks.
The lowest price of a turnout for a Peer and his wife in
Coronation robes and accessories is a trifle under £200.
To do the thing well the bill will run up to £500.

It is said that the theatrical costumiers are doing a
roaring business, hiring out costumes to impecunious
Peers, who by this expedient save more than half the cost.
Robes that have lent added dignity to some portly Peer
at the Coronation of King Edward VII will, when duly
returned, grace the stage in scenes from *Hen y V,
Richard III,* or *Henry VIII.*

May 24.

There is current a curiously persistent rumour alleging
a mysterious malady that has smitten the King. Many
estimable people are certain there will be no Coronation
in June, the date fixed being preceded by a Royal funeral.
It is not a new thing, the story springing into birth shortly

after the accession.[1] At one time it was found desirable
to put forth a semi-official contradiction. It must be
admitted that for a stricken man His Majesty is pretty
lively. Every day brings its appointed work, with calls
that could be met only by one of robust constitution.
Much of the work in the way of public ceremonial His
Majesty formerly did has been relegated to his successor
in the princedom of Wales. Even in this Whitsun week,
set apart for holiday and rest by other eminent public
men, the King has been on the go through a greater
part of the twenty-four hours. Apart from public appearances His Majesty devotes constant attention to the
Coronation preparations. No detail escapes his eye or
his care.

In the comparatively short rest taken at Windsor in
the early part of this week, he entertained an interesting
house party. It included such diverse persons as Lord
Rosebery, Arthur Balfour, and Lord Roberts. The
Commander-in-Chief shines more on the battlefield than
at the dinner table. Like another great soldier of an
earlier epoch, he has no small talk. There are no more
delightful dinner guests than Lord Rosebery and Arthur
Balfour.

June 12.

Personally conducted by a reverend canon I have had
the advantage of visiting the interior of Westminster
Abbey, jealously guarded from intrusion of the public
during the process of preparation for the Coronation.
It was significant of His Majesty's energy and all per-
vadingness that before we entered it was felt judicious
to inquire whether the King was in the building. Scarcely
a day passes without His Majesty driving down in his
private brougham and spending some time in the Abbey.
What struck me most was the fact that of the six or seven
thousand persons bidden to the Abbey, very few will see

---

[1] A month later His Majesty suffered an attack of appendicitis, which
necessitated a serious operation and postponement of the Coronation.

13

the ceremony of the Coronation. It will be performed in the space beneath the lantern where in ordinary times the lectern stands. That, the chairs and the pews have all been removed. In their place stands a large platform appropriately known as "the theatre." It is built on two levels—one five steps high, on which the King will stand, one lower by two steps for the Queen.

Round this comparatively small space are erected boxes for the Royal family, one for the King's particular friends, and galleries for Peers and Peeresses, Privy Councillors, Members of the House of Commons and their wives. Of these, save the occupants of the boxes, the only spectators who are assured of a full view of the ceremony are the Privy Councillors. The gallery allotted to the House of Commons directly fronts the theatre. But the structural peculiarities of the Cathedral are such as to interfere with the view of all but those in the front rows of seats.

For the great multitude of ticket-holders there will not be even a pretence of seeing what is going on in the Sacrarium. The main body, including the sons and daughters of Peers, will be in the nave. They will, however, be comforted by an excellent position for seeing the Royal procession entering the Abbey, and will hear the music, not the least beautiful adjunct to the ceremony. Absolutely the best place, commanding a bird's-eye view of the whole business, will be the organ-loft. Every day rehearsals of the music and of portions of the ceremony are performed. One must not say anything of the spectacle of a great dignitary of the Church walking with stately step from corner to corner of the theatre, with outstretched hand leading an imaginary Sovereign, and presenting him to a loyal, but ghostly, audience, who are supposed to break forth in shouts of " God save the King." Actually at this rehearsal the silver trumpets from the orchestra on top of the choir screen pealed forth a brilliant fanfare.

Of the temporary structures erected in connection with the Coronation procession, the annexe at the west front eclipses all. It is the most marvellous piece of stage effect ever built. If, daily walking past it to the House of Commons, I had not watched its growth from lath-and-plaster stage to its present look of hoary antiquity, I would have been incredulous of the fact that two months ago the place on which it now stands was an open roadway. Regarding it, close by or afar off, it is impossible to distinguish it from the historic pile to which it has been temporarily attached. Not only has every architectural feature of the Abbey been skilfully reproduced, but the weather-stained colour centuries have been silently busy in laying with reverent hands on the walls of the temple built by Henry III is faithfully copied. Inside, equal skill and expense have been lavished. The interior forms a beautiful octagon hall, upon which the light streams through leaden paned windows copied from the oldest parts of the Abbey.

My guide, to whom every inch of the old building is familiar, looking sadly round, asked what I thought of the new one.

" It is very clever," I said.

" Yes," replied the canon, with almost savage emphasis, " it's wickedly clever."

The pity of it is that this work of modern art will have completed its destined career within the space of two or three hours. It is designed with intent that in the octagon room the Royal procession shall be formed. When the King and Queen descend at the Abbey door here will be in waiting the Prebendaries and the Dean of Westminster, with the Regalia. On the day before the Coronation the latter will be brought from the Tower under escort and deposited in the Jerusalem Chamber, where through the night sentries will keep watch and ward over the treasure.

June 16.

On Saturday I ran over to Bruges to see the marvellous collection of pictures by early Flemish painters appropriately gathered in the ancient city. I was twice honoured by a long conversation with the King of the Belgians, who, escorted by a troop of Lancers, welcomed by the acclamation of his people, came down in state to open the exhibition. I was much struck by His Majesty's admiration, even affection, for everything English. His kingly courtesy led him to express this feeling in marked degree towards *Punch*. He told me that for forty years he never missed reading it, looking forward with special delight to its arrival. He expressed his regret that the etiquette that governs kings deprived him of what would have been the great pleasure of being present at the Coronation next week.

" They don't want me," he laughingly said, " but they have asked my nephew." I said something about the rare collection of pictures on the walls of the old hall in which we stood.

" Yes," said the King, " but there you English are to the front again. For some of the best work of our old Flamand painters we have to go borrowing from you."

This is quite true. Of the works of Hans Memling, comprising fully one-half of his known paintings, some of the best come from Chatsworth, others being lent by Lord Northbrook, the Duke of Norfolk, Lord Crawford, and other well-known British collectors. At first, in resentment of the unfriendly feeling shown in Belgium towards this country in connection with the war in South Africa, there was some difficulty in obtaining the loan of pictures. In the end more generous feelings prevailed.

June 20.

Colonel Saunderson, who has just returned to his parliamentary duties after long sojourn on the Continent, brings with him a pretty story. Arriving in Berlin, he found himself the object of marked attention by the public in the streets. Wherever two or three were gathered together disposition was shown to raise the welcoming " Hoch ! hoch ! " Everywhere he was respectfully saluted, more especially by passing soldiers and officers of the army. The secret was out with next day's papers, which announced the arrival of Lord Roberts. There is certainly some facial resemblance between the gallant Colonel and the famous Field-Marshal. But the Colonel has the advantage of height by some inches.

Invited to dine with the Emperor, he was after dinner taken to the opera and seated in the Imperial box on the right hand of His Majesty.

" This," the Kaiser laughingly said, " will settle it. My people will know now you must be Lord Roberts."

The prophecy was abundantly fulfilled in the papers of the following day, all announcing that Earl Roberts had been present with the Emperor in the Imperial box at the opera.

June 20.

The sudden illness of the King, culminating in resolve to remain in seclusion till, next week, the great day dawns, sent a thrill of alarm through London. It is not a matter to which it has seemed proper to allude, but it would be idle to further ignore the fact that there are countless people in London, of all sorts and conditions, who are firmly convinced that His Majesty is the victim of some hapless disease. With only a week for their predictions to run, there are many who confidently assert that there will be no Coronation next Thursday. This is, of course, a phantasy based solely upon imagination and superstition. From some who come in personal touch with the King I learn that, prior to an attack of lumbago directly traceable to our genial June, His Majesty was in excellent health and highest spirits.

Another more ominous breakdown is that of the

Premier. Here, again, wintry June is directly responsible for the chill which has compelled Lord Salisbury to abandon his engagements and keep to his room. For some time there has been evidence in his public appearance of desire and necessity for rest. He was in the House of Lords on Tuesday night, fast asleep on the Treasury Bench, whilst his son-in-law, the First Lord of the Admiralty (Lord Selborne), was learnedly discoursing on the plating of His Majesty's ships. The Premier's heavy gait when walking, his lethargic appearance when seated, his growing inability to command his voice when addressing the House of Lords, are painfully suggestive. In both political camps it is regarded as a certainty that shortly after the Coronation this loyal servant of his country will claim the guerdon of well-earned rest. His retirement will be followed by a peculiarly interesting reconstruction of the Ministry.

A function second only in importance and interest to that in which the King and Queen play the principal part, is the luncheon in Westminster Hall, to take place immediately after the ceremony of coronation. For this thirteen hundred places have been booked in advance. In addition, eight hundred breakfasts will be served between seven and nine in the morning. The Peers will feed apart, the Royal Gallery and the Queen's Robing Room pertaining to their House being turned into a banquet hall. There was much moaning at the bar when a charge of two guineas was fixed for the meal. Hankering after the simple sandwich and the wholesome whisky and soda was openly expressed. It prevailed so far that arrangements were drafted for setting up a buffet, at which Peers and the ladies they escort might stand up, taking refreshments at a less extravagant price. It turned out that the demand for two-guinea tickets proved so extensive that there was no room for the buffet. The motto of the Peers on Coronation Day will accordingly be " One Meal, One Price."

Peers and Peeresses will attend Westminster Abbey, and go on to luncheon in their robes and coronets. After long deliberation, alternative sartorial style is permitted to Commoners and their wives. Members may attend in uniform, Court dress, or morning dress ; in the latter case, black frock-coats being indispensable. Ladies may go as they please, in Court dress or morning dress. In the former case trains are not permitted, nor in the latter are hats or bonnets.

Profound mystery broods over the Coronation dress of Her Majesty. Whilst most other details of the Coronation have been described in advance, no information has been forthcoming in respect of this interesting matter. The fact is, infinite care has been taken to keep the secret till Her Majesty walks up the nave of the Abbey on Coronation Day. Precautions have been carried to such length that the making of the robe has not been entrusted to an ordinary dressmaking firm. The task is even now going forward in the private house of a personal friend of Royalty, where, with locked doors, a bevy of girls are working.

The portentous secret has leaked out to the extent that one knows the embroidery of gold thread has been designed and wrought by the Ladies' Work Society, of which Princess Louise is president. The Princess, whose native and trained art is well known, is, indeed, taking general supervision of the creation of this work of art. The general design of the gold embroidery is a display of the Cross of St. George, round which are entwined the rose, shamrock, and thistle. Competition for the making of this gown was very keen amongst the principal houses of London and Paris. More than one offer was received by Her Majesty practically to make it for nothing, returning to the Queen, for disposal upon whatever charity she thought fit, her cheque for the charges.

There has been a little trouble among His Majesty's judges in the matter of place at the Coronation. All the judges received command to attend in the full glory of wig and gown. When, however, the question of places in the Abbey came to be discussed, it was found that the judges were to be divided into two sections. One, being Privy Councillors, had seats assigned to them in the choir, commanding full view of the " theatre." Others, not right honourable, will be bunched together in the nave. Their position, it is true, is at the entrance to the choir, but they will not see anything save the procession.

An informal meeting of the second section of judges was held, at which some disposition was shown to resent this preference by abstaining from attendance. The situation was saved by the caustic remark of one of the junior judges, who, five years ago, used to enliven the House of Commons with frank speech, and now keeps lively court in the King's Bench Division of the High Court of Justice.

" When," he said, " we take into consideration the fact that C—— and W—— [1] are among the members of His Majesty's Privy Council, we may regard our position the more honourable, being seated apart elsewhere."

Their lordships laughed, and agreed to say nothing more on the subject. It speaks volumes for the public estimation of the two right hon. gentlemen alluded to.

June 24.

The sudden striking down of the King by an attack of appendicitis, gives uneasy point to the story entered among these notes a month ago, alleging a mysterious malady that would preclude Coronation. The superstition is founded on a story dating back to the visit of the King to India whilst he was still Prince of Wales. Consulting a native seer, he was told he would in due time come to the throne of England, but would never be crowned. Bearing in mind the fact that this is not a phantasy born this week,

[1] Well-known Members of the House of Commons, henchmen of Mr. Chamberlain's.

the condition of affairs to-day takes on a certain un-
canniness. Forecasts of this nature have a tendency
to bring about their own fulfilment. If the one reported
was ever made, it was likely enough to be in the King's
mind, and with a man of nervous temperament, which
His Majesty is not, might have had discomposing effect.

On this matter I have personal testimony of interest
and value. A friend, who visited His Majesty at Windsor
last Saturday, and spent some time in his company,
found him apparently in good health, certainly in high
spirits. He talked about his health, complained that
the doctors fed him on " slops," but evidently had no
idea that he was stricken with a grave malady. By
curious coincidence, to the same gentleman, visiting him
ten days earlier, the King, talking about various forms
of illness, referred to appendicitis, and showed disposition
to discuss it.

It was after my friend left the Castle, other visitors
arriving, including some ladies, His Majesty, with his
accustomed graciousness, conducted them about the
grounds, overstraining his strength. On Sunday he was
better again, and the doctors authorised his journey to
town on Monday.

That led to the conclusion of the matter. On Monday
afternoon His Majesty had to abandon his intention of
presiding at the state banquet in the evening. He went
to bed early, and at one o'clock on Tuesday morning was
seized with severe pains. The doctors summoned in
consultation straightway decided on the necessity for an
operation. Of the family and household the Queen was
the only one informed of the impending ordeal. The
King submitted with that patient courage that has always
distinguished him. After an interview with the Prince
of Wales, he asked for a cigar, and was much comforted
by its soothing influence.

At this present time of writing the King is reported in
the bulletins to be progressing satisfactorily. The events

immediately preceding His Majesty's breakdown are, however, not of a character that induces the public to place unreserved confidence in the published statements of the doctors. It would be a serious libel upon their professional acumen to assume that up to Monday night, when the King's temperature ran up to 102, those eminent experts had not diagnosed their patient's true condition. However it be, the public remember that Tuesday morning's papers contained assurances, avowedly based on the opinion of the doctors, that there was nothing serious the matter with His Majesty. This made all the more crushing the blow that fell on the Metropolis soon after the stroke of noon on the same day, when it was made known that the Coronation was postponed consequent on the deadly sickness of the King.

June 25.

Comedy and tragedy are ever within touch. Depressed under the national calamity that has obscured festive preparations, I recall the humours of the final rehearsal of the high personages who were to have taken part in the Coronation, which I had the rare privilege of witnessing in Westminster Abbey. In its way, though of course less picturesque and dignified, it was almost as interesting as would have been the actual event. The procedure ordered to take place on the stage where the two chairs stand was gone through in every detail. With the exception of His Majesty, all the *dramatis personæ* were the Peers who had parts assigned to them on the occasion of the Coronation. The part of the King was filled by Sir Spencer Ponsonby Fane, Comptroller of the Lord Chamberlain's Department. The Duke of Norfolk, in his capacity as Earl Marshal, directed the proceedings much after the manner that the author and manager of a new piece about to be placed on the stage conduct rehearsal.

For the most part the Peers were in morning dress, which, with the adjunct of a coronet, had a comical effect.

In this style appeared the Duke of Devonshire. After his custom he arrived a little late. With right hand in his trousers pocket, and an inexpressibly bored look on his face, he strolled about the stage at the bidding of the Earl Marshal. Quite different was the manner of the venerable Lord High Chancellor (Halsbury). He, too, was in morning dress. That circumstance was not permitted to interfere with the grace and mobility of his movements. Advancing to pay homage to His Majesty he could not have been more reverential in manner had the personage in the chair really been Edward VII, instead of Sir Spencer Ponsonby Fane aforesaid. Bowing low, the Lord Chancellor fell on both knees and kissed the King's hand, afterwards, with inexpressible gravity, going through the ordered formula of touching the lay figure of His Majesty with his finger on either side of the forehead.

Such of the Peers as wore their Coronation robes had pages carrying their trains. The Peeresses taking part in the rehearsal did not wear Court dress. Shawls trailing behind, and in two cases white drapery that looked like a tablecloth, served for the train, giving their pages opportunity of rehearsing their graceful duties. Once as the procession was moving down the ladies fell a-whispering, a tendency checked by firm command from the Earl Marshal to preserve silence. Several bishops in their robes, which are conveniently stored in the Abbey, solemnly acted their parts.

There was something pathetic in the appearance of the Archbishop of Canterbury, by reason of his almost blindness led on to the dais. It was part of his appointed function after the Coronation to conduct the King to the four quarters of the platform and proclaim him to the people. How this would be accomplished, in the painful circumstances affecting the Primate's eyesight, was a matter of some concern to his colleagues in the great function. It was regarded as probable that, with his great tact and unfailing kindness of heart, it would come to pass that His Majesty would lead the Archbishop instead of the Archbishop conducting the King. Like Lord Halsbury and other Peers of Parliament, Dr. Temple, also on his knees, performed the act of homage. He afterwards read aloud some portions of the Coronation service committed to his charge.

June 26.

The Chancellor of the Exchequer did not attend the dinner given last night by the Prime Warden and Wardens of the Goldsmiths' Company " on the occasion of a Trial of the Pyx." Nominally this dinner is in honour of the Chancellor, who is Master and Worker of the Mint. When Lord Goschen was at the Treasury he usually accepted the invitation of the Prime Warden. But the pleasures of the table have no attraction for Sir Michael Hicks-Beach. The Home Secretary, however, managed to make the most of the dinner interval at the House of Commons, spending it at Goldsmiths' Hall. Among other guests were the Premier of Natal, the Kanwar, Sir Harnam Singh, and Sir Redvers Buller, looking none the less cheerful for recent tribulation. Unlike similar functions with other of the great City Companies, the Goldsmiths' do not invite representatives of the Press with intent to have their proceedings reported. This has a natural tendency in the direction of shortening the speeches and lessening formality.

In conversation with Sir William Roberts-Austen, chemist and assayer, I learned that this year the Pyx has triumphantly sustained the really severe trial it undergoes. In addition to coinage issued from the Royal Mint, the produce of branches at Sydney, Melbourne, and Perth are assayed. Of all, including the mother Mint on Tower Hill, the purest metal was turned out from the youngest and smallest of the Mints—Perth, in Western Australia.

In accordance with ancient custom each Warden is

entitled to invite a guest, who sits beside him in his appointed place at the tables set at right angles with that
at which the Prime Warden presides under the light of
the famous Flaxman candelabra. This ancient ordinance
last year led to an awkward incident. One of the Wardens
invited the Grand Duke Michael, then visiting London,
to be his guest at the Pyx dinner. The invitation was
accepted, and being notified to the Court, a seat was fixed
for the Grand Duke next to the places at the table pertaining to his friend. When the company proceeded
to the dining-hall, and the Grand Duke discovered where
he was expected to sit, he bluntly refused. At the head
table sat the Prime Warden, with, as it happened, Lord
Wolseley in the place of honour at his right hand. It
would never do for the Heir Presumptive to the Throne of
all the Russias to take a lower seat. There were some
moments of pained confusion. In the end the Grand
Duke was conducted to the upper table, and Lord Wolseley
was dispossessed of the place of honour, where the future
Czar seated himself and enjoyed a more or less pleasant
evening.

June 27.

Met Sarah Bernhardt at an At Home given by Mrs.
Labouchere in the corner house of the Old Palace Yard.
"Labby" left the House of Commons early to assist his
wife in doing the honours of the place, and was in much
request by the crowd of fair women, finely dressed, who
filled the room. As for Sarah, she was in the highest
spirits, "in her wild-flower mood," as someone said.
No one, to look at her as she stood laughing and chatting
with all comers, would imagine she was a grandmother !
She has altered considerably since first coming to London,
having quite grown out of that extreme slightness of form
at one time the source of perpetual jesting among ribald
French newspapers. I remember when years ago I dwelt
in the Quartier Latin reading in the *Figaro* a grave description of Sarah's controversy with her medical attendant.

He had prescribed a pill.   She preferred a powder, explaining that if she took a pill its rotundity would, temporarily at least, spoil her figure.

She was dressed like a girl of sixteen, in a gown of soft white China silk with a deep edge of Valenciennes lace. Her hat was large and rather flat in shape, fashioned of pleated pale-green tulle, crowned by a great pale pink rose—emblematic, I suppose, of the sweetness and serenity of her later life.   She recited two pieces, or, rather, read one and recited the other.   The first was a story of two lovers wandering through a wood taking their last farewell. Over their imaginary grief Sarah mourned in the richest, softest, most musical voice ever heard from woman. Whether it was Nature or art I am not sure ; certainly when she had finished the story the tears were running down her unpainted cheeks.

It is an old controversy whether famous actors and actresses really feel the emotion they simulate in their presentation of varied character.   Upon this point Miss Ellen Terry is an interesting and important witness. Talking about the revival of *Charles I*, she told me she was never able to play the part of the Queen with dry eyes.   On the first night of the revival many of the audience literally sobbed through one of the scenes.

" But," said Ellen Terry, " no one in the theatre cried more helplessly than I did."

June 29.

Supped last night with Johnny Hare and a lively company at the Garrick.   Occasion made memorable by a comedy unrehearsed, played off the stage without accessories, and witnessed by a company of distinguished actors.   Gathering in the hall of the Garrick about the time named for supper, the company chatted and the host led the way to the supper-room.

The guests being seated, it was discovered that a chair was filled by one whom nobody knew.   In such intimate society the appearance of a stranger was noteworthy.

He must be somebody, or Johnny Hare would not have invited him. Whispered inquiry going round the table failed to discover his identity. The most puzzled man of all was the host, who had never in his life set eyes on the stranger, who made himself thoroughly at home, enjoying the wines, the meats, and not least the conversation.

Towards the close of the feast wags seated near the Unknown suggested that it would be a nice thing if he, on behalf of the company, would propose a toast to the health of the host. Nothing loath, he rose, and in prosy fashion extolled the great actor. During the speech, loudly cheered by wicked guests, Hare's face was a sight to see. There is nothing he detests more than speech-making. To have the necessity of making a reply forced upon him by an intruder at his supper-table was a little too much. However, entering into the spirit of the joke, he made due acknowledgment, and the company soon after breaking up, the still Unknown went home, pluming himself on having spent a pleasant evening.[1]

[1] As far as I have heard the mystery of the unbidden guest was never fathomed. It is surmised that he was a country member of the club who, joining the supper-party on the way to the feast, found an empty chair and sat down in it.

CHAPTER XVI

July 1, 1902.

IN connection with the Coronation honours surprise is expressed in the House of Commons at the assumed choice by the Prime Minister of two Liberals, one made a peer, the other a baronet. Why Lord Salisbury should specially delight to honour these worthy gentlemen is a question some of their political friends, whose names do not appear in the honours list, cannot quite make out. The fact is, neither Lord Salisbury nor Mr. Arthur Balfour had anything to do with the selection beyond confirming it. What happened was that the King expressed a wish to the Prime Minister that the Coronation honours should in their distribution not be based upon party grounds. In obedience to this command, honours were divided, the Leader of the Opposition in the Commons being invited to nominate two new Peers.

The case of Sir William Harcourt the King took entirely in his own hands. He wrote a holograph letter of four pages, offering a peerage in the friendliest personal terms. When the veteran Commoner asked leave to be left in the Chamber of the Legislature where for thirty-four years he has been a prominent figure, the King wrote another letter of graciously expressed consent, adding warm acknowledgment of the long service Sir William has done to the State. It was expected that while Sir William would, if he simply consulted his own inclination, decline a peerage, he would be ready to sacrifice himself on the altar of paternal affection, and for Loulou's sake wear the badge. Sir William tells me that his son no more hankers after a

peerage than does his father.[1] Loulou intends to enter the
House of Commons and devote himself to active public life.
He has accomplishments that should command success.

July 2.

Invitations to the great function at the India Office
to-morrow-night were engraved before the illness of the
King upset everything. They bear the announcement
that " Their Majesties the King, Emperor of India, and
the Queen, have graciously signified their intention of
being present." A printed slip enclosed notifies that
" By Command of His Majesty Their Royal Highnesses
the Prince and Princess of Wales will represent Their
Majesties on the occasion." The earlier form has a special
significance. As far as I know, it is the first time His
Majesty has been officially styled Emperor of India. It is
true that in the latest coinage of the reign of Queen Victoria, the style *Ind. Imp.* appeared at the end of the sovereign title, and is preserved in the coinage under the new
Sovereign. But in parliamentary and official documents the
understanding entered into when, piloted by Disraeli, the
Royal Titles Bill passed an unwilling House of Commons,
is honourably observed. It was then insisted upon that
Queen Victoria's added title, Empress of India, should be
used only in India, never in this country. Lord George
Hamilton would probably plead that to-morrow night's
function being inaugurated and conducted by the India
Office, the style customary in India is permissible here.

July 3.

If one of the prognostications of the Budget be verified,
and a tax imposed on imported timber, it will make a
serious difference to the contractors for the multitudinous
constructions planned for viewing the Coronation procession. In extent and seating capacities these will
exceed anything done in that direction in Jubilee times.
One, a fair sample of the larger constructions, is being

[1] On the break-up in 1917 of the Coalition Government presided over
by Mr. Asquith, and the formation of a new one by Mr. Lloyd George,
Mr. Harcourt became Viscount Harcourt.

14

planned at the corner of Pall Mall and Waterloo Place,
facing the Athenæum Club. It is on the site of the old
Wanderers' Club, lately pulled down. The stand will
seat 900 persons, paying an average of six guineas each.
Supposing the seats are all let—and the rush for seats
continues unabated—this means a turnover of £6,000
per day, and there will be two days for sight-seers.

Six guineas is a moderate price for a good seat, ten
being the more common figure. I have seen the list of a
firm of agents who have the letting of some of the best
private houses in St. James's Street and Pall Mall. The
figures are amazing. For a second floor in St. James's Street
two hundred and fifty guineas has been paid for occupation the first day, two hundred guineas for the second. In
the same street a first-floor balcony has brought five hundred guineas. In Pall Mall a balcony lets for the same
almost fabulous sum. Portions of a roof bring a hundred
guineas. It will be understood that these are not offers
to let. They are bargains actually concluded.

July 4.

The scene at the India Office, when the Prince of
Wales, on behalf of the King, received the homage
of the Indian princes, was as impressive as it was
unique. On a daïs at the eastern end of the lavishly
decorated, brilliantly thronged hall stood the Heir
Apparent and his Consort. The Viceroy's bodyguard,
in scarlet or yellow uniform, carrying lances with red
and white pennons, formed a lane through which the
Indian princes advanced, arrayed in the drapery of the
East, flashing with jewels. Their very names suggested
pages of history. There was the Maharajah of Jaipur,
who traces his regal line back to the Sun God—a pedigree
compared with which our kings and queens are but
as yesterday. In the glittering line were the Maharajah
Sindhia of Gwalior, whose kingdom extends over thirty
thousand square miles; the Maharajah of Kolhapur,
whose far-off ancestors founded the Mahratta Empire; the

Lion of Rajputana, Sir Pertab Singh ; the Maharajah of
Bikanir, who begins to count his pedigree from Umalrai,
fifty-sixth in descent from that great Rajput, Rama ;
and the Maharajah of Cooch Behar, whose family have
for four hundred years reigned in unbroken succession.

These were only a few recognised in the procession
making its haughty way through the lines of sowars.
Some of the chiefs are of gigantic height, all of soldierly
bearing. Arrived on the daïs, each, drawing himself
up to full height, saluted the representative of the Emperor
of India. Then, advancing a step, holding his sword
horizontally by hilt and point, he proffered it to his liege
lord. The Prince of Wales, advancing half a pace,
lightly touched the sword, whereat the chieftain, again
drawing himself to full height, saluted and, turning
sharply about to the right, marched off, giving place
to another ruler of an ancient Indian state, who went
through the same ceremony. As a spectacle it was magnificent. For all it meant as the latest chapter in the
history of India it was an episode never to be forgotten.

Earlier in the evening there was an incident noted
and understood only by some of the Anglo-Indians
grouped on the daïs awaiting the coming of the Prince and
Princess of Wales. There were plenty of chairs about ; the
night was sultry ; the Prince tarried long. But none of
the waiting Maharajahs took a chair. The reason for
this abnegation throws a flood of light on the condition of
native India, even in this twentieth century. Amongst
those on the platform were the Maharajah of Jaipur and
the Maharajah of Kolhapur. For ages there has existed
between these two houses question of precedence. Kolhapur, as I have said, traces his lineage back to the founder
of the Mahratta Empire. The Maharajah of Jaipur has
a pedigree a hundred and forty generations long, with
the legendary hero of the Rajputa to begin with. That
is hard to beat ; but the massive Maharajah of Kolhapur
will not acknowledge supremacy. In anticipation of

the ceremony at the India Office, the point was, by common consent, remitted to the arbitrament of the Secretary of State. The idea of Lord George Hamilton settling a matter at issue between the lineal descendant of Rama of Rajputa and the great Mahratta soldier-king is a delicate and delicious bit of comedy to be revelled over in quiet moments. He shrewdly declined the commission, with the result that, neither of the rival Maharajahs being at liberty to sit down first, all the Maharajahs remained standing.

Money was lavished on the spectacle on a scale that shocked old Treasury men. But the India Office has nothing to do with the Treasury. The wealth of India is at its command, and as a highly placed official, who took me into his confidence on the subject : said, " When we want anything done we've only to ask, and there you are." This is all very well for the British clerk. But lo ! the poor Indian with his plagues, his famines, and his subsistence on three farthings a day.

July 5.

A notable interview, illustrating the far-reaching influence of the British Empire, has just taken place in London.   The parties to it were the emissaries of the King of Abyssinia and Apolo Kagwa, Prime Minister, actually the ruler, of Uganda.   Denizens of the same vast continent, possessing at home only the vaguest idea of each other's existence, these representatives of two swarthy nations, brought hither upon the occasion of, the King's Coronation, met in a London drawing-room, and with the assistance of interpreters bearing commissions in the British Army, talked with each other.   Apolo Kagwa, the stately Ugandian, made a pretty speech in which he welcomed the Abyssinian Ambassador on the common ground of being a friend of the English King and people.

A week ago I met Apolo and his secretary on a gunboat placed at their disposal for a view of the fleet at Spithead. He does not speak English, but his secretary is tolerably conversant with the language. Apolo is over six feet high, of extremely powerful build. His face of mahogany hue is of the negro type, but instinct with intelligence. Very little escapes his eye, whether on land or sea. The young English officer who, familiar with the country and the language, has him in personal charge, told me the first day he took Apolo out for a drive they went to the Park, along Piccadilly by Knightsbridge. Coming back, meaning to look in at the House of Commons, they turned down Sloane Street. Instantly Apolo told the captain the coachman was going wrong.

"He didn't come this way," he said; "right along there," pointing towards Piccadilly.

Considering he had been driven for the first time by devious ways through crowded thoroughfares, it is a high tribute to the trained observation of uncivilised man that he should have picked out Sloane Street from the congeries of cross-roads passed on his way westward. A sense of humour is evidently the birthright of the Ugandian. I never saw a merrier couple than Apolo and his secretary, chatting together on the deck of the gunboat, their quick eyes noting every surrounding incident.

The Foreign Office have made arrangements whereby the Uganda Premier and his secretary will be personally conducted on a visit to some of the centres of industrial activity in England and Scotland. They have been duly impressed with the sights of London. It is thought politic that they should be enabled to carry back and communicate to their people impressions of the industrial activity and resources of Great Britain. The lesson will not be lost upon Apolo Kagwa. The officer in charge of the dusky visitors, who has seen two years' service in Uganda and speaks the language fluently, gives me an interesting account of how the Premier received his curious Christian name. The Ugandians are fond of finding names for themselves out of the Bible. The Premier's secretary, for example, was christened Ham.

That is plain sailing. The selection of the name is appropriate enough for one of negro race. But where in the Old or New Testament is Apolo found ? Nowhere in this precise form. But there was Apollos, a friend of the Apostle Paul's, " eloquent and mighty in the Scriptures." Kagwa desired to be called after him. The difficulty was that in the Ugandian tongue the letter " s " must needs be followed by a vowel, which would overload Apollos. After some consideration Kagwa solved the difficulty by leaving out the " s." Whilst he was pruning he also struck out one of the " l's," and remains Apolo.

July 12.

It is generally recognised that the hurrying on of the date of the Coronation is, from the point of view of the King's health, a most desirable proceeding. With fullest command over himself it would be impossible to prevent His Majesty from chafing under the ominous delay. Whether the reported prophecy that he would come to the throne, but would not live to be crowned, be or be not an invention, it is not the kind of thing even the most phlegmatic of men would like to have hovering over a sick-bed. The apparent imminence of its realisation on the very eve of what promised to be its falsification invests it with an eerie influence. Apart from this fanciful consideration, by no means to be slighted in a sick chamber, there are others that make it desirable the Coronation should be accomplished with the least possible delay. Assuming it to take place in August, the colonial premiers and the Indian princes, who have journeyed far to be present on the occasion, will be able to extend their visit to the necessary limit.

July 13.

The appointment of Schomberg McDonnell, private secretary to Lord Salisbury, to permanent office at the Board of Works goes to confirm the persistent rumour of the retirement of the Premier from active service. For fourteen years the brother of the Earl of Antrim has been Lord Salisbury's right-hand man. One of the best-

known and most popular figures in London Society, he is an
ideal private secretary. Others one has known in his position
affected an air of mystery and reserve when public matters
were touched upon in their presence that was more amusing than imposing.   Schomberg McDonnell has a breezy
manner and a volubility that comforts the unaccustomed
caller with the impression that he is quite off his
guard, and that ministerial secrets will be cheap to-day.
When he leaves at the conclusion of the interview, he
will find his stock of information has not been appreciably
augmented.

A new light was thrown upon the character of this
interesting middle-aged young man when, things looking
very bad in South Africa, he went to the Front on active
service.   A man-about-town of sybaritic tastes and not
very robust health, he seemed the last in the world
likely to volunteer to share the privations of an army
in the field.   Moreover, by quitting his post at the
right hand of the Prime Minister, he ran the risk of
supersession in the coveted appointment.   Nothing, however, could keep him from the Front, where he did good
service, winning a step in rank and coming back to
be reinstated in his old position in Arlington Street and
Hatfield.

There is a close precedent for his appointment to the
post of Secretary to the Board of Works.   When, in 1886,
Gladstone was driven out of office, one of his last acts
was to appoint his private secretary—Henry Primrose—
to this same berth, a snug one, yielding revenue of
£1,200 a year.   There is also prospect of promotion.
Gladstone's former secretary, now K.C.B., is to-day
Chairman of the Board of Inland Revenue, with a salary
of £2,000 a year.

July 19.

The marvellous recuperation of the King, making it
possible to fix the date of the Coronation for August 9,
has greatly cleared the air of troubled London.   The

worried stand-contractors, and their not less irritated ticket-holders, now know exactly where they are. After all, the stands put up in anticipation of the Coronation procession on June 26 will be utilised. Most of them remain as they were set up, though naturally a little dingy as far as colour and decoration are concerned. It will be necessary in these respects to touch them up before the happy day. Not the least gratifying prospect is that of their final removal. In certain clubs in Pall Mall that event will be second only to the close of the war in re-establishing severed friendships. A number of members, being the majority who either did not want to obtain seats to view the procession or failed at the ballot box, growl all through the summer day at the presence of the huge wooden structures that cover the face of the club. They certainly bestow on the interior a funereal air, and lead to lighting up at an abnormally early hour.

July 24.

Rumours are current touching the circumstances under which the Marquis of Salisbury severed his long connection with State affairs. It is said he submitted to the King a list of Coronation honours, which promptly came back to him with many alterations scored in His Majesty's own hand. Amongst the late Premier's suggestions was the proposal that two eminent solicitors, one long connected with the Bank of England, should be knighted. This was crossed out, and there was substituted the name of a well-known practitioner, long a personal friend of His Majesty's, deservedly popular in all relations of life.[1] It is only a short time since, on the initiative of the King, this gentleman was knighted. In the Coronation *Gazette* he will be found advanced to the position of a baronet.

According to gossip of the hour, this was the last straw that broke the back of Lord Salisbury's loyal resolution

George Lewis.

to remain at his post till the Coronation was actually accomplished. He forthwith tendered his resignation, and it was promptly accepted. This is the story told in political circles. It may be purely imaginative ; it is certainly persistent.

At his garden party last Saturday Lord Salisbury had the air of an overworked man to whom welcome holiday had come at last. He looked already better for his rest, and was in unusual high spirits, talking in jesting mood with the long succession of guests. As with all great workers, manumission from office will not for him mean idleness. He has his loved laboratory at hand, and has already set apart a fixed portion of the day for working in its prized seclusion. There is no doubt that his retention of office during at least the past two years has been due to impulse of loyalty to his Sovereign and his party. In the counsels and personal regard of Queen Victoria he had come to fill the place held during the closing years of his life by the once-contemned and distrusted Dizzy. The death of Queen Victoria seemed a fitting epoch for his retirement. But the Boer War was still going forward, and his resignation would have led to serious ministerial crisis. He accordingly stayed on, not, it is to be hoped, to receive the final rebuff which gossip alleges.

Since his retirement he has not been seen in the House of Lords, nor is he likely hereafter to haunt its stage. He had no particular love of the place, was visibly bored by the speech-making, taking part in it only upon extreme compulsion. Should he by chance look in on any special occasion, he will have to find a seat on some unaccustomed bench. Probably he will seek one at the corner of the front bench below the gangway, where he would find himself immediately *vis à vis* with that other Premier retired from business—the Earl of Rosebery.

A very old Cabinet colleague of Lord Salisbury's, one who owes his peerage to his favour, tells me that during the last two years a marked change came over the ex-Premier's manner when presiding in Downing Street. Through his first and second Administrations he was absolutely the dominating figure at the Council. For at least two years before his final retirement he was accustomed to sit silent, letting others talk, Chamberlain, in the main, leading. This mental habit of aloofness was visible to the vulgar eye in the House of Lords. For the greater part of a sitting Lord Salisbury sat with head sunk on his breast, his closed fists dug into the cushion on either side supporting him whilst he slumbered. That was a condition which, on the whole, was comforting to his colleagues. They were uneasy whilst he was awake, since at any odd moment he might rise, and, once on his legs, Heaven only knew into what blazing indiscretion he might flash. This condition and attitude on the part of the head of the Government probably account for much of the wobbling that marked the course of Ministers in Parliament and outside during the past three years.

On the same high personal authority I learn the secret of an incident which at the time excited much comment, and still mystifies the public. It will be remembered how, a day or two after the resignation of Lord Rosebery's Ministry, Schomberg McDonnell, Lord Salisbury's private secretary, personally waited on Campbell-Bannerman, and demanded the seals pertaining to his Secretaryship of State. The proceeding was most unusual, and, by the retiring Secretary of State for War, was resented as unwarrantable. The usual course in such circumstances is for the retiring Ministers of the Crown to proceed in person to wherever the Sovereign may at the time be resident, and place the seals in the Royal hand that bestowed them.

The reason for Lord Salisbury's extraordinary procedure was, I am told, founded upon apprehension that Campbell-Bannerman would take advantage of the closing hours of his official life to bestow the chief command of the British Army upon Redvers Buller. On the very night the cordite explosion took place in the House of Commons, dislodging Rosebery's Ministry, Sir Henry announced the resignation of the Duke of Cambridge. Lord Salisbury and his friends had reason to believe that this was a step preliminary to planting Redvers Buller in the office, a promotion they were resolved at any cost to frustrate. Hence the anxiety to gain possession of the seals without whose instrumentality the suspected intention could not be carried out.

CHAPTER XVII

CABINET Ministers taking their turn in attendance on King Edward during his stay at Balmoral find the situation considerably improved as compared with experience under the late Queen. Notably, there is withdrawal of the prohibition against smoking, a sore deprivation to some of the Queen's councillors. One told me that his only chance of a smoke after dinner on wet nights—and it is often wet in the Highlands—was to sit at the open window of his bedroom and blow his clouds of smoke outside. Even then he was in terror lest a whiff of the detested perfume should escape into the corridor. To prevent that calamity he, being of a practical turn of mind, stopped up the keyhole, and tucked a mat well round the foot of the door.

The accommodation for guests was limited. The best suite of rooms in the Castle, formerly occupied by the Prince Consort, remained shut up, with everything in its place as the vanished hand left it. The King has had these rooms added to daily use. But the bedroom and private sitting-room of the late Queen are held sacred rfom intrnsion. Some alteration, including thorough redecoration of the Castle, was made in anticipation of the King's autumn visit. There was one thing His Majesty promptly proceeded to do on his coming into possession. The place was redolent of the memory of John Brown. Amongst other mementoes was a life-size statue of the faithful, but bumptious gillie. This was dislodged without a day's delay. Many years ago the Queen bestowed upon the favourite a residence at Balnachoil, in convenient contiguity to Balmoral.

On the death of John Brown his family took up their residence there. His Majesty has now succeeded in purchasing the place, and has completed what, in Cromwell's time, was called a purge.

July 24.

Curious testimony to the vitality of superstition, even in the twentieth century, is forthcoming in connection with the launch of the Caister lifeboat, built to replace the one wrecked in the winter of 1901. The Countess of Selborne, wife of the First Lord of the Admiralty, kindly undertook to perform the ceremony of naming the *Nancy Lucy*. Friday, the 25th inst., was the day fixed for the ceremony. On this being made known on the Norfolk coast, there was great stir among the gallant fishermen. As has been shown on many a dark and stormy night, notably in the November storm of two years ago, when Caister men, scorning to "turn back," lost their lives in the effort to rescue the unknown crew of a nameless ship, they are ready to face any peril. But they shrink from putting out to sea in a boat launched and named on a Friday. Urgent representations on the matter being made to Lady Selborne and the donor of the new lifeboat, the ceremony was accomplished to-day (Thursday).

October 3.

Death of the Duke of Richmond announced to-day. His withdrawal from the parliamentary and political arena was long ago completed. He was not the type of man, albeit a Peer, out of which even Conservative Ministers are constructed in these days. That is a pity, for though neither pushful nor brilliant he was a capable business man, sagacious, and thoroughly honest, in many respects the very opposite in character to the Royal Stuart family whose blood was in his veins. When Disraeli came into power in 1874 his unerring instinct discerned how valuable to him would be the colleagueship of the sixth Duke of Richmond, sublimation of respecta-

bility. So he made him Lord President of the Council,
and gave him the lead of the House of Lords.

I remember how, when Beaconsfield took his seat on
the ministerial bench in the House of Lords, he was
careful to place the placid Duke of Richmond between
himself and his loving friend and colleague, the Marquis
of Salisbury. He always had a hankering for something
substantial fixed between himself and fiery orators. It
will be remembered how, when he and Gladstone, both
in their prime, were nightly fighting each other in the
House of Commons, he publicly thanked Heaven that
between him and the right hon. gentleman, then Leader
of the Opposition, there interposed " a substantial piece
of furniture "—the clerks' table, to wit.

The Duke of Richmond was the type of councillor, varied
only by preference for Disraeli, to whom Queen Victoria,
in time of trouble, turned instinctively. Such a time came
when, towards the close of the session of 1884, conflict
between Lords and Commons was threatened over the
Redistribution Bill. Lord Salisbury was resolute in denouncing the measure, and it seemed inevitable that the
Lords would throw it out on the second reading. Her
Majesty, anxious to avoid what promised to be unseemly
conflict, out of which the Peers must inevitably come the
worse off, sent for the Duke of Richmond, and besought
him to use his influence with the Peers to bring about a
compromise.

The episode is one about which Sir Charles Dilke could,
if he would—probably some day will—relate some
interesting matters. He was at the time President of
the Local Government Board, and was by Gladstone
deputed to conduct the negotiations with the leaders
of the Opposition in the Lords that resulted in the
amicable passing of the threatened measure.

October 31.

Evidence of Queen Victoria's personal dislike for
Gladstone is abundantly forthcoming in John Morley's

monumental life of the great Liberal statesman. Before
its appearance the world was familiar with the efforts
Her late Majesty made to avoid the inevitable result of
the general election of 1880, which pointed to him as
Prime Minister. She first sent for Granville, then
for Hartington, and would not accept that implacable
person's refusal. When the worst had happened, and
Gladstone was installed in office, she several times, with
almost motherly concern for his health, pressed a Peerage on his acceptance.

It is a notable coincidence that the nearest parallel
to this personal prejudice is found in her earlier objection
to Disraeli. This existed and was strongly manifested
up to the death of the Prince Consort, whose ascetic
sense of morality was offended by some traits in Dizzy's
character. It is one of that masterful man's triumphs
that years after the Prince Consort passed away, he
not only overcame the Queen's repugnance, but trans-
formed it into a feeling of unqualified admiration, even
personal affection.

A glimmer for the reason of Queen Victoria's distaste
for the companionship of Gladstone is found in her
half-pathetic, half-humorous complaint, " He addresses
me as if I were a public meeting." A member of the
family, who was intimately acquainted with Gladstone's
own views on the subject, hints at an earlier and more
deeply cutting offence. During his first Administration,
following on the general election of 1868, Gladstone,
his mind already concentrated on the problem of the
pacification of Ireland, conceived the idea that much
might be done in that direction by the appointment
of the Prince of Wales to the post of Lord-Lieutenant.
He communicated the proposal to Her Majesty, and
was amazed at the warmth of her resentment. She
would have nothing in her realm approaching the condition of things created by the temporary reign of the
two Kings of Brentford.   To delegate semi-royal authority

to a Peer or Commoner was one thing. To place the Heir Apparent to the Crown in state in Dublin Castle was quite another. The offence thus innocently given was, according to the belief entertained to this day by the Gladstone family, never forgotten or forgiven.

December 7.

Nothing is heard of W. S. Gilbert now, either in literature or on the stage. Nor is he often seen in the London circles—Bohemian and otherwise—where his wit used to sparkle. He has retired to a little estate in Middlesex, resting from labours that have brought him a handsome competence. But the fire of his wit still occasionally flashes under the embers of advancing years. Paying a flying visit to London, and strolling in the Park, he came upon Joe Parkinson taking his morning ride. This he does because the doctor orders it, not because he likes it. He feels most at home when the horse is walking, and rarely ventures upon anything beyond a melancholy trot. Gratefully pulling up when he saw Gilbert, he was greeted with the remark:

"At it again, old fellow. If you don't mend your ways I'll have you summoned for furious loitering."

December 8.

Lord Rowton, occasionally dropping into personal reminiscence of Disraeli, shows how interesting would be the biography if he could be induced to write it. He tells me he remembers the day at Hughenden when there arrived the gift of a friend, a brace of peacocks. Disraeli was much interested.

"What are they, to begin with?" he asked his faithful secretary. "Look up my father's encyclopædic work, and see if you can find anything about the origin and habits of the peacock."

Monty Corry, as he then was, looked up some work of D'Israeli the elder, and there found the following description of the bird: "It has the form of an angel, the voice of a devil, and the guts of a——"

The last word cannot well be printed out of the volume of a philosopher and a student.

In the course of the same conversation, Lord Rowton mentioned that Disraeli made the acquaintance of the lady who subsequently became his wife during a chance visit to Glamorganshire.

" I remember," Disraeli added, " that I stayed at an inn which bore the remarkable name The Cow and Snuffers."

Does The Cow and Snuffers still exist, I wonder ?

December 9.

Yesterday Herbert Spencer died at Brighton, whither he had retired to nurse in solitude a shattered nervous system. He suffered a long and hard life, his natural temperament being such that many things other men got along with placidly give him acute pain. To put the incontestable fact in another way, he was perhaps the most irascible man who has ever been faced by the inconvenience of other people presuming to inhabit the same globe.

One thing delightful about him was his perfect freedom from the trammels of ordinary affectation. He had not for some years been in the habit of going out to dinner. Whilst he was still sufficiently graceful to trifle with this weakness, he suffered acutely from the inanity of ordinary conversation at the table. In order to overcome this difficulty he invented a pair of ear-clips. When he found himself between two commonplace persons whose chattering seared his soul, he adjusted his ear clips and ate his dinner amid grateful silence.

Previous to this recent attack of illness he had been a pretty constant attendant at the Athenæum Club, a locality whose atmosphere is soothed by the presence of many bishops, archdeacons, deans, and the like. There was something in the calm of the gaiters and the serenity of the broad-brimmed hat that subtly soothed him.

Up to recent date the Athenæum, like the Carlton.

15

preserved the exclusiveness which forbids the entertainment of strangers within its gates. Against this restriction some of the younger members of the Athenæum kicked. The result of a long agitation was reached in a compromise whereby one member might invite to dinner a single guest. On this concession an ingenious system was built up whereby four, six, or more members clubbed together, each inviting a stranger, and so making up a dinner party.

Herbert Spencer regarded this innovation with horror. He fought against it tooth and nail while it was discussed, and absented himself from the club for a long time after the custom had been established. One evening he chanced to look in at a time when a well-known author was entertaining a small party of equally eminent men at dinner. Spencer, passing the ante-room, saw the strangers gathered, and furiously cross-examined a waiter as to what they did there. A few moments after the circumstances had been explained to him the strangers, their host, and the other members of the club who completed the party, were startled by the appearance of an irate elderly gentleman bursting into the room, trundling an arm-chair behind him. This he propelled into the middle of the group surrounding the host, and producing a copy of the *Standard*, opened it to the widest extent of its sheet, and proceeded to read the news of the day.

CHAPTER XVIII

January 2, 1904.

OPINIONS differ as to whether Monsieur Lebaudy is such a crank as he looks. Certainly he plays his extravagant part with delicious gravity. It is an odd coincidence that a comedy of such peculiarly Gilbertian conception and quality should find its stage at the Savoy Hotel in close contiguity to the little theatre where *The Mikado* delighted mankind. Lebaudy's latest move is to renounce his family name, Jacques Lebaudy. He will henceforth, dating from to-morrow, be known as Jacques I, Emperor of the Sahara. " When His Majesty's titles are intentionally omitted it will be regarded as an unfriendly act, and will result in diplomatic negotiations being broken off with the author." This proclamation concerns the outside public. Within his costly suite of rooms at the Savoy Hotel, rented and maintained from the savings of his worthy father, the sugar refiner, Lebaudy is always addressed as " Your Majesty," approached and withdrawn from with the ceremony exacted by crowned heads.

" The Emperor " is fortunate in having secured the services of Colonel Gouroud, sometime Edison's agent in this country, a man born for the performance of the part he daily fulfils with excruciating gravity. His style in the Imperial household is Acting Governor-General of Sahara. The qualification "Acting," he explains to his friends, is due to the aversion of a citizen of the world to commit himself with undue haste to great responsibilities. There are some questions of policy (possibly of salary) to settle with His Imperial Majesty before the Governor-General-designate finally throws in his lot with the twentieth century monarch.

Meanwhile he has attended to certain essential preliminaries. He has designed an Imperial banner—a
tasty thing in light yellow silk, embroidered with the
crescent. He has invented a gold lace uniform for the
Governor-General when in official attendance on His
Imperial Majesty, and is now engaged upon a map
of the Sahara cut up into squares, each being a tempting
allotment for desirable settlers prepared to take oath
of fealty to Jacques I.

This is a bare, unillumined record of proceedings
at the Imperial Court on the Savoy Embankment.
Delight comes in on hearing Gouroud descant on these
and similar details, as if he spoke of a real, everyday
world. A soldier of fortune who bears scars won in
the American Civil War, who brought to this country
and pushed with great energy one of the greatest scientific
discoveries of modern times, a man equally at home
in London and New York, His Excellency, now somewhat advanced in years, has at last found his true
métier—guide, philosopher, Acting Governor-General of
the Emperor of the Sahara.

January 14.

Sargent back from Washington, where he has been
painting the portrait of President Roosevelt. Takes
mine in hand again. Began by brushing out all he did
last October. Sat for two hours. He tells me a charming
story about a Chelsea pensioner. Having noted the
picturesque figure of the old man as he hobbled through
the grounds of the Hospital with his wooden leg, Sargent
engaged him for a sitting for a picture he had on the
easel. He looked forward with pleasure to a chat with
the veteran, who would be sure to fight his battles o'er
again, and tell the doubtless thrilling story of the loss
of his leg. The model being posed, Sargent cheerily
opened the conversation with inquiry—

" And where did you lose your leg ? "

" Just round the corner, sir," the veteran replied,
" at Mrs. Walbank's."

It turned out on further inquiry that after serving
his time in the Army, the old soldier, whole-limbed,
had taken service with Maple, the furnisher. Delivering
some heavy goods in the neighbourhood of Tite Street,
where Sargent lives, a wardrobe fell upon him, breaking
his leg, after which he found refuge in Chelsea Hospital.

The lack of looked-for stirring romance was a sad
discouragement to the painter.

January 23.

Whilst their present Majesties were still Prince and
Princess of Wales, once a week during their residence
at Marlborough House a brougham, with coachman
and groom in private livery, drove up to the Albany,
and a tall lady, with figure remote from suggestion
of the status of grandmother, descended with light step
and entered the building, remaining often for an hour.
It was the Princess of Wales paying her accustomed
visit to her old friend, Sir Henry Keppel, whose remains
were yesterday buried with full honours in a Berkshire
village. From a time dating shortly after the Danish
Princess came over the sea to marry the Prince of Wales,
Admiral Keppel enjoyed the honour of her intimate,
affectionate friendship.

Among the old Admiral's prized possessions in his
rooms at the Albany is a photograph, from the camera
of a private practitioner, representing the old Admiral
and Her Majesty (it was taken last year) standing together.
The Queen has passed her right hand under the Admiral's
arm, he grasping it with expression of beatific pleasure
beaming on his wrinkled countenance.

For many years the Admiral lived at the Albany, his
modest means suggesting the desirability of his apartments being on the top floor. The Albany is too con-

servative to trifle with so modern a device as a lift. Anyone, including the Queen of England, going upstairs must
needs walk. A couple of years ago the Admiral, dis-
tressed at the inconvenience his Royal afternoon caller
was put to, opened a campaign with the design of getting
a lift built in the chambers. The suggestion was that a
levy should be made proportionate to the rent paid for the
several suites. The other lodgers, especially those on the
ground floor, demurred, and to her last call the Queen
walked up and down stairs to cheer her old friend with
her presence.

January 30.

His friends hear with surprise that Henri Georges
Stefan Adolphe Opper de Blowitz, dying in his seventy-
eighth year, has left behind him in this country personal
estate valued at only £187 10s. It was understood that,
following an example common with public persons in
France from emperors downward, the famous corrres-
pondent of the *Times* had invested in this country a
fortune said to be considerable. For more than thirty
years he filled the handsomely paid position of *Times*
correspondent in Paris, and, were he so disposed, and
possessed the capacity, had many peculiar opportunities
of making money. He was a frequent visitor to London,
where he had many personal friends.

The last time I met him was at luncheon at Countess
Tolstoi's, where he was so much at home that he always
found at his disposal a chair specially designed for his
comfort. It was built something after the fashion of the
tall arm-chair for a child when it is first privileged to sit
at table. Blowitz on an ordinary dining-room chair
could scarcely have been discovered by the other guests.
Mounted in his arm-chair, his massive head and broad
shoulders were seen to advantage. He talked English
moderately well, but preferred French, in which tongue
he held forth with exceeding fluency.

March 1.

Drummond Wolff on Patriotism

28, CADOGAN PLACE, S.W.
February 28, 1904.

MY DEAR MR. LUCY,

I am going to address to you what you will consider a well-deserved reproach. You have stigmatised Lord R. Churchill, Gorst and myself as patriots. Now a patriot is a man who has his price. Poor R. C. is beginning it. Gorst may still find a successful connoisseur; but I am a battered old piece of second-hand goods, who could not find a customer even at an alarming sacrifice.

Having thus delivered myself I write to ask you some day to come and see me. I am a gouty, rheumatic old mountain, who cannot visit Mahomet. I am always at this tenement until 12, though perhaps only in curl-papers, always at luncheon 1.30, and after 5.30 p.m. My telephone number is 937 Victoria, and I should be very glad if you would give me the opportunity of some reminiscences any day at these periods.

Yours very sincerely,

H. DRUMMOND WOLFF.

March 5.

The retirement of Sir William Harcourt from parliamentary life has an interest beyond the purely personal. That of itself is considerable. For more than thirty years he has been a leading figure alike in the House of Commons and on the public platform. Since in the last days of Gladstone's first Administration he was made Solicitor-General, he has not been omitted from the composition of a Liberal Ministry. Oddly enough, he never took his seat on the Treasury Bench in the position of Law Officer of the Crown—his first appointment. Between its date and the next meeting of Parliament Gladstone, rushing into a general election, was badly beaten, and Disraeli reigned in his stead.

Sir William gives a lively account of the efforts made by himself and the present Lord James of Hereford to evade the dignity of knighthood which goes with the law offices.[1] They were Radicals in those days, and lightly held titular honours, especially one shared with sheriffs and the like. They had a personal interview with the Premier, and besought him to let them enter upon their new offices as plain Henry James and Vernon Harcourt. Gladstone, punctilious in these matters, was inexorable. It was, he said, desirable that to the ancient offices should pertain the dignity of knighthood. The Attorney-General pointed out that there was in the Government one notable exception to that rule. "Who is that?" asked Gladstone sharply. "The Prime Minister," was the response. Gladstone laughed. All the same his promising young recruits had to submit to the accolade.

Another honour more unique than a peerage was proposed for his acceptance. When he made known his intention of not offering himself for re-election to the House of Commons, a movement was inaugurated on the Unionist side to entertain him at a farewell dinner, the hosts being drawn from both camps, thus representing the House of Commons as a whole. The proposal was enthusiastically received, being regarded as a high tribute to personal character. Harcourt, pleased but punctilious,

---

[1] In the following letter Lord James of Hereford laughingly refers to his relations with Sir William Harcourt, when they jointly held the posts of Law Officers of the Crown :

"BREAMORE HOUSE, NR. SALISBURY.
"December 8, 1909.

"DEAR SIR HENRY LUCY,

"Your 'Toby Diary' was very pleasant reading for me this morning. But the proudest bar in my legal shield is slightly bent. In the recess of 1873 I became Attorney-General, whilst W. V. H. became Solicitor-General. You reverse these positions.

"Strange as it appeared to me then, still stranger does it appear to me now that Sir W. H. should have consented to serve under me. If I possessed one-half your powers of description, I could indite a most charming chapter by recounting the acts of affectionate insubordination displayed by the Solicitor-General towards his chief.

"But those were happy days for both of us. Of course, the reversion of our positions is not of the slightest consequence.

"I am looking forward with intense interest to the coming campaign. The Lords, in my view, are playing a madly reckless game—stakes far too high. "I am,

"Yours very truly,

"JAMES of HEREFORD."

not altogether liking the idea of being fêted by the other side, begged to be excused, and the proposal was reluctantly abandoned.

Disinclination to become the guest of the political foeman, even when the ranks of the entertainer were leavened by a sparkling of Liberals, did not extend to social amenities. Gladstone's colleague in the Home Rule Cabinet, the inventor of the death duties, the statesman who, by rare exception, did not permit age to wither or custom to stale his infinite Radicalism, was more often seen in blue-blood Tory town and country houses than any other member of the Front Opposition Bench.

Wherever he went he was the life and soul of the party. His wit was often mordant, but his heart was ever kind. Over a wider circle than the House of Commons his familiar presence will long be missed.

In later years Sir Henry James, growing accustomed to dignities, accepted a peerage, conferred by Lord Salisbury's hands. As everyone knows, Harcourt, more consistent, refused a similar honour, though personally pressed upon him by his Sovereign. Amongst the prized possessions at Malwood are two letters written in the King's own hand at the time of his Coronation offering the veteran statesman a Peerage. Sir William cherishes the letters, but declined the coronet.

Twenty-four years ago, when on a great wave of popular enthusiasm Gladstone returned via Midlothian to Downing Street, it was understood that Harcourt fancied the Woolsack. Clad in wig and gown he would have made a notable figure, adding both to the dignity and the gaiety of the House. Roundell Palmer, founder of the Selborne peerage, was preferred, and Sir William went to the Home Office, where presently he was greatly perturbed by Fenian outrages. The country has occasion to be grateful to the providence that directed his footsteps from the Woolsack to the Treasury. It is as Chancellor of the Exchequer, creator of the death duties, that he will live in history. To himself it has been a subject of grim pleasantry that he of all men should have been the means of enabling a Unionist Government to subsidise the clergy, relieve landlords, endow denominational schools, and, above all, go to war with the Boers.

March 7.

People are chuckling over a story, which, I believe, is true, about a vivacious member of London Society. At a dinner party, at which were gathered many notable people, she found herself seated immediately opposite a gentleman whose almost pompous seriousness of manner and conversation contrasted with the general gaiety of the company. He at once fascinated and irritated her. After the dinner had proceeded towards its later course, the company was startled by the lady exclaiming in angry voice :

" Mr. ——, take your feet off my lap ! "

The other guests, attracted by her cry, were horrified to find the tips of a pair of pumps showing above the table immediately over the lady's knees, upon which, apparently, the heels rested, the patent leather fronts gleaming on the tablecloth. The glimpse was only momentary, as almost at the sound of the remonstrant voice the pumps disappeared.

A look of bewilderment mounted the countenance of the serious man, who faltered denial. A burst of merry laughter revealed the fact that the sprightly dame had been up to one of her not unfamiliar tricks. She had borrowed from the gentleman who took her down to dinner a pair of pumps. Holding these deftly by the heels, her hands concealed beneath the cloth, she produced the exact appearance of feet resting upon her lap. Her *vis à vis*, preserving his characteristic to the last, was he only person of the company who did not see the joke.

CHAPTER XIX

March 14, 1904.

ONE of the oldest Members of the House of Commons, now translated to " another place," sends me the following interesting notes on the Cecil family :

I read with interest and general agreement your article in the *Observer* of Sunday about Lord Hugh Cecil, comparing him with his father in early days in the House of Commons when Lord Robert Cecil.

I must be one of the few now living who was in the House at that time. I have a perfect recollection of Robert Cecil. He was then conspicuously tall, slim and thin, angular in his attitudes ; badly developed and unkempt in general appearance. His speeches had not the finish of style of Lord Hugh's. They were remarkable chiefly for their virulence and insolence. They did not seem to be inspired by any practical convictions, but rather by party spirit. It is most difficult to understand how he developed into the large, massive, ponderous personality of his later days. His style of speaking altered as much as his personal appearance. It became measured and dignified, though not without a subtone of sarcasm.

In those days Robert Cecil and his wife lived in Mansfield Street. I was often at their house at evening parties, and seldom met there any but Liberals. I found him delightful and sympathetic in private life, a complete contrast to everything in his public life.

You doubtless know the story of his marriage. Miss Alderson, the daughter of the Judge, a very clever and agreeable young woman, was much taken up by Lord Salisbury (*père*), and was a frequent guest at Hatfield. When Robert Cecil fell in love with this clever woman, the father was very irate and refused his consent.

He would not increase the moderate allowance he gave to his second son, though it was absolutely certain that Robert Cecil would succeed him, owing to the ill-health of the oldest son.

As a result, Robert Cecil and his wife after marriage had to eke out their slender income by writing for the *Saturday Review*. They contributed largely to the special style and tone of the *Saturday "Reviler,"* as it was then called.

But what a fortunate marriage in its products! It is the fashion to depreciate the eldest son, the present Lord Salisbury—I think unjustly. He is overshadowed by Lord Hugh and Lord Robert, but he has good stuff in him, and has considerable powers of debate. The three make a remarkable group of politicians. They will maintain their family tradition.

In appearance, apart from their slimness and gestures, they remind me more of the mother. They have not the dark complexion of their father and of their uncle Eustace, which is very distinctly marked in the Balfour and Beresford-Hope families.

I continued to be intimate with the Salisbury's, and was often their guest at Hatfield till the Home Rule Bill of 1885. This made a complete breach. I still went occasionally to their parties in London, but they were very different from old days. One seldom met a Home Ruler there.

April 10.

" C.-B." greatly amused the House last night, during debate on the pen behind the Speaker's chair, now assigned to the use of private secretaries of Ministers, by reminiscences of a Member who used to retire thither after dinner and divest himself of some of his garments preparatory to a snooze. The Member in question was Edward Bates, a shipowner, who sat in the House thirty years ago, and was brought into prominence by Plimsoll's historic outburst leading to amendment of the Merchant Shipping Laws.

" C.-B." will not forget another Member of the same Parliament seated on the back bench behind Disraeli and his colleagues. He was an Irish landlord of high stature and corresponding girth. On summer nights he had a habit, resented by his immediate neighbours,

of furtively removing his boots preliminary to an inevitable bout of noisy sleep. One night, when thus resting, a division was called. Happily regardless of the
summons, he slept on whilst the House was cleared.
Observing his condition, a mischievous Member stole
back, quietly removed the boots, hiding them under
the topmost bench.

The incident of a sleeping Member being reported to the
Government Whip, an emissary was dispatched to wake
him up and get him in the right lobby. The first part
of the instruction was easily accomplished. But when
the hon. Member, feeling for his boots, found they were
not, he positively declined to budge. In the end he,
like Agag walking delicately, went forth in his stockinged
feet, making the full round of the division lobbies
in the unconstitutional condition. When he got back
to his seat ten minutes later he found his boots in the
very place he had dropped them before going to sleep,
a circumstance that completed his puzzlement.

April 12.

John Bright's objection to donning uniform was
lifelong. In his diary, printed for private circulation,
Evelyn Denison, Speaker of the House of Commons
from 1857 to 1872, notes that on the occasion of his re-
election to the chair in 1866, "Mr. Bright, rising after
proposer and seconder, and before I spoke, made a
speech against Court dress for Speakers' dinners."

From Mr. Albert Bright
REFORM CLUB, PALL MALL, S.W.
March 21, 1904.

DEAR MR. LUCY,

I see you say in the *Strand Magazine* that my
father wore a Windsor or ministerial uniform, but not
a sword. He never wore a uniform, but was allowed by
the Queen to wear a plain velvet suit with black buttons,
etc., which I now have.

Yours faithfully,
JOHN A. BRIGHT.

April 18.

The death of Sir Henry Thompson removes a prominent figure from life in London. Long ago he retired from active pursuit of a profession whose highest range he reached. Almost up to the last he still saw private friends as patients. Recognised as the greatest surgeon of the day in the particular phase he practised, he chiefly fancied himself as an artist. He had taste and some skill, but did not rise beyond the status of the amateur. He also wrote, being a pretty constant contributor to the high-class magazines. His longest-lived fad, lived up to the latest, was his reputation as a host. His " octaves " have been famous through more than one generation. The name he derived from the circumstance that his guests numbered eight, generally presenting a skilful, attractive mixture of men well known in various professions and divers walks of life.

During at least the last ten years Sir Henry systematically observed almost ascetic moderation in eating or drinking. But he spent infinite pains in ordering and overseeing the cooking of the dinner for his guests. The *pièce de résistance* was invariably chevreau, a kid familiar in Central Germany. Sir Henry always had a saddle sent over for his octaves. As the years rolled by, and his hospitality was unlimited, one grew to know all about that kid, its history being invariably recounted when the dish was handed round.

Another unaltered custom was, at a certain stage of the meal, to rap on the table with the handle of a knife and ask what wine the guests would like to drink. No one ever expressed a preference, and champagne duly iced appeared. King Edward, whilst Prince of Wales, not infrequently made one of the eight. Early this year His Majesty was present at what Sir Henry Thompson proudly heralded as his three-hundredth octave. I saw him last at what chanced to be his final hospitality. It was on the 24th of last month. Though deafness was increasing

he, with his marvellous complexion, looked in wonderful
health. But he was eighty-four, and that, as Mr. Gladstone used to say, is an incurable disease.

July 15.

Tim Healy dismisses Arthur Balfour's Ministry:

GLENAUIN, CHAPELIZOD, CO. DUBLIN.
July 14, 1904.

MY DEAR LUCY,

It is so good of you to remember me. How you
find time for all your work is a standing puzzle to me.
Isn't the political posture quite the oddest (in both islands)
you have ever known? Even the world itself, in East
and West, seems to be donning new robes. We dunno
where we are! We dunno where we aren't. Yet we
strut our little hour 'mid goodly pageantry got up
for our diversion all over the earth's surface. The
entrées weren't bad, but the *hors d'œuvre*! I fancy the
"Unities" require that this Government should soon
go out, with blue fire and minute guns (10-centimètre
would do!), so that John Burns and Lloyd George should
come in with spacious airs to round off our enjoyments.

Give me the whole bally comedy, or I'll demand my
money back! On the whole I conclude that the English
are a more amusing race than the Irish. Not so spiritual,
no doubt, and quite unpractical, *mais quel rein!*

As a member of what Mr. Redmond joyously diagnoses
as "a dying race," I, who am about to die, salute thee.
(also the missus!)

Faithfully yours,
TIM HEALY.

P.S.—I lost 6d. on you yesterday buying *Observers*.
Next to your Flavin afflatus, the Cross-bench article
was one of your best.

Do you work these out easily, or inspirationally, or
obstetrically?

August 12.

The release of Mrs. Maybrick on the termination of
her service of penal servitude is followed by an agitation
for the bestowal of a free pardon. It is once more urged

that she was sent to penal servitude as punishment for a specific crime upon which she was never indicted, and particulars are recalled of the alleged mental incapacity of the judge who presided over the trial. It is said that the King is among the believers in Mrs. Maybrick's innocence, and that His Majesty would cheerfully sign the free pardon if the act were recommended to him by the responsible Minister. That report is unconfirmed, and is probably nothing more than a rumour.

Certain facts within my personal knowledge appear fatal to the fresh demand of Mrs. Maybrick's friends. Some years ago I was staying with George Curzon and his wife at Reigate Priory. The house party included Lord Llandaff, who, known as Henry Matthews, was Home Secretary at the time of Mrs. Maybrick's conviction. In the course of an interesting conversation he told me that when the case was referred to him with demand for respite of the convict, he shut himself up for three days with verbatim reports of the evidence submitted, the speeches of counsel, and the summing up of the judge. He had, further, the advantage of personal communication with Fitzjames Stephens, who passed the sentence of death. Coming to consideration of the case with an open mind, prejudiced by instinctive dislike of the prospect of bringing a woman to the gallows, he was convinced that Mrs. Maybrick, systematically and with murderous intent administered arsenic to her husband. The only doubt—at which he clutched in desire to save her life—was as to whether death supervened directly from absorption of the poison. Giving Mrs. Maybrick the advantage of the doubt, he commuted the death sentence into one of penal servitude for life.

Lord Llandaff may have been wrong in the conclusion arrived at. Even Home Secretaries are not infallible. But it happened that upon the appointment of every Home Secretary during the last fourteen years, the case has been revived. Approached with demand for Mrs.

Maybrick's release, the new Home Secretaries have in succession, as Henry Matthews did, called for the documents relating to the trial, dispassionately considered them, and come to the conclusion that on their conscience they could not let her go free.

October 3.

I was much struck by persistent inquiry as to the probable future of Lord Rosebery made by a prominent American man of affairs, who, after some weeks' sojourn in London, has gone home to take part in the Presidential campaign. By a course of severe cross-examination he extracted from me the personal opinion, given for what it is worth, that while in the next Liberal Administration, under whatsoever Premier, there will be a strong section of Roseberyites, the head and founder of the clan will himself coldly stand aside pursuing the labour self-allotted in his lonely furrow.

" Very well," said this shrewd observer, looking on British affairs with the advantage of perspective provided by the Atlantic, " If that is so, Roscbery is played out. His talk about the ' lonely furrow ' reminds me of a chant I used to hear as a child, when before the war I lived ' way down Virginny. It goes like this :

> 'I toils in de furrer
>   For to make ma bread,
> When de sun mak' a blistah
>   In de sky oberhead.
> En Ah won't git res'
>   Til de worl' turn roun',
> En Gabrel make a fluttah
>   En de trumpet soun'.'

" If Rosebery doesn't stir himself in the flood-tide of Liberalism that will sweep the country at the next election he ' won't git res',' at least not in Downing Street, till ' Gabrel made a fluttah en de trumpet soun'.' I'm not going to quote Shakespeare with his reference to the tide

16

in the affairs of all men. But obviously, even a man of supreme capacity like Rosebery can't go on past middle-age irresolutely letting opportunity slide."

October 13.

The marvellous progress made by Japan during the last forty years is strikingly illustrated by the personal experience of Sir Charles Cayzer, M.P. for Barrow. He began a career which has landed him in the position of one of the wealthiest shipowners of Great Britain by shipping before the mast of a sailing vessel. One of his voyages brought him to Nagasaki, then grudgingly opened to foreign vessels by the tottering Government of the Shogun. At a distance of four miles from the town a barrier was drawn which Europeans crossed at their peril. In Nagasaki itself foreign devils were subjected to the fullest limit of contumely. Compatible with safety.

Those were the days of the two-sworded man, and the abject slavery of the peasant population. Barbaric laws of almost incredible ferocity were daily administered. Sir Charles frequently came across men with the fingers of the right hand cut off at the knuckle. Others convicted or accused of offences an inch or more venial had the hand taken off at the wrist. One day he came upon a wretch with his mouth literally sewn up. He had been found guilty of perjury, and to the gentle, simple, practical Japanese mind this homely process recommended itself as thoroughly effective in the prevention of further crime.

December 3.

The following letter from Tenniel addressed to my wife differs from his ordinary habit of correspondence. His rare letters were invariably brief. This one affords a pathetic but pleasant peep at him in his honoured retirement, where " beside the Silent Sea " he " waited the muffled oar." The reference to the Kruger cartoon is to an original drawing he presented to me in token of long friendship. It was one of the last of his contributions to *Punch*, appearing in the number dated September 19, 1900.

10, Portsdown Road, Maida Hill, W.
December 2, 1904.

Dear Mrs. Lucy,

Pray accept the best of thanks for your most kind letter—with 1,000 apologies for the delay—absolutely unavoidable—in acknowledgment.

It is always delightful to find oneself, " tho' lost to sight," not entirely forgotten. No need, therefore, to tell you that your letter was and is a great happiness to me in my old age. That I do thank you very heartily, and, moreover, am very proud that my poor little cartoon of " Kruger scuttling away from the sinking ship " should be now hanging in front of Lucy's desk, reminding him, perhaps occasionally, of the happy bygone days which, together with the many delightful times I had in Ashley Gardens, you, and he, may be quite sure are never likely to be forgotten by me !

Trusting you are both well in the full enjoyment of the bracing breezes of your Hythe Hill-top, and possibly pitying us poor mortals groaning in the miseries of Fog, Frost, Darkness and Dirt. I will only say of myself that I am wonderfully well, my chiefest trouble and dread being failing sight ; I dare not leave home after dark—and never by daylight if I can avoid it. In point of fact, the conviction was long since forced upon me that the properest place for this person is his own hearth-stone, and I accept the inevitable with such cheerful philosophy as I am gifted withal ! And with ever kindest regards to Lucy and yourself, I remain,

Very sincerely yours,
John Tenniel.

CHAPTER XX

Mr. Balfour's successor in the Premiership (when he arrives) will find himself heritor of an alteration of procedure for which gratitude will be due to His Majesty. As far back as the memory of man goes, it was the duty and practice of the Leader of the House of Commons to wind up the labour of an arduous day by writing a letter to the Sovereign reporting, if he were so gifted describing, proceedings at the sitting. It was necessary not only that this should be done, but it should be done by the hand of the Leader himself. In his last Premiership exception to the rule was, by special favour, made in the case of Disraeli. Queen Victoria, otherwise an uncompromising stickler for etiquette in this matter, allowed her favourite Minister to delegate the task to Lord Barrington. Sir Robert Peel, with characteristic conscientiousness devoting all his energies to the task, sometimes sorely felt the burden. Gladstone tells how, shortly after his resignation in 1846, the weary Titan spoke sadly of his correspondence with the Queen. "All requiring to be done with my own hand, and carefully done."

When Mr. Morley came to write the life of his old friend and chief, the Queen graciously placed at his disposal whole volumes of Gladstone's parliamentary sketches, carefully stored in the library at Windsor Castle. Close by them are stacked Disraeli's, dating from the period when, fresh to the leadership, he devoted as much pains to this literary work as he bestowed upon *Lothair*. In Theodore Martin's *Life of the Prince Consort* there will be found several striking pen and ink sketches of Parliament done by Dizzy in his prime.

It was a sight to see W. H. Smith, when Leader of the

House, applying himself to the task. It was generally entered upon at approach to midnight, " Old Morality," with reverential air, placing the quarto sheet of letter-paper on his blotting-pad, and, with absorbed attention, beginning to write.

One of the most dramatic scenes I have witnessed in the Commons was Gladstone, at half-past one o'clock in the morning of June 8, 1885, sitting down to write his letter to the Queen, having wound up a momentous debate by a fiery speech. He wrote on whilst the contending hosts, returning from the division lobbies, refilled the benches. Before he finished he had opportunity of informing Her Majesty that in a House of 516 members her Ministry had been defeated by a majority of 12.

February 13.

The death of Dr. Robson Roose, which took place yesterday, did not come as a surprise to his friends. It was the cutting short of a career which, at its close, touched the gloomy depths of tragedy. A little more than twenty years ago, Roose had a small and growing practice as a family doctor in Brighton. He had the good fortune to attend Edmund Yates, then in residence in that suburb of London. Yates was so struck by his capacity that he induced him to take the critical step of moving to London. A few discreet paragraphs recording " What the World Says " brought the new settler some distinguished patients, and his success in their treatment quickly spread the area of practice. It is mentioned in some obituary paragraphs that among the number was Gladstone. That is a mistake, Roose having no personal knowledge or intimacy in that quarter. But there was hardly another man of note in the political and social world who at one time did not benefit by his care. Amongst them were Randolph Churchill, Chamberlain, Michael Hicks-Beach, and George Wyndham. These and others were habitually met at the dinner-table Roose delighted to have spread either at his house in Hill Street, Berkeley Square, or at his club.

As a consulting doctor he commanded the highest fees, and was constantly sent for from the country. Whilst he was honoured and trusted by the great and rich, he had a clientele of his own, of which he never spoke, who added nothing to the weight of his purse. One of the kindest-hearted men that ever lived, he was ready, and not unaccustomed, to sacrifice a lucrative call, devoting his time to the care of some poor man, woman, or child, whose hard case had been brought under his notice. At one time, certainly so recent as three years ago, his income must have been very large. Unfortunately he, a mere child outside the working pale of his profession, was led into Stock Exchange transactions that drained his resources, and finally left him penniless, with broken spirit, helpless against the advance of a fell disease.

At the opening of this year poor Robson Roose, who through a busy life had spread around the largesse of kindness, found himself bankrupt, practically homeless, sick at heart, death-stricken in body. One of his old friends, Lord Burnham, appealed to others who had known him in days of prosperity with the view of raising a fund that by purchase of an annuity would secure some measure of comfort to his declining days. The immediate hearty response that greeted the suggestion testified to the profound regret created by his story. Even while the subscription list was daily swelling Robson Roose, characteristically anxious to the last not to give trouble, quietly died.

March 28.

Sir Benjamin Stone, Photographer-Extraordinary to the House of Commons, searching for fresh food for his camera, has happened upon a valuable discovery. There is a chamber in Westminster Abbey, a remnant of the original structure, hidden from the curious visitor. It is called the Chapel of the Pyx. Once known as the Treasury of the Kings of England, the vault was up to last year used for the guardianship of the gold and silver standards used every five years by the Mint authorities for what is known as the Trial of the Pyx. In Plantagenet times, and earlier, the iron-bound vault stored the most precious possessions of the State. Amongst its treasures were the regalia of the Saxon monarchy, King Athelstan's sword, the dagger that wounded Edward I at Acre, and the iron gauntlet worn by John of France when taken prisoner at Poitiers. To this day, set in a framework of iron bars facing the door, are to be seen fragments of human skin. In the reign of Henry III burglars in search of treasure broke into the vault. They were caught *flagrante delicto*, flayed alive, and portions of their skin nailed to the door by way of encouraging others.

The vault is accessible through double doors, opened only by six keys. Permission to enter requires the signature of the Chancellor of the Exchequer, the Financial Secretary to the Treasury, and the Comptroller of the Exchequer. Fully authorised, Sir Benjamin visited the chapel and found it empty, save for a number of iron-bound chests lying about on the stone flooring. Opening one, he found it half full of what at first sight looked like a collection of chips. On closer inspection the pieces of wood were recognised as Exchequer tallies. In olden times, when reading and writing were not common accomplishments, money paid into the Exchequer was acknowledged by a strip of wood known as a tally, half being given to the disburser of cash, the other half retained by the Exchequer authorities.

The wood was notched, indicating the amount dealt with, the name of the payee being roughly scratched on its surface. Many of the tallies Sir Benjamin's enterprise has brought to the light of the twentieth century are inscribed in Hebrew. Among the names is that of the Jew of York whom Ivanhoe knew.

The Mint authorities lately abandoned their occupancy of the Chapel of the Pyx, the gold and silver standards being transferred to Tower Hill.

March 18.

Bishop Potter, who has created some sensation by, in modified measure, " consecrating " one of the new beer saloons opened in New York, is one of the most popular men in the States. All kinds of stories are told about him, mostly poking fun. When in Boston last winter I heard one that may be new on this side. The Bishop is accustomed to go about preaching in out-of-the-way places. Halting one Sunday evening at a small town in the Adirondacks, he held forth with his accustomed energy and good humour.

At the close of the service a tall, gaunt backwoodsman came up, with outstretched hand and eager smile. He had, it seemed, ridden ten miles over the hills in order to be present at the service. Twice before he had enjoyed the opportunity, and had brought away new knowledge.

" As usual," he said, " I larned somethin' to-night."

" And what was that ? " asked the pleased Bishop, warmly shaking the horny hand.

" Why, Bishop," said the backwoodsman, " I found out for the fust time that Sodom and Gomorrah wuzn't twins."

April 1.

With reference to Lord Salisbury's denial of Mr. Chamberlain's right to claim the late marquis among the supporters of his fiscal policy, I recall a personal incident bearing on the subject. In the summer of 1903 I happened to sit at dinner next to a sister of the present marquis. In the course of conversation I spoke of the continued absence of her father from the House of Lords, a chamber in which for years he had filled so large a space. She replied that Lord Salisbury did not think it desirable in the public or party interest that, having finally retired from office, he should as a private member resume attendance. But, she added, a few days earlier, talking in the family circle about Mr. Chamberlain's fiscal policy, then newly declared, her father said that, should he be alive when the matter was submitted in legislative form

to the House of Lords, he would at any personal cost
drag himself down to Westminster in order to lift up his
voice against the proposal.

April 3.

Colonel Saunderson maintains his reputation as one
of the wittiest speakers in the House of Commons. In
debate on the second Home Rule Bill, he was remonstrated with for his opposition, since in a Parliament on
College Green he was " sure to come to the top of the tree."

" Yes," growled the Colonel, " drawn up with a rope
round my neck."

His humour is sometimes unconscious. Speaking last
night on the subject of disorder at Irish elections, he
said : " They throw stones at Cavan. When I was
Member for the borough one hit me on the head. It
weighed 4 lb. 8 oz. (Cheers.) Luckily, my head is very
thick. *So I had it made into a paperweight."*

The Colonel looked puzzled when the House broke
into a roar of laughter.

April 13.

The death of the judge whom it is so hard to call
Lord St. Heliers makes a great gap, not only on the
judicial bench, but in social circles. Sir Francis Jeune,
to use the more familiar name, was a fascinating personality, with a singularly wide range of sympathies.
Before he married, his wife, then Mrs. Stanley, was
coming to the front as one of the most assiduous and
most popular of London hostesses. With fuller opportunities and larger means, this hospitable tendency was
systematically extended. Only ten days ago Lady
St. Heliers, quite certain, as she said, that her husband
was out of danger and would speedily recover his old
habits of activity, asked some old friends to a little
dinner got up on the spur of the moment to meet a
celebrity passing through London.

Privileged to know his wife before her marriage, I
enjoyed the pleasure and advantage of intimacy with

Sir Francis Jeune for twenty-four years. In a pretty wide range of acquaintance I never knew a man whose knowledge was so extensive and intimate, or anything so modest and charming as his manner of communicating it. The last time I saw him was in the autumn, the occasion being one of those delightful sea trips to which the chairman and directors of the P. and O. Company make occasion to invite their friends on the launching of a new steamer. Jeune was one of the earliest of the little band so favoured, and has been one of the most constant and most popular passengers on successive trips.

At the last home dinner party he was, to all appearance, in his usual good health, certainly in the full flow of his high spirits and gentle good humour. It seems that the hand of death was even then approaching him. He has passed away at an age which on the judicial bench is regretfully regarded as young.

April 29.

Captain O'Shea was one of the men who, having at a particular epoch concentrated public attention on themselves, pass out of memory, their existence paradoxically recalled by the announcement of their death. It is strange that, after all, he should die at Brighton. Thither his wife proceeded after the divorce, and there for a brief while she lived as the wife of Charles Stewart Parnell.

Mrs. O'Shea—Kitty, as she was in early days affectionately, later with bitter derision, called by the Parnellites—came of good family, among her kinsmen being Lord Chancellor Hatherly and Sir Evelyn Wood. But she brought little into the settlement when she first married. At the time of her second marriage, both she and her grim spouse were financially derelict.

May 10.

Sir Edward Chandos Leigh, counsel to the Speaker of the House of Commons, has had a great find in his library. For many years there rested on his shelves a copy of

Shakespeare, published in 1747. That is not old enough to make it of especial value amongst book collectors. But on the fly-sheet was written the name "William Dodd." This was the reverend forger whose sombre history is told in the records of the mid-eighteenth century. Whilst still a comparatively young man, Dodd stood high in the world's esteem as a gifted divine. He was Chaplain to the King and Prebendary of Brecon in 1763, nine years later Rector of Hockliffe and Vicar of Chalgrove. His devout frame of mind was indicated by service through seven years as editor of the *Christian Magazine*. But his chief literary work was a volume entitled *Beauties of Shakespeare*, the materials of which were doubtless extracted from this volume.

Amongst the reverend doctor's former pupils was the fifth Lord Chesterfield, whose name he forged on a bond for £4,200. He was tried, found guilty, and hung at Tyburn in the year 1777. His Shakespeare, companion of many a busy hour, has found a purchaser willing to give for it £131.

May 15.

In bridge circles, which grow increasingly wide, there is current a pretty story about the King. Playing a game with a French pack of cards, where, differing from ours, the court cards are a little lacking in individuality, His Majesty's partner attempted to explain an unexpected stroke of play by complaining of the ambiguity.

"It is so hard," she said, smiling sweetly on His Majesty, "playing with these cards to know a king from a knave."

May 20.

I have seen a manuscript letter by Sir Philip Francis, dated March 31, 1795, which contains two new stories about Sir Boyle Roche—whose name, by the way, Sir Philip spells "Roach." Some ladies went to the Irish House of Commons to hear a particular debate which was postponed.

" Indeed, ladies," said Sir Boyle, " I'm very sorry for your disappointment, but why didn't you come to-morrow ? "

One day Sir Boyle rose to order.

" Mr. Speaker," he said, " an hon. gentleman who sits behind me is perpetually laughing in my face. I beg to move that before he laughs at me again he will be pleased to tell me what he is laughing at."

October 20.

An esteemed friend from the country visiting London has had his pleasure marred by loss of a watch, cherished more on account of personal associations than of its considerable intrinsic value. Walking the full length of Bond Street, emerging on Piccadilly he wondered to himself whether he should turn east or west. Mechanically feeling for his watch to see what time it was, he found it was not. The chain hung limp and loose, lamenting separation from an old companion. The watch was safe in Oxford Street, for he had there consulted it. Evidently the bond had been loosed in Bond Street. Anxious for return of his treasured heirloom, he put an advertisement in the paper, offering a liberal reward for its return. Promptly came a reply fixing an appointment. Arrived at the place of tryst he found a respectable-looking man who responded to the arranged countersign. The watch was forthcoming in undamaged condition, and my friend cheerfully paid the fine.

There was, however, one favour he had to ask of his newly found friend. How was it done ? In Oxford Street the watch was safe in his pocket. When he reached Piccadilly it was gone. He was absolutely unconscious of any contact with a passer-by in Bond Street.

" Come now," he said, " I have kept faith with you. I've got the watch; I might now nod to that policeman who is passing, and give you in custody. But I play fair. So tell me how you did it."

" Well, guv'n'r," said the man, edging up to him

with genial effusiveness, "I don't mind tellin' yer. Do you remember when you was looking at a picture in Agnew's shop you felt something touch you on the left ear? You turned round and snicked at it with your right hand. At that moment, your elbow being up, I from the right-hand side put my hand in your pocket and sneaked the watch."

My friend was so delighted with the ingenuity of the trick, and with the frankness with which it was disclosed, that he gave the man an extra half-crown, and went off chuckling. Having made some progress on his way homeward, he put his hand to his pocket to pull out the doubly treasured watch. The pocket was empty! In that moment of genial approach the thief had sneaked it again.

This true story reminds me of another, more tragic in its details. It was told to me years ago by Mr. White, at the time Chaplain of the House of Commons. Late one night, just as he was going to bed, a knock came to the door. Opening it, he found a poorly clad woman who in sobbing voice entreated him to accompany her to see her dying husband. He lived in a by-street off Westminster Bridge. It was a dark and stormy night, not inviting for such a journey. Mr. White, wondering why he of all men should have been summoned, consented to accompany the woman.

Arriving at the house he found in a squalid chamber, lit by a tallow candle, a man lying on a truck-bed, evidently dying. At his request he prayed with him. Then leaning over the bed so as to catch the faltering whisper, he asked why the man should have sent for him, as far as he knew, having no knowledge of him. In simple words the man told how, twelve months earlier, he had strayed into St. Margaret's Church when Mr. White was in the pulpit. The sermon chanced to deal incidentally with cases of men tempted like him. He admitted that he had for years lived by thieving. But the preacher's counsel heartened him so that he straightway resolved to amend his ways. He triumphed, for a full year going straight. He had just made money enough to keep his wife and himself when he was stricken down by fatal illness. Dying, he felt a strong desire to see and talk with the man who had been his salvation. Hence his wife's errand.

The death-rattle in his throat interrupted his story. Mr. White, rising from bending over the bed, found himself clutched by the watch-chain. The temptation of proximity had been too much for the dying thief. In the very agony of death he had tried to steal the chaplain's watch.

October 31.

Atkinson, Attorney-General for Ireland, rarely visits his native land without bringing back to Westminster one or two good stories. His latest relates to a trip he took in the west of Ireland in company with the Chief Secretary and Sir Henry Robinson, Vice-President of the Irish Local Government Board. In pursuance of their mission the three Ministers stayed a day or two at a small country inn. Thither came special messengers or postmen with big Government envelopes addressed either to the Right Honourable Walter Long, M.P., or the Right Honourable Sir Henry Robinson, K.C.B.

Atkinson did not happen to have any letters to his name, nor was it entered in the guest book. For all the purposes of the inn he was known by the number of his room—28. On arriving he, by a timely tip, made friends with the factotum who combined the business of boots with a miscellaneous assortment of kindred avocations. This faithful retainer did not at all like hearing and seeing two of the guests distinguished as Right Hon., while his special patron was apparently plain "Mr." On the second morning he approached Mr. Walter Long, and said, with a brogue I do not attempt to reproduce, though it adds unction to the Attorney-General's story :

" If you please, sir, the Right Hon. 28 has sat down to breakfast, and wants to know if you are coming."

December 11.

On Friday last the *Times* startled the political world, depressed the Liberals, elated the Unionists, by definite announcement that Sir Edward Grey had declined to accept office, and that as a consequence it would be necessary to reconstruct the Cabinet. The evening papers were enabled to come out with a declaration from Sir Edward that the statement was " inaccurate and unauthorised." This was, of course, true at the moment it was made. So was the *Times* announcement at the time it was written. Up to a late hour on Thursday night Sir Edward Grey was implacable in his determination to stand by his refusal of the Foreign Secretaryship offered to him by the Prime Minister.

It is a curious story, which doubtless the next generation will be privileged to read in the detail of some Minister's diary. Meanwhile, the main facts may be briefly but authoritatively stated. The wing of the Liberal party the leadership of which is shared by Sir Edward Grey, whilst loyally accepting the Premiership of Campbell-Bannerman, thought it desirable that he should strengthen the force of the party in the House of Lords by taking his seat in that House, leaving the leadership of the Commons in the vigorous hands of Asquith. Early in last week, during the preliminary appointments to Cabinet office, it was understood that " C.-B." assented to this condition. Traces of this understanding will be observed in the leading articles of London morning and evening papers more or less directly in the confidence of new Ministers. On Wednesday " C.-B." took occasion to make it clear that he had no intention of going to the Lords. Thereupon followed that succession of prolonged visits to 29 Belgrave Square of Asquith, John Morley, Lord Tweedmouth, and others whose several appointments, already publicly announced, did not require further conference with their chief.

Asquith, Henry Fowler, and Haldane, representatives of the Liberal League, finally assented to the Premier's view, though I fancy it was upon the assumption that, whilst naturally anxious to figure as Premier in the assembly with which he has been so long honourably associated, he would not over-tax his strength by remaining in the Commons beyond the first session of the new Parliament. Edward Grey was, however, obdurate. He did not hesitate to declare his belief that experience of the Front Opposition Bench under the conditions obtaining during the last five years, threatened trouble if they were, in the matter of personal leadership, transferred to the Treasury bench. He was won over from what seemed an immovable position by the personal intervention of Arthur Acland, Vice-President of the Council of Education in the Administration of 1892–5. It was only at a late hour on Thursday night that this much-esteemed *amicus curiæ* was able to convey to Belgrave Square the intelligence that Sir Edward had given way and would accept the Foreign Secretaryship.

Meanwhile the *Times*, unaware of the final development of the crisis, went to press with the news of what was an actuality up to an advanced hour of the evening.

December 20.

Lord Rosebery's speech at the meeting of the Liberal League on Monday showed where the shoe pinches in his relations with "C.-B." He fully admitted what, as he said, "no one out of a lunatic asylum could deny," that the present Cabinet and the new Parliament will have no truck with a Home Rule Bill. The presence in the Cabinet of four vice-presidents of the Liberal League was to him sufficient pledge of safety on that score.

What he complained of was that, having at Bodmin publicly explained his reading of "C.-B.'s" Stirling speech,
the Premier, addressing a public audience immediately
afterwards, absolutely ignored an incident of which the
political world was exclusively talking. He claimed
as a matter of courtesy, if not of right, that, having
made a deliberate statement on a crucial question,
either affirmation or denial of his reading of the Stirling
speech should have been forthcoming.

Silence was in the circumstances certainly a little
odd. There are cynical persons who ascribe to innocent-
looking "C.-B." Machiavellian tactics. Not being disposed
to have two kings on the Cabinet throne, he at Stirling
candidly threw a fly with an eye to Lord Rosebery's
whereabout. The bait being taken, he was the last
man inclined to relieve the fish of consequent embarrassment.

In support of this theory a wicked story is current
in the clubs. Shortly after the delivery of the speech
in which Lord Rosebery genially hailed " C.-B." as
" my old friend," Chamberlain (so the story runs) met
the Liberal leader at a Mansion House festival. Saluting
him, he mischievously inquired :

" And how is 'my old friend' ? "

" There is," replied "C.-B." with the twinkle in his
eye that precedes a genial humorous sally, " an Italian
proverb, which I cannot quote textually. Roughly
translated, it means, ' When a man comes up, slaps you
on the back, and calls you "old friend," he is either going
to pick your pocket or stab you in the back.' "

The story is doubtless more or less well invented. It
is current in a circle in close touch with Lord Rosebery,
who has almost certainly heard it repeated, a circumstance not calculated to smooth out his relations with
a former colleague succeeding him in the Premiership.

December 31.

The oddest episode in a career full of varied interest

17

is Labouchere's sudden retirement from the House of Commons, and his voluntary exile in Florence. Up to the period of his departure there seemed to be no man to whom London was more indispensable. Reasons for the step are suggested in the following letter:

From Henry Labouchere.

VILLA CRISTINA, MONTUGHI, FLORENCE.
December 28, 1905.

MY DEAR LUCY,

Many thanks for your kindly remarks in *Punch* and in your letter. The fact is, that one gets bored even with Parliament, and this boredom is all the stronger when one is wanted to electioneer, instead of enjoying life here. I hope that Herbert Paul will get in for Northampton, but the working-men there are a very queer lot, and the Socialists voted generally for me and for the Liberal ticket, when I was to the fore. At present the result depends a good deal on the riding. Anyhow we seem likely to get a big majority in the country. I have known "C.-B." well for years. People do not realise that he is one of the pawkiest of Scots, and capable of putting all the Asquiths and Haldanes in his pocket in a game of beggar my neighbour. The real difficulty of the present lot will be Home Rule. But my impression is that it is not so much of a bogey as the Unionists seem to imagine it to be. It has done good work for them in the past, but they will have to find a new one. Mrs. Labouchere begs me to say all sorts of things to you and Mrs. Lucy. You should come down here for a holiday. If ever you and she do, you must remember us, and put up with us. In this happy place few have heard that there is a General Election. "C.-B." and A.B. are unknown, and Joe was never heard of.

Sincerely,

H. LABOUCHERE.

CHAPTER XXI

February 7, 1907.

AMONG the side-issues of the probably momentous parliamentary session which opens on Tuesday, may be the resurrection of Lord Rosebery. If, as seems inevitable, the Government straightway open their campaign against the House of Lords, the ex-Premier must be forced from the seclusion which remains one of the mysteries of modern politics. Reform of the House of Lords has ever been his watchword. He has a personal grudge against the venerable institution, since it compels his membership, seriously handicapping him in the political fight. Had he remained plain Archibald Philip Primrose, there is no doubt he would have won and maintained against all comers (after Gladstone) the leadership of the Liberal party. The opposition offered by the Radicals to his Premiership thirteen years ago had a souring influence, increasing rather than diminishing. Their objection was based directly and solely on the fact that he was a peer. Otherwise even Labouchere admitted his full capacity for the post.

This is a matter not seriously urged as of consideration. The fact remains that in several powerful speeches delivered within the House of Lords and outside its walls, Rosebery has denounced a condition of things brought to a climax last December, whereby a body of hereditary legislators override the opinions and actions of the representatives of the people, even when fresh from the polls. Some folk enjoying his intimate confidence are convinced that his apparent retirement from the fighting line of Liberalism is not consonant with his aspirations, hopes, even his intention.

The course of events and his own line of policy have certainly left him in an undesirable position. He would have been a welcome addition to the Ministry formed by Sir Henry Campbell-Bannerman. He made that impossible by an unexpected speech which " C.-B.," with characteristic canniness, instantly took advantage of. But his personal following in the House of Commons found appointment to some of the highest posts in the new Government. It seemed as if he might occupy a position behind the Throne more powerful than the Throne itself. He might have been to the Liberal Cabinet what Chamberlain was to Balfour's Cabinet after he had purged it of Free Traders, inducted his son into the office of Chancellor of the Exchequer, himself humbly retiring to the glades of Highbury. That dream, if ever dreamt, has not been fulfilled. Rosebery's middle-aged young men installed in Cabinet position have become integral members of the Government, even enthusiastic extollers of the chief whom one, a brief year ago, insisted should be relegated to the safe obscurity of the House of Lords.

Meanwhile, the Premier is daily strengthening his position, growing in favour with M.P.'s and commoner mortals. The latest proof of his popularity is a proposal, started yesterday in the Reform Club, to have his portrait painted and placed in the Club House as a mark of the eminent services rendered by him to the national cause. Subscriptions are limited to a guinea, and there is no doubt that sufficient funds will be forthcoming to carry out the proposal. *Ave, Cæsar !*

To some who were witnesses of " C.-B.'s " struggle through years of hopeless leadership of a rent opposition this turn of the tide is as amazing as it is pleasing. Through a somewhat long experience I have never seen the House of Commons play so low down as it did with him, notably in the closing sessions of the last Parliament. The worst aspect of the miserable business was the lack of support he received from his own side, including colleagues on the front bench. It was natural enough for the Ministerialists to make mock of him, That was a gentlemanly game in which they were supported by the lead of Balfour and Chamberlain, who openly sneered at his habit of preparing his speeches and practically reading them from manuscript. At least, he might have looked to his own followers for angry resentment of this rudeness. If he did, he looked in vain.

Fortunately for him, happily as it turns out for the party, he had at his back the support of the country as distinguished from the metropolis and the House of Commons. With the advantage of perspective, provincial Liberals took a juster view of the character and capacity of the long-suffering Leader of the Opposition, and when the hour struck they hailed him as the man. It was the country that, in spite of cabal and backstair intrigues in town, made " C.-B." Prime Minister.

March 5.

George Prince of Wales, with the honours of full Admiral rank fresh upon him, sat in the Peers' Gallery of the Commons to-night, an attentive listener to Robertson's statement on the present condition of the Navy. Tweedmouth, First Lord of the Admiralty, and his predecessor in the office (Lord Cawdor), sat on the back bench. Contrary to his Royal father's habit when he visited the Commons, the Heir Apparent does not seat himself in the recess immediately over the clock, a position that brings him in close contact with any Foreign Minister who may be in the Diplomatic Gallery. On Tuesday H.R.H. sat lower down on the front bench, which he had all to himself.

It was mute testimony to the reverence that hedges about the Throne, that none of the Peers in attendance on debate presumed to sit on the same bench with Royalty. In the House of Lords this etiquette is occasionally varied. There the Prince of Wales has come into reversion of his Royal father's place at the corner of the front bench. His present Majesty was seated there on the memorable night when Wemyss, holding forth from the second cross bench, in the fervour of oratorical passion, brought his clenched fist down on His Majesty's hat. Not unfrequently, when the Prince is seated at the right-hand corner of the bench, other Peers, notably Rosebery and Roberts of Kandahar, take their place beside him.

March 12.

Staying at Arbury, the ancestral home of the Newdegates, I was struck by the reckless manner in which, in her first book, *Scenes from Clerical Life*, George Eliot gave away her cherished anonymity. As everyone knows, her father, Mr. Evans, was bailiff or land-agent of the Arbury estate. His daughter would be privileged to gain occasional peeps at the interior of the Hall. Her quiet eyes, roaming through its stately apartments, retained pictures faithfully preserved when she came to try a 'prentice hand on novel-writing. In *Mr. Gilfil's Love Story* there is an almost photographic picture of the dining-hall at Arbury, a room " so bare of furniture that it impressed one with its architectural beauty like a cathedral." With its lofty groined ceiling, its richly carved pendants, " it looked less like a place to dine in than a piece of space enclosed simply for the sake of beautiful outline. The small dining-table with a party round it seemed an odd, insignificant accident, rather than anything connected with the original purpose of the apartment."

It is many years since I first read *Mr. Gilfil's Love Story*, recurring to it only after leaving Arbury. It was therefore a coincidence, not a memory, that impressed on my mind precisely the same feeling of the oddness of the small dinner-table set in the centre of what, in proportion and beauty of roof, resembled a cathedral aisle.

The memory of George Eliot is kept green in the Warwickshire hamlet upon which she conferred immortality. The *Mill on the Floss*, where Maggie Tulliver lived, is still there, though the water no longer has a wheel to turn. The present owner of what the novelist wrote of as Cheverel Manor is careful to preserve the legacy left by the daughter of his kinsman's land-agent. He is preparing to erect in the park a granite pillar, bearing the simple record of the birth and death of the Marian Evans who came to be known to all the world as George Eliot.

March 16.

Bereavement of Lord Ripon by loss of his wife will doubtless result in a readjustment of ministerial positions. There is no reason why, if he cares to retain the post, he should resign the office of Lord Privy Seal. He draws no salary, and his counsel would be welcome at Cabinet gatherings. But the post of Leader of the House of Lords is irksome for a man on the verge of eighty, even had he been spared the stroke of domestic sorrow. At this time of the year the Lords are, in a labour sense, at best half-timers. Ten minutes frequently suffices for the accomplishment of their appointed task, and they safely count upon getting away in good time to dress for dinner. All the same, there is the tie upon the Leader. Well or ill, fresh or fatigued, he must be in his place and see business through. Lord Ripon, having had his long services to the Liberal party acknowledged by appointment to the leadership in the Lords, may be expected gratefully to lay the burden down, relapsing into the condition of a private Member.

A year ago the prospect would have led to expectation that the Prime Minister would be disposed to seize the opportunity of exchanging the arduous duty of leadership of the Commons for the more leisurely work of the Lords. Some of his friends and colleagues dear, with whom the wish was father to the thought, openly anticipated such conclusion to be arrived at about this period in the history of Parliament. Whether " C.-B." ever harboured the thought is doubtful. When the rumour was buzzed about in January last year, he, imitating a classical example, "lay low and said nuffin." Meanwhile he found opportunity, and successfully used it, of demonstrating that, though still bland, he is not nearly so childlike as he was counted in the bleak days of Opposition. He has quietly, but perceptibly, established a position in the Commons which, in the matter of autocracy, was not exceeded by Gladstone or Balfour. Personally he likes the work, being thoroughly at home in the assembly, where he has lived and laboured almost longer than any contemporary. He has no sympathy with the Lords, and they no liking for him. In such circumstances it is not probable that the Marquis of Ripon's retirement from the leadership will affect arrangements in the other House.

Lord Ripon's successor will unquestionably be the Earl of Crewe. His management of the Education Bill last session was a revelation of capacity that surprised many, deceived by his habitually cold, constrained manner, and the level flow of his unadorned speech. This icy exterior really guards an ambitious character conscious of its own capacity. Twice a guest at the Viceregal Lodge in the early 'nineties, I had repeated opportunity of observing him at close quarters, and was struck by the patient, tactful, dignified manner in which he discharged exceptionally arduous duties. Representative of a Government pledged to Home Rule, he was tabooed by his own class, who boycotted the Viceregal Lodge during his tenancy. I remember, on the Queen's birthday, being seated at luncheon next to an officer of a crack regiment, at the time garrisoned at Dublin. He told me he was invited to the State banquet in the evening, but compromised by attending the less formal luncheon. I met him again in the late afternoon, and observed his arm was in a sling. He explained that, riding back to barracks after the luncheon, his horse stumbled on the cobble stones, throwing him, and seriously spraining his arm.

"It serves me right," he said. "It is a direct punishment for showing myself at a Home Ruler's luncheon."

This sort of thing might have been suffered without resentment had there been the compensation of popularity with the class in whose interest the cross was borne. But the Nationalists of Dublin were almost as openly hostile to the Viceroy as were the Unionists. No Irish Member called to pay his respects either at the Castle or the Viceregal Lodge, and when the Viceroy rode abroad in state, to Punchestown races, for example, he met with a chilly reception. All this Lord Houghton, as the then Lord President of the Council ranked, bore without wincing. Only in moments of rare confidence did he betray sign of his deep hurt.

March 23.

In forming his Ministry "C.-B." proposed to Winston Churchill that he should take the post of Financial Secretary to the Treasury. Though it ranks among the minor offices, only just above an ordinary Lordship of the Treasury, it is actually of first-rate importance, often proving a stepping-stone to Cabinet rank. W. H. Smith, "Old Morality," starting on his way to be one of the most successful Leaders of the House of Commons known to his generation, began as Financial Secretary to the Treasury. So did Austen Chamberlain, though his subsequent promotion to the Chancellorship of the Exchequer was mainly due to paternal influence.

In setting this offer aside, and asking to be sent to the Colonial Office, Winston, whose private coffers do not overflow, sacrificed £500 a year. Whilst the Financial Secretary to the Treasury draws £2,000 paid quarterly, the salary of the Under-Secretary for the Colonies is only £1,500. But the post has its compensations, as is shown in the prominent position in parliamentary life reached by the present incumbent. Within twelve months of his joining the Ministry an even greater temptation presented itself. When Bryce accepted the post of Minister at Washington, there were rumours current that Winston would succeed him at the Irish Office. These were somewhat tardily denied, and the event seemed to prove that they had no existence in fact. I happen to know on the best authority that the post of Chief Secretary was actually offered to Winston before it was passed on to Birrell. It was a long climb up the ladder for the young Minister. Not only would his salary have been trebled; the post carried with it a seat in the Cabinet. Moreover the prickly thorn bush of Irish Government had strong allurements for a man of fighting disposition, with a strong belief in himself.

Winston asked time to consider the offer, and took it to a length that excited much remark in outside circles, where the circumstances were not known. Nearly a month elapsed between Bryce's nomination to Washington and the announcement that Birrell would leave the Education Board for the Irish Office. The occasion for the delay rose from the circumstance that after due reflection Winston, having intimated his willingness to accept the Chief Secretaryship, doubt and difficulty beset the mind of the Premier. A candid friend, hearing what was to the fore, brought under his notice extracts from certain public utterances delivered on Irish politicians and politics at a time when irresponsibility loosened a tongue not at the best of times abjectly subject to authority. On full consideration it was felt that Winston would never do at the Irish Office, and the new session found him at the post where the old session left him.

His admission to the Cabinet is only a matter of time. It is possible that before another year has sped redistribution of the ministerial cards may bring him to the War Office,[1] a dream he never dreamt when he camped out on the

[1] In Jan. 1919 Mr. Churchill was appointed Secretary of State for War.

veld in South Africa, or, earlier, rode as a non-commis-
sioned volunteer with the troop that captured Omdurman.

March 25.

The Blue Book of rules governing procedure in the
House of Commons is not a quarter in which one would
instinctively seek for flights of humour. But there is
among them a Standing Order which would more accu-
rately be described as a Standing Joke. Five years ago
when, under Arthur Balfour's leadership, the problem of
procedure was attacked, a clause of Order 18, providing for
the suspension of a Member guilty of obstruction, ran
thus :   " If any Member be suspended under this Order,
his suspension on the first occasion shall continue for
one week, on the second occasion for a fortnight,
and on the third, or any subsequent occasion, for a
month." It was proposed to alter these particulars,
and as a preliminary to introducing an amendment,
all words after " occasion " were struck out. Other
business pressing, Balfour was obliged to intermit consideration of new rules, and the opportunity of renewing
it has never to this day presented itself.

The consequence is the sub-section, like the unfinished
window in Aladdin's tower, unfinished has remained.
In the current edition of the Standing Order it reads
thus :   " If any Member be suspended under this Order
his suspension on the first occasion——" That and nothing
more. It follows that if a Member be suspended under
the rule his exile would be indefinite, unless it were
terminated by a special resolution.[1] As an example
of the way we are governed this little incident, which
has apparently passed out of the memory of the authorities
and the House, is unique.

March 27.

Lord Rosebery's reappearance in the political arena

---

[1] The dilemma presented itself in a later session. Mr. Dillon being
suspended under this Order, it became necessary, in due time, to pass a
resolution authorising his return.

is not calculated to add to the serenity of the Premier's
Easter holiday. His speech yesterday addressed to
members of the Liberal League was not avowedly hostile
to the Government either in tone or spirit. It had the
even more disturbing effect of the speech of the candid
friend. With the significant exception of the work of
Haldane, Edward Grey, and Asquith, all, as he reminded
the meeting, vice-presidents of the Liberal League,
Rosebery differed from all points of view with the Government. He is a master of picturesque phrases that
describe a situation or a policy. In talking about " the
umbrella of Liberalism " which covers a multitude of
political problems, he reverts to a famous phrase uttered
when, taking note of signs of revolt against the pre-
eminence of the then Premier, he remarked, " Mr.
Gladstone's umbrella is big enough for me." Of his
speech yesterday he surmised that some would regard it
as " the croaking of a retired raven on a withered branch."
Unfortunately for the Government, it is more closely
akin to the cry of an exceedingly virile hawk hovering
before its swoop.

It is easy to read between the lines of this notable
discourse that the object of Rosebery's personal antipathy
is the Premier. Closely regarding the parliamentary
scene, it has always been a marvel to me to note " C.-B.'s "
capacity for creating and sustaining a feeling of animosity.
Genial by nature, courteous in manner, suffused with the
atmosphere of dry humour, he seems the last man in
public life to awaken such feeling. Yet it strongly existed in the last Parliament, Balfour and Chamberlain
habitually assailing him with a contemptuous manner
that added insult to injury. In the altered circumstances
of to-day, when positions are reversed, and a Premier
sustained by an overwhelming majority may not be
contumeliously treated, Arthur Balfour is, on the slightest
provocation, ready to pour on the unoffending head
the vials of his wrath.

Rosebery has this one link in common with the Leader of the Opposition. He can't abear " C.-B." If other than he had formed the Liberal Ministry last year, the ex-Premier would have been content and pleased to take a seat in the Cabinet. " C.-B." was inevitable; Achilles, accordingly, retired to his tent and has sulked ever since. It cannot be supposed that the Premier urgently desired to have in his Cabinet a colleague of the potency and occasional moods of Lord Rosebery. Undoubtedly, had the latter pleased he might have returned to his old post at the Foreign Office.

There was an epoch when misunderstanding and disagreement seemed on the verge of settlement. At the time when the fall of the Balfour Ministry was imminent, Lord Rosebery received friendly intimation from " C.-B." of the desire to look in to luncheon at Berkeley Square. The suggestion was cordially met. The guest duly arrived, luncheon for two was served, and nothing was said. Whether " C.-B." had arrived with formal proposition of friendly alliance, and whether in the presence of his esteemed host he abandoned intention of communicating it, is not known. However it be, he chatted about the weather, the inconvenience of having the streets up, and cognate interesting matters, leaving his mystified host without even passing reference to the political situation.

April 20.

Among Foreign Ministers accredited to the Court of St. James's is a gentleman who, after the manner of Sir Richard Calmady and his prototype, a once well-known Member of the House of Commons, was born without the customary allowance of length of leg. It was all right down to, and for a short way below, the knee. And there the limb ended. This calamity would appear sufficient to debar a man from active life, not to mention the prominence of the estate of ambassador to one of the oldest monarchies of Europe.

His Excellency, however, did not take that view of the situation. He called in art to continue the work of halting Nature. What may be called "continuations" were carefully modelled in the way of calf, ankle, and foot, and His Excellency was equipped for the daily round of life.

Walking behind him, one might notice a certain swinging stride. That is no uncommon peculiarity with a man ordinarily gifted in the matter of leg. The Ambassador not only walks, but, as were Sir Richard Calmady and Mr. Cavanagh, M.P., he is a fearless horseman. It is said that he can do anything the average man more fully blessed is accustomed to perform—save ride a bicycle. He regretfully draws the line at that exercise.

April 22.

Black Rod, entering the House of Commons this afternoon, bearer of a message from the Lords bidding attendance in the other House to hear the Royal Assent given by Commission to several bills, Members with one exception bared their heads. The exception was Mr. Ward, the Labour Member for Stoke-on-Trent, whose abstention may perhaps be accounted for on the ground that his soft wideawake hat is of such colossal size that it is not convenient to dispose of it otherwise than on his head. However that be, notice was taken of the incident by cries of "Order! Order!" in deference to which he hurriedly removed his far-spreading roof.

He was, however, quite right in the first instance. The rule governing the situation is put in a sentence of a private letter addressed to me eleven years ago by the present Prime Minister. Note was taken in some of the papers that, whilst Members generally uncovered as the Speaker, on the opening day of the session, fresh from the House of Lords, read the Queen's Speech, Sir Henry Campbell-Bannerman, seated on the front Opposition bench, kept his hat on.

"I did it purposely," he wrote, "maintaining the

constitutional rule of the House, which has always been that Members uncover to hear a direct message from the Queen, but never to hear a message read at second hand from the Chair. When I first came into the House, this distinction was universally observed. It was observed to the end by Gladstone, Northcote, Lowe, Hartington, and all the *vieille école*. If I am the last survivor of the true faith and practice, I am proud of the fact."

The situation could not be described more lucidly or upon higher authority. The message Black Rod brought to-day was not direct from His Majesty, but from the Royal Commissioners. Therefore the baring of the head was surplusage of deferential loyalty. Difference arises when, as happened on the opening day of the current session, His Majesty, seated on the throne in the House of Lords, personally dispatches Black Rod to summon the Commons. The only other case is where an officer of the Crown having a seat in the Commons—usually the Comptroller of the Household—brings a message from the Sovereign in reply to an address from the House. Thereupon as, arrayed in court dress, he stands at the Bar and proclaims " A message from the King ! " Members uncover and remain bareheaded till the Royal messenger retires.

When the Parnellites were in their prime, with Joseph Gilles Biggar to the fore, he and a number of his compatriots were accustomed to raise howls of anguish from the loyal majority by keeping on their hats when a message from a Royal Commission seated in the other House was read. It would have added a pang to the death throes of Joey B. if he learned before he departed that in this matter he was acting strictly in accordance with rule and predecent, and that the apostles of Law and Order were in the wrong.

April 24.

Sir Wilfrid Laurier will take the opportunity of his

visit to London to press forward a question which
stands apart from the appointed business of the Colonial
Conference, but lies close to the heart of the Canadian.
A little more than two years ago, staying at Government
House, Ottawa, with Lord and Lady Minto, the Canadian
Premier talked to me frankly about the results of the
Alaska boundary question just settled by the Commission
presided over by the Lord Chief Justice of England.
The three claims put forward by the United States
were all conceded. The incident renewed the old demand
made by Canada that the Dominion should have the right
of making her own treaties with Foreign Powers. This
seems, on the face of it, an impossible condition of Empire.

In conversation with me, Sir Wilfrid pointed out that
it is not absolute power of treaty-making the Canadians
claim. Proposed treaties would still be subject to
the veto of the Sovereign acting upon the counsel of
his responsible Ministers. If such veto were pronounced,
there would be an end of the matter.

What the Canadian Premier insisted upon was that
the Dominion must be permitted to arrange the preliminaries of all treaties affecting its trade and territory,
leaving to the Sovereign the responsibility of vetoing
the proposed arrangement, should his Ministers think
it desirable in the interests of the Empire. The question
arose so far back as 1882 in connection with the Alabama
claims. Canada suffered grievously from the Fenian
raid organised and launched from the United States.
When the Washington Treaty settling the Alabama
claims was negotiated, the Canadian Ministers urged
the Imperial Government to insist on insertion of a
clause that would have brought Canadian claims for
damages under purview of the Court. The demand was
ignored, and Canada left to bear her own burden.

At a forthcoming interview with Sir Edward Grey,
Sir Wilfrid will renew the demand for the modified
form of treaty-making power indicated.

CHAPTER XXII

May 4, 1907.

THE death of "Ian Maclaren" (Dr. Watson) has eclipsed the gaiety of two hemispheres. As a writer and as a lecturer he was equally popular in Great Britain and the United States. The latter, being of larger geographical area, and its inhabitants perhaps more exaggerated in manner, his American welcome was even more hearty than British audiences were accustomed to bestow. There is another phase of his many-sided character in degree obscured by his brilliant success. He was a great preacher, a perfect manager of parish work. He created Sefton Church, Liverpool, and left it in a state of spiritual and financial prosperity equally abounding. Little more than two years ago he resigned his ministry with the pathetic cry " I am worn out. I cannot go on. My strength seems to be nearly exhausted." But the call of duty and the impulse to work were irresistible. After a brief interval of comparative rest he began again, generously answering calls made upon him to fill the pulpit in the churches of friends.

His first visit to the United States in the character of a lecturer was an immediate success. He went under the guidance of Major Pond, the typical lecture agent, of whom he in his inimitable manner told many stories. A born mimic, he had at his command the intonation of the Yankee as completely as he had the musical burr of the Lowlands of Scotland where he first laboured, where he met the Doctor and others whose names are now enshrined in literature.

Looking over a heap of his letters, I come upon one,

a quotation from which will illustrate the fact that, unlike some eminent writers, he did not keep all his good things for his books. It is dated June 1903, at which time a well-known literary journal had put forth the suggestion that I should write the life of Samuel Smith, an honest, but somewhat dull, Member of the House of Commons, a leader in the religious world, recently deceased. On another page of the same number it was affirmed that Doctor Watson was the most suitable person to prepare the biography of Major Pond, also just passed away. The incongruity of the two suggestions greatly tickled Watson's sense of humour.

" The two books," he wrote, " will probably come out about November for the Christmas season. But, alas ! for what different classes of readers. Your book, *A Covenanter of Commerce*, will be immediately added to the libraries of the Young Men's Christian Association, and be largely quoted at Exeter Hall. Mine will be entitled : *An Impressario : being the remarkable career of Major Pond, Indian scout, guerilla fighter, operatic manager, and director of stars*, by his companion-in-arms John Watson, D.D The vision of prophecy being upon me, I quote some of the reviews : ' *The Covenanter of Commerce* should be in the hands of every deacon.'— *Baptist Trumpet*. ' A valuable work for street preachers.' —*Primitive Methodist Whistle*. ' Glad to welcome "Toby, M.P.," into the ranks of serious literature.'—*Mr. Samuel Smith*. ' From this to passive resistance is but a step.'— *Dr. Clifford*.

" Very different is the revelation of prophecy regarding reviews of the other book : ' It is lamentable to think that this worldly book has been written by an ex-moderator of the Presbyterian Church.'—*The Supralapsarian*. ' Exposure of circumstances in Dr. Watson's life which ought to have been concealed.'—*Temperance Gazette*. ' It is a painful fact which has recently received a striking illustration that heresy and immorality are closely connected.'—*The Moderator of the Original Seceders*."

It is sad to think that this gay, kind heart, as full

of loving-kindness as it was of laughter, had its beating stilled far from home, midway in what should have proved a triumphant progress.

May 28.

At Sotheby's to-day there fell under the hammer a pathetic letter from Lord Byron, which comes to light nearly a hundred years after it was penned. It is dated from the " *Volage* frigate, at Sea, June 29, 1811," the poet being on his return home after a long sojourn in Greece.

" In a week, with a fair wind, we shall," he writes, " be at Portsmouth, and on July 2 I shall have completed to a day two years of peregrination, from which I am returning with as little emotion as I set out. I think, upon the whole, I was more grieved at leaving Greece than England, which I am impatient to see simply because I am tired of a long voyage. Indeed my prospects are not very pleasant. Embarrassed in my private affairs, indifferent to public ones, solitary, without the wish for social intercourse, with a body a little enfeebled by a succession of fevers, but a spirit, I trust, yet unbroken, I am returning *home* without a hope, almost without a desire."

On the faded manuscript the bitter italicising of the word " home " is marked by a sharp stroke.

June 1.

Goschen's personal estate, returned at a gross value exceeding £141,000, marks an exception in the case of British statesmen. Men of supreme ability, their time devoted to the service of the State, have not opportunity to pile up riches. Gladstone, for example, having through a long period of his life had control of national finances, in his gift posts of honour and profit, left behind him a fortune at whose moderation a tea dealer would turn up his nose and a soap boiler sneer. Goschen's case was an exceptional one, since when he first entered political life he was a member of a city firm. He retired from it with a decent fortune, and his training and intimate acquaintance with public affairs doubtless suggested opening for sound investments.

Another statesman who recently died leaving behind him a big estate was Lord Cranbrook, better known in history as Gathorne-Hardy, a member of Disraeli's first Government. But his possessions were hereditary, coming from Yorkshire mining fields. One of his colleagues thirty years ago, happily still with us (Viscount Cross), has for many years been able, according to his statutory declaration, to maintain a position suitable to an ex-Minister of the Crown only by assistance of the bounty of the Civil Pension list. Now that Villiers is dead (leaving behind him, by the way, a vast fortune), Cross has reached the proud position of being the oldest recipient of this form of a grateful nation's bounty.

A kinsman of Goschen's sends me the following interesting personal notes about the late peer: " He was in reality a play-actor rather than a statesman, and it was at his house in Portland Place where, as a youngster, I met several of his *confrères*—i.e. Henry Irving, Charles Wyndham, George Grossmith, *et hoc genus omne*. It may interest you to know that when I was ten years old his butler took me to my first political meeting. It was at Gravesend, and the great man was the chief attraction. I was rather surprised when the butler from the back of the hall started interrupting his master. It was only later on that I discovered that this was a regular practice, invented to give the speaker an opportunity for those ' specially prepared impromptues,' which delighted his audiences.

"Have you anywhere recorded the story of his visit to Oxford (I think), just after he had reduced the interest on Consols from 3 per cent. to 2¾ per cent. ? At the end of the proceedings the usual vote of thanks was proposed and three cheers called for, whereupon a wag in the audience promptly shouted out, 'Make it two and three-quarters!'"

June 8.

The present year sees the Jubilee of the Savage Club, an institution whose fame has, I fancy, crossed the ocean. It started in a humble way, offering opportunity for the nightly gathering of working journalists and dramatists content to dine off a mutton chop, drink beer out of mug tankards, and smoke clay pipes. To-day it is located in a lordly club-house off the Strand, and at its weekly dinner entertains the British nobility and foreign ambassadors. One likes best to think of it in its earlier habit, Bohemian in all respects, not excepting looseness in the matter of paying subscriptions. There is an old club tradition of Edmund Yates meeting Sala and asking for particulars about the new club, then located in a room at the Crown Inn, Vinegar Yard.

" What is the subscription ? " Yates asked.

" Just whatever members choose to owe," was Sala's witty, though matter-of-fact reply.

When I was elected a member, I regarded with profound respect Henry S. Leigh, author of *Carols of Cockaign*, one of the most constant frequenters of the club, round whose head shone the halo of the reputation of never having demeaned himself by paying a single year's subscription. At that time the club had advanced as far as Evans's on the road of respectability that has landed it in the Savoy. My membership was proposed by George Grossmith, father of "Gee Gee," merry with us to this day. He was one of the original members, and his death marked a tragedy in the long series of Saturday night dinners. Presiding at one in the spring of 1880, he was stricken with a fit of apoplexy, and died in a room adjoining that which, an hour earlier, he had filled with laughter greeting his humorous talk.

June 10.

It is not often that tragedy and comedy suddenly meet as they did during the opera at Covent Garden last night. Even as Their Majesties, accompanied by the King and Queen of Denmark, entered the Royal box, welcomed by hearty cheering from all parts of the house, King Edward's old friend and long-time servant, Sir Arthur Ellis, breathed his last in the ante-room to which he had been carried from the stalls where, ten minutes earlier, the hand of death struck him. Such an ending under his own roof would have been terrible enough. Coming amid the brightness and gaiety of this gala night it was inexpressibly distressing. For those immediately concerned, the brightness was made more painful by the necessity of comporting themselves through the full length of the opera as if nothing had happened. Their Majesties were not informed of the sad event till the curtain fell.

A friend of Sir Arthur's tells me that last August he was one of a shooting party, which included the late Comptroller in the department of the Lord Chamberlain. The condition of his heart even then was known to be such that men were afraid to go out shooting with him, fearing what might happen before the day sped. An enthusiastic sportsman, Sir Arthur was not to be denied, walking out with his gun as if he were as hale as the rest of them. Widely known, everywhere popular, his tragic end has cast a gloom over the festivities this week in full swing at Court.

June 11.

A number of autograph letters on sale at Christie's this week raises an interesting point in the life of Disraeli. Amongst them is a long letter in Dizzy's handwriting addressed to Macready, the actor, offering to submit a play for his consideration. The shyness of the budding dramatist is testified to by the mark " Private and

confidential " at the top of the page. The play was
evidently submitted and as certainly rejected. After
considerable interval, Disraeli writes again, asking for
return of his precious manuscript. It is noteworthy that
whilst the first letter is couched in friendly terms in the
first person, in the second the affronted author " presents
his compliments to Mr. Macready " and begs that the
manuscript may be returned. As far as I remember, no
reference to this play-writing episode appears in published
records of Disraeli's life.

June 20.

Mark Twain was undoubtedly the hero of the Windsor
garden party, the King of Siam being quite a secondary
personage. The position has been retained throughout
a busy week. The popular humorist, who by three
years has passed the limit of age after which, according
to the Psalmist, life is but labour and sorrow, has been
in constant demand for the various morning, afternoon,
and night functions which London Society provides for
him whom it delights to honour. In his drawling voice
Mark wants to know what's the matter, what has happened since he was last in London, passing unobserved
among the throng, entertained only in the houses of
personal friends ? That was half a dozen years ago.
His fame was then firmly established. He has not done
anything in the interval notably to widen its base. Yet
he finds all London at his feet.

He lunched with us at Ashley Gardens on the day
after his arrival. The American Ambassador, Whitelaw
Reid, appropriately led off the larger hospitality by
giving in his honour a dinner at Dorchester House. It
was a notable gathering of some two dozen men, more or
less well known in literature and art. There was quite
a muster of R.A.'s, including the P.R.A., Sir Lawrence
Alma Tadema, Edwin Abbey, and Hubert Herkomer.
The editors of two London morning papers, and the

proprietors of two others, were among the representatives
of journalism, Sir Conan Doyle and Anthony Hope adding
to the carefully mixed salad the flavour of fiction. The
guest of the evening, accustomed to post-prandial habits
on the other side of the Atlantic, was surprised to find
there were to be no speeches. When cigars were lit and
the coffee went round, there was an ominous movement
on the part of the host. But he rose from his chair only
to ask Mark Twain, seated at the other side of the table,
to exchange places with him.

Accustomed to have speeches extracted from him on
all occasions, Mark regarded this representative gathering
under the roof of the American Minister as especially
one where he would be called upon. Meeting him again
a couple of days later, he confided to me that he had
been at some pains to prepare a discourse worthy of the
occasion. He selected the subject of International
Copyright as one that seemed appropriate to a gathering
that included many distinguished literary men. He
embellished it with some bits of as yet unpublished
autobiography. He brought the notes of his discourse
to the dinner-table, and carried them off unused.

"But," he added, with a twinkle of wonderful bright
eyes, "I made something more than a speech out of it.
I made a pot of money."

News of his having prepared the speech reaching New
York, one of the papers cabled him an offer of £120 for
exclusive publication. This was accepted, and he was
richer by so much for an undelivered speech.

"I reckon," he said, "it would have taken me a quarter
of an hour to say it all. That works out at £8 a minute,
which is rather expensive oratory, even though it be
mine."

July 8.

Mark Twain has turned his face homeward, physically
a little weary with the strain of hospitality to which he

has been subjected during the last three weeks, but with
a heart full of gratitude. Of the multiform successive
honours done him, there are two which, according to his
own testimony, have most deeply touched him.   One
was the bestowal upon him by the University of Oxford
of an honorary degree.   The other the dinner given to
him by the *Punch* staff in their own dining-hall at the
historic table upon which are carved the initials of
Thackeray, Leech, Keene, Dicky Doyle, Du Maurier,
and some others whose names the English-speaking race
would not willingly let die.   The honour certainly was
unique, since in the long history of *Punch* there is no
precedent for the admission of a stranger within the
sanctum.   Mark Twain had originally intended to leave
for home last Saturday, but outstayed his time in order
to dine in Bouverie Street.

The proceedings, which were especially joyous, began
with a pretty incident.   As the party entered the dining-
room, a cupboard door opened, and, lo ! there emerged
a veritable fairy, carrying in her hand a framed picture.
The dainty apparition was the eight-year-old daughter
of Phil Agnew, one of the proprietors of *Punch*, and her
gift the original drawing of Bernard Partridge's fine
cartoon, published a fortnight earlier, representing Mr.
Punch and Mark Twain hobnobbing over a punch
bowl, the former giving a toast " To a Master of his
Art."

This little episode, as unexpected as it was graceful in
conception and execution, profoundly moved the guest.
When, in his speech delivered later, he alluded to it, his
voice was for a moment broken with emotion.   Another
peculiarly pleasing incident of a personal character was
the presence of Frank Burnand, returning to old familiar
haunts for the first time since he retired from the editorship of *Punch*.   The warmth of his reception by old
colleagues testified to the enduring link of admiration
for the genius and affection for the man.

July 9.

Yesterday I captured an addition to my stock of " bulls" presenting themselves, whether in the china shop at Westminster or elsewhere. The speaker was a wealthy stockholder in the leading British railways. The topic of conversation was the pending strike. His parable was the absolute impossibility of the directors meeting the men's demands, which, he said, would, if conceded, further diminish depleted dividends by something like 2 per cent.

" There could not," he moaned, " be a worse time for such a movement. Why, the railway directors, as things stand, can keep their nose out of the water only by the skin of their teeth."

For " nice derangement of epitaphs " that is hard to beat.

August 8.

Sudden outbreak of dramatic incident is common enough in the House of Commons. In the more chilling atmosphere of the House of Lords it is exceedingly rare. This made the more striking the incursion of Lord Clanricarde in debate on the Irish Evicted Tenants Bill. For three decades his name has been accepted in speech and writing as the embodiment of all that is bad in Irish landlordism. Thirty-three years ago he succeeded his father, the first marquis, a reputable if not brilliant man, who for a couple of years was Ambassador at St. Petersburg, and in the middle of last century held office as Postmaster-General. The English Peerage is comparatively new, but the Irish Earldom of Clanricarde goes back to 1543. The present marquis is a nephew of the first Earl Canning. He entered public life in the Diplomatic service, but did not rise higher than a second secretaryship, and retired more than forty years ago. For a few years he sat in the Commons as Member for Galway, where he owns an estate of 57,000 acres.

The county was peaceful and prosperous enough in his father's time. With the accession of the heir a new state of things came into being. It was brought to the notice of the world by assassination of the agent, who was made the instrument of the landlord's tyranny and greed for rent. Lord Clanricarde was not to be intimidated by the murder of a man whom he paid to act in his absence. Safe in snug quarters in the Albany, Piccadilly, he closed a firmer hand on his hapless tenantry. For more than a quarter of a century, whenever debate on the land question in Ireland has been opened in the House of Commons, the doings on the Clanricarde estate have served as illustrations of what is possible in that distressful country. Only this session a bill was brought in avowedly designed to deliver the Clanricarde tenantry from the tyranny under which they are ground. Birrell, whilst declining to adopt it as a Government measure, admitted that if anything justified the novel and drastic proposal, it was the condition of the Clanricarde tenantry.

Lord Clanricarde, who in his seventy-fifth year is unmarried, lives a solitary life in London, a soul apart, occasionally having opportunity of reading in the Irish papers and in the parliamentary reports what his fellow-men think of him. A quarter of a century ago T. W. Russell, not at the time having reasonable prospect of being a Minister of the Crown, visited Galway, and wrote in the *Times* a long article relating the squalid story of the Clanricarde estates. In the course of it he observed that for thirty years Lord Clanricarde, whether as heir or successor, had not visited Portumna Castle. On the next day there appeared in the paper a curt communication, comprised in seven lines, in which Lord Clanricarde convicted Russell of inaccuracy. He had, within the period mentioned, been once under the roof of his ancestral home. It was on the day of the funeral of his father.

This was quite true. He arrived at the Castle on the morning of the funeral, left Galway from the side of the vault into which his father's coffin was lowered, and has never revisited the place.

He is not infrequently seen at the Reform Club, a shabbily dressed, grey man, who speaks to no one, and no one speaks to him.   It is the same in the Lords, about whose benches he flits, a grey shadow, nameless to the majority of its peers.   When, last night, he rose from a corner seat separated by the gangway from that on which ex-Ministers sit, there was general inquiry, " Who is this ? "   When it was known that he was the famed and feared Clanricarde, a chill fell on the assembly.   A House largely composed of landlords listened in grim silence to his tirade against the evicted tenant, his denunciation of a measure that proposed generous restitution.

An Irish Member tells me a Clanricarde story which, happily humorously, illustrates the terrorism that exists on that forlorn estate.   About four years ago there ran through the countryside a rumour that " himself " was coming.   The prospect of seeing face to face the man who dominated and devoured their pitiful homesteads created profound sensation.   Nothing else was talked about.   One day the train, having stopped at a local station to put down passengers, was making ready for a start, when the driver saw a man running towards the station at the top of his speed, shouting :

" Lord Clanricarde ! Lord Clanricarde ! "

His lordship had, then, arrived, and doubtless was coming down to take the train on the way to visit another portion of his far-reaching estate.   Time was precious and time-tables imperative.   But the great man must be waited for.   So the train halted till the almost breathless pedestrian, recognised as a local farmer, rushed in, got his ticket, and entered the train.

" Where's his lordship ? " asked the bewildered station-master.

" Bedad, I don't know," said the late-comer.   " I only wanted to catch the train."

August 10.

Sir George White has settled down in his quarters as Governor of Chelsea Hospital, almost forgetful of Ladysmith days and the craving he had towards the later weeks of the siege for a piece of white bread. Lady White was At Home yesterday, her guests having exceptional opportunity of inspecting the stately building of which Charles II laid the foundation-stone, Sir Christopher Wren serving as architect. The old pensioners, whose quaint garb lightens the neighbourhood with patches of scarlet, were spending the afternoon in the stately hall used as a club-room. At many tables they were seated, mostly smoking short pipes, playing cards or dominoes, some reading the papers. Their quiet games go on under tattered colours drooping from the walls, each the record of a battle whose story is enshrined in English history.

Here, through a week of drear November, fifty-five years dead, the Duke of Wellington, coffined in state, lay whilst an endless throng of mourners reverently passed. There was one too many among the visitors of the week. At Talavera, Hugh Gough, afterwards Lord Gough, was in command of the 2nd battalion of the 78th Highlanders. He was severely wounded. Before he fell he captured the colours of a French regiment who, up to Talavera, proudly called themselves the Invincibles. As he could not secure the flag and go on fighting, he unscrewed the eagle from the top of the lance, put it in his pocket, and had another go at the enemy. Returning to England, he presented the eagle to Chelsea Hospital, and the place of honour was given it in the hall. When the body of the Duke of Wellington was carried forth and the crowd dispersed, discovery was made that the eagle from Talavera had also flown away. It was believed at the time that a Frenchman, obtaining admission with the crowd, seized an opportunity of quietly pocketing the eagle, thus avenging not only Talavera, but Waterloo.

Amongst the precious possessions retained by the Hospital, locked up in an iron chest, excluded from heir-looms shown to the public, is the magnificent Communion service. Of silver-gilt, age has burnished it to the colour of old gold. Its money value is estimated at £30,000. It is not for sale at that or any other price. It was presented to the hospital by King James II, whose royal stamp is impressed on plates, goblets, and cups. Lady White's guests were permitted to see this treasure-trove, which does not often glimmer in the light of day.

I had some interesting talk with the picturesquely clad, many medalled veterans. After war's fitful fever they doze well. Each man has his oak-panelled room whither he may bring any cherished possessions long life has left him. Here he takes his breakfast, dinner, and tea. There is no restriction upon the pensioners' movements through the day. They may go out and come in as they please, so that they are in at the appointed bed-time. If they want to take a holiday they may have leave to the extent of two months of the year, receiving an allowance of 10d. a day. There are some 560 of these relics of ancient wars, awaiting in quiet and comfort the last trumpet-call. Meanwhile, stick in hand, pipe in mouth, they saunter about the streets of Chelsea, at the approach of winter changing their red coats for blue, but always wearing the cocked hat worn by foot regiments at Waterloo and earlier.

CHAPTER XXIII

August 15, 1907.

THERE has just died at Caister an old fisherman whose name will ever be connected with one of those tragedies of the sea in which obscure men suddenly leap into the niches of heroes. Caister, on the Norfolk coast, fronting the track of vessels ever going north or south, has earned evil renown as among the most dangerous spots on the East Coast. On a wild night in mid-November 1901, the familiar signal brought the lifeboat's crew together. In teeth of a terrible gale, with a sea that tossed the *Beauchamp* lifeboat about as if it were a bit of cork, they put out. Amongst them was the old fisherman Haylett, who had not for many years missed the call to duty. With him was his son, a man in his prime. For more than an hour they battled with the storm, finally approaching the wreck, but found it impossible to get alongside. Presently there came a wilder gust of wind which swamped the lifeboat, and nine of her crew were drowned. Among them was the younger Haylett, his father, with the good fortune that had stuck to him through many similar adventures, escaping.

He was a witness at the inquest, and gave a graphic account of the terrible struggle to reach the doomed vessel.

"Why," asked the Coroner, "when you saw it was hopeless, did you not turn back?"

"Caister men never turn back," was the old sailorman's reply, grand in its simplicity.

The Norfolk family which presented the *Beauchamp* to the National Lifeboat Association, not feeling disposed to renew their gift, I was privileged to send a new lifeboat to Caister. When it was built, I had painted within the

277

rail at the stern the old fisherman's simple saying. Thus it comes to pass when the lifeboat, *Nancy Lucy*, puts out to sea, howsoever dark be the night, its crew, bending to their oars, are cheered by the knowledge that they are faced by the proud motto : " Caister men never turn back."

August 20.

The Lord Chancellor (Loreburn), acting upon the advice of his medical man, is about to proceed to Canada in search of three weeks' rest. He sails immediately, and intends as far as possible to maintain the privacy of his visit. The event is notable as being the first time within recent memory that the holder of the Great Seal has set foot outside the United Kingdom. In Lord Loreburn's case the holiday has been authorised by placing the Lord Chancellorship in Commission. I am told the legal document necessary to the occasion, of folio size, is as thick as one of the volumes of Morley's *Life of Gladstone*.

Among the Commissioners appointed to act in the Lord Chancellor's absence is Lord Justice Fletcher Moulton, one of the judges of the Court of Appeal, the area of whose own holiday is consequently circumscribed. I remember, on the downfall of Lord Rosebery's Ministry in 1895, Lord Herschel, then Lord Chancellor, spoke with boyish glee of his opportunity of travelling abroad. His pleasure had a tragic ending. He went to America as one of the members of the Anglo-American Commission, and died at Washington in the prime of life, as statesmen count their years.

One reason for the restriction limiting the holiday opportunities of the Lord Chancellor is that, in accordance with ancient custom, if not with statute law, he is obliged to carry the Seal about with him wherever he goes. It is regarded as unsafe that the precious instrument should face the dangers of the sea. When a new Seal—to be precise, a new pair of dies—is made, the old one becomes the property of the Lord Chancellor. On retiring from office he is privileged to take the Seal with him. Thus

it has come to pass that Lord Halsbury has a rare collection of Great Seals. In ancient days, when circumstances necessitated the ordering of a new Seal, the old
one was damasked by being broken to pieces with a
smith's hammer in the presence of the Sovereign. That
was a waste of rare ornamental material well enough in
barbarous times. Some earlier Lord Halsbury suggested a better way. The old order is still observed,
insomuch that damasking is done by gentle tap of the
hammer administered by the Sovereign, the Seal
forthwith becoming the perquisite of the Lord Chancellor,
one of whose titles is Keeper of the Great Seal. Lord
Halsbury's collection of damasked Great Seals is unique
in number. They are set as salvers, one pair of dies
serving for two.

August 31.

There is to-day no longer talk of Campbell-Bannerman
presently going to the House of Lords, leaving Asquith
to lead the Commons. The apparently pliable, always
genial-mannered septuagenarian has turned out to be
in fact as well as in name the head of the Cabinet,
the First Minister of the Crown. He is a master of the
varying situation, and his predominance is based upon
esteem and affection rather than any principle of discipline.
A little incident coming under personal observation
illustrates this happy state of affairs. Three weeks
ago one of the newly made Peers entertained the Premier
at dinner at the Reform Club, bidding to meet him some
score of representative Members of the House of Commons,
and one or two personal friends. The proceedings
being social and private, the occasion was not one for
speech-making. But the health of the Premier being
informally proposed by the host, a colleague in the
Cabinet was not restrained from rising to join in the
tribute, bearing testimony to the absolute unanimity of the
Cabinet, their unqualified trust in, and personal affection
for, their leader. This unpremeditated outburst was the

19

more notable by reason of the fact that the speaker was a hard-headed, unemotional lawyer who, preceding the formation of the Ministry, was a principal confidant of Lord Rosebery, and was numbered among the group in the Cabinet who were counted as his men.

September 10.

Week-ending in Surrey, we motored over to Winchester to see the old college built 500 years ago by William of Wykeham. Its chapel, cloisters, and some other of the buildings, stand to-day as they were when they were last looked upon by the pious founder. Eton and Harrow are, in respect of age, infants in arms compared with Winchester. On a summer day, with trees in full leaf, the quaint, shady courts seemed removed by a breadth of a continent from the busy world of everyday life.

The dining-hall was at the time of our visit prepared for the mid-day meal. The simplicity of the arrangements is extremely severe. No cloth covers the much dented surface of the long, narrow oaken tables. For every boy is set a wooden platter and a mug, covers laid for Wykehamists ever since the days of Richard II. Whilst the form is observed, variation necessary as a consequence of modern civilisation has been introduced. The boys do not now have their meat served on wooden platters, as was the wont in Plantagenet days. These are reserved for bread, meat being handed round in ordinary dinner plates. One kindly custom hallowed by time is strictly preserved. At the foot of the table stands a big, iron-bound oaken chest. After every meal scraps from the table, remains from the dishes, are swept into it, and are in due course distributed among the poor of the town.

Among the house party paying the visit was a distinguished Oxford don, who left Winchester for college just sixty years ago. It was delightful to watch him going over the old familiar ground. He told us how, in his time, there were two " mutton days " in the week. On each two sheep were killed, the carcasses duly apportioned for the mid-day dinner. For the head boys there was the succulent saddle ; for the forms below, the legs were carved. " We small boys got the rest," said the don, a note of infinite pathos unconsciously pervading his voice as he recalled his earliest terms at Winchester.

Another injustice suffered by the minors was in connection with what are known at Winchester as toe-pans. In the don's time the boys slept ten in a chamber. Every Saturday morning it was among the multifarious duties of the fags to prepare an ordinary hot-water foot-bath. As there were ten boys and only one toe-pan allowed per morning, someone had to suffer. It was, of course, the small boys, the three fags who, having laboured to provide luxury for their masters, were themselves unprovided for. The difficulty was met by the small boys being permitted to take a dip in the lukewarm and not absolutely pellucid contents of their masters' foot-bath.

This weekly washing of feet was, the don testified, the only form of bathing stately Winchester authorised or provided for its young gentlemen. In the summer time they raced off to get a dip in the river Itchen, on whose banks the ancient city is built. But from October to May neither masters nor boys suffered a bath, wherein they kept up the traditions of William of Wykeham, who probably did not even have a toe-pan.

This toe-pan served a double debt to pay. The don, habitually the most modest of men, warmed by the excitement of old associations, confessed that when he was a boy he was a great hand at making a plum pudding His chamber companions put their pocket-money together to buy the ingredients, which were secretly conveyed and concealed under the bed till the master had made his last round and Winchester slept. Then the accomplished cook arose, and, by the light of a single candle, surrounded by a circle of eagerly expectant youth, compounded the pudding in the solitary toe-pan with which the room was endowed. The work completed, the pudding was hidden away till the following night, when the pan was again dragged out, filled with water, and placed on a surreptitiously made fire. Before morning it was cooked to a nicety, concealed with increased care, since it was now edible, and at night there was great feasting.

One night when the pudding was bubbling on the fire, the master paid a surprise visit. The sudden storm of snoring which, on his entrance, rose from all the beds, did not drown the cheery noise of the boiling water. Taking in the situation at a glance, the master ordered the oldest boy to bring " that thing " round to the court-yard. This said, he stalked forth, awaiting obedience to his command. The boys were equal to the occasion. Getting the pudding out of the cloth at the cost of scalded hands, they soaked stockings and handkerchiefs sufficient to fill the cloth, which, tied up, was conveyed to the irate master, waiting in the courtyard.

" Dash it down," he commanded. With right good will the order was obeyed.

" Again," said the master, puzzled at the unexpected result of his discipline. Down went the dripping bundle with a force that untied its bonds and disclosed its contents.

" Go to bed," said the discomfited master, and went off to his own.

September 20.

A common sight through the parliamentary session is the appearance of a messenger entering from behind the Speaker's chair carrying a red dispatch-box, addressed on a slip of paper peeping forth from below the closed lid. The Minister whose hand it reaches produces a duplicate key and proceeds to attend to the correspond-ence selected and sent on by his private secretary.

The inference—as a matter of fact, the custom—is that
the enormous correspondence reaching a Minister day
by day, and all through the day, passes first through the
hands of the secretary, who reads all, endorses some,
and retains a minimum for the personal consideration
of his chief.

I learned by accident the other day that there is a
limit to this confidence between Cabinet Ministers and
their secretaries. There are some letters and documents
it is not desirable should, at particular stages of negotiation, be seen even by the most faithful and prudent of
secretaries. There is accordingly established in the confidence of every Cabinet a certain masonic sign which,
appearing on the envelope, arrests the hand of the
secretary as he is about to open it. Such communications—there are, I believe, not very many in the course
of a year—are handed intact to the Minister, to be read
and considered in secret.

September 28.

The Navy is among the most conservative of national
institutions. It jealously preserves daily customs going
so far back that their origin and purpose are, like the
birth of Jeames, "wropt in myst'ry." Dining last night
on the flagship of the Channel fleet, I was struck by
a bluejacket entering the saloon and saluting the Flag
Captain, saying "Five minutes to nine, sir." Turning
to the Admiral, the Captain in a low voice repeated the
communication, whereat the Admiral nodded. The
same thing happening on the following night, I ventured
to inquire what it might portend. No one seemed quite
to know. It had been nightly done as far back as memory
went, and will doubtless continue as long as the Union
Jack flies from a masthead.

The bluejacket was dispatched on the errand by the
officer in command of the watch on deck. It was a
preliminary to the firing of the nine o'clock gun, which

takes place on every one of His Majesty's ships when in harbour, at home or abroad. At sea the ceremony is dispensed with. On the flagship the signal is fired from one of the smallest guns in the ship's armament. In Nelson's time and later, on the stroke of the hour, a marine let off his musket. This gave rise to a legend to the effect that the marine was trying his gun to see it was all right, and as a warning to any who might be prowling about the ship with nefarious design.

Another—a prettier and less obscure ceremony—marks a morning hour. A bugler approaches the officer in command of the watch, and saluting, says, " Eight o'clock, sir." " Sound it," curtly responds the officer. The bugler, facing for'ard, blows a call, at which the watch stand at attention, with hand to cap, saluting. Two signalmen run up the flag at the stern, whilst the band plays " God save the King," officers and watch meanwhile standing motionless at the salute. The music ceasing, the band marches off, the bugler disappears, and the watch set about their ordinary duties. When, as happened during my visit, some eighteen battleships are in harbour, one hears from far and near the familiar strain of the National Anthem, and sees the flag simultaneously run up from many quarter-decks.

November 30.

The tragic death of Sir Henry Colvile, who, after facing perils by land, sea, and air, was killed by collision with a friend's motor-car, recalls the story of a career shattered at the moment it seemed most promising. Colvile was of the rare type of Fred Burnaby, whom he resembled in several particulars. A soldier by profession, he was a captain in the Grenadiers, whilst Burnaby, at the time of his famous ride to Khiva, was a captain in the Blues. Times of peace bored him, and he sought danger in fields of private enterprise. Again, like Burnaby, he was a daring balloonist. He beat the Horse Guardsmen's record by spending the earliest hours of his honeymoon in a balloon. From the church door he and his bride drove off to the shed where his balloon was awaiting him, and forthwith they ascended. That was his first wife. The lady who now mourns irreparable loss is of French birth, a slight, pretty accent betraying her. During his time with the Grenadier Guards, where he rose to the post of command, Colvile generally managed to be at any spot where fighting was going on. Five times he was mentioned in dispatches, and on State occasions wore a medal with five clasps. He did splendid work in the Soudan, where he won his C.B. and his colonelcy.

The outbreak of the war in South Africa found him with the rank of Major-General in command of the infantry brigade at Gibraltar. But he was not the man to be left out when fighting was to the fore. Lord Roberts, knowing his worth, called him to the front, giving him command of the Guards Brigade. Here, as usual, he distinguished himself, being mentioned in Lord Methuen's dispatches and thanked by the Commander-in-Chief for his services at Paardeberg and Poplar Grove.

Then came sudden catastrophe and final fall. The loss of guns at Sanna Post, and the failure to relieve the Yeomanry at Lindley, happened in the darkest days of the Boer War. There was ominous growling at home against an Administration which, after being in office, with brief interval, for a period of fourteen years, had landed a British Army in the field under conditions that, but for Sir George White's stand at Ladysmith, would have resulted in the loss of Cape Colony. A victim was needed, and would be useful in diverting the scent ominously centring on Downing Street. So Henry Colvile was "broken." The bitterness of his fate was intensified by the fresh muddle of reappointing him to his command at Gibraltar, and immediately afterwards recalling him.

There is a good deal written and talked about just now touching telepathy and other mystic matters. An occurrence, doubtless purely accidental, certainly curious, happened in my personal experience with regard to Colvile's death. A very old friend, it happened, as it frequently does in the whirl of London life, that we had not met for more than a year. Dining alone with my wife on Sunday night, the conversation suddenly turned upon Colvile, whom I do not remember chatting about for many preceding months. We recalled our first meeting, where he joined our ship at Port Said, homeward bound from Japan. He, then captain on leave, was returning home from surveying a desert portion of Palestine through which a group of London financiers were talking of making a canal that should compete with the one at Suez. This was in January 1884. We speedily became friends. I have now a number of photographs given me by him, the earliest products of the newly invented Kodak, assiduously used during his travels.

The chance acquaintance was renewed and strengthened on his return to London. Once I dined with him when he was captain of a detachment of Guards on duty at St. James's Palace. Another time, on the eve of the Soudan expedition in the autumn of 1884, I was one of a party of four, dining at his rooms in Ebury Street. Two, one an officer in an infantry regiment, started off the next morning on their mission as special correspondents to London morning papers, and one was killed on the battlefield.

We talked of a hurried visit Colvile paid to us in the country after his recall from Gibraltar. He came loaded with maps of the scene of operation at Sanna Post and Lindley, with copies of the orders directing his movements. A man studiously quiet in manner, I remember his eager face as he knelt by the maps outspread on the study floor, and showed how, struggling with contradictory commands and consequent misunderstandings, he had done his best to save the guns at Sanna Post and relieve the Yeomanry beleaguered at Lindley.

On his retirement from active service, finding it impossible to live far beyond sound of the trumpet and the drum, he bought some twenty-six acres of rather swampy land in close proximity to Aldershot. He amused himself by draining it and planning miniature bridges under which the superabundant water passed away. He built for himself and Lady Colvile a pretty bungalow, and was as happy as a soldier in his circumstances, still in the prime of life, could be.

We recalled a delightful week-end visit paid to them there some two or three years ago. The only other member of the house party was a niece of the King, an attached friend of Lady Colvile's, in whose gracious presence lived again the face and figure of her grandmother, Queen Victoria, as presented in pictures and engravings done sixty years ago. A little incident temporarily drew Colvile out of the gloom that naturally settled down upon him in his enforced retirement. On the Sunday morning, H.R.H. produced her diary, which she said she faithfully wrote up every day. On this particular date she deputed to me the task of filling up the page. This I did in some detail, writing down what purported to be the reflections of the diarist on current events, with some passing comments on the company in which she found herself.

Last Sunday night we, for more than an hour, thus chatted about Henry Colvile, whilst all unknown to us he lay unconscious in the Brompton Hospital, stricken down a few hours earlier by the hand of Death.

December 12.

To Folkestone to lunch with the Bancrofts. Tram to Sandgate (in fine weather a beautiful drive), skirting a rainy, desolate sea. Found the Bancrofts charmingly housed. They have had the good fortune to pick up an admirably built house with frontage to road, at the back tree-shaded terraces leading down to the sea. It is furnished with perfect taste in respect of decoration and comfort. Lady B. did not appear at luncheon, being confined to her bed with a cold. We were six, including Mrs. Forbes-Robertson, whose husband is in the States coining money with Jerome's *Passing of the Third Floor Back*. Meanwhile she lives in Folkestone, happy with her children.

When I say we were six, that was the number seated at the table. As conversation proceeded we discovered that, as in the family circumstances of the little maid Wordsworth knew, we were seven. From the next room came an inquiring whistle, followed by the adjuration, "Halloa, Bogey!" Bogey being the endearing abbreviation of the name of the head of the household. It was the parrot, on no account to be left out of current conversation. It contributed to it constantly, if with some irrelevance. After much coaxing Bancroft induced it to say, "God save the King." Having thus observed the *convenance* of the occasion, it added, *sotto voce*, the deplorable commentary, "Rats!"

Talking about plays and the remuneration of authors, Bancroft said that during the full run of their management at the Prince of Wales's, and afterwards at the Haymarket, he and his wife paid the author a fixed fee of five pounds a night. In the full tide of fortune, the start of which they felt was due to Robertson, they proposed a more liberal scale of payment. Not to be outdone in chivalry, Robertson declined to depart from the time-honoured system of the nightly fiver. Bancroft added that it was Boucicault who introduced the system of percentage that to-day makes the successful dramatist rich beyond the dreams of avarice.

The *pièce de résistance* at luncheon was called "mixed grill." As the name suggests, it was a composite dish. Someone said it reminded him of the contents of the witches' cauldron in *Macbeth*.

"Yes," said Bancroft, rummaging among the kidneys,

sausages, and cutlets for a toothsome bit, "but the mixture is not quite the same.   Here be no

> ' Toad, that under cold stone
> Days and nights hast thirty-one
> Swelter'd venom sleeping got.
> Fillet of a fenny snake,
> Eye of newt and toe of frog,
> Wool of bat and tongue of dog,
> Adder's fork and blind-worm's sting,
> Lizard's leg and howlet's wing.' "

We were all glad of that.

As I inspected this dish, of which Bancroft, having compounded it, was pardonably proud, I thought of the opportunity lost to Arthur Cecil owing to too early death. I frequently met him coming on from the theatre to the supper-room at evening parties. He had a way, which hugely delighted his friends, of going about closely examining the various dishes displayed on the buffet, humming an uncertain tune as he went. If there was nothing to his taste the performance was prolonged. If the variety was rich it was abbreviated. Just as a bee buzzes round a flower preparatory to setting upon its sweetness, so Cecil hummed his way along the buffet. When the tune suddenly stopped we knew he had found something to eat.

This mixed grill would have made short work of his song.

After luncheon my wife and I paid an afternoon call on Lady B. We found her in a dainty bedroom with spacious bay-window looking on to the sea. In spite of her cold she was in high spirits. Mention made of Forbes-Robertson in *The Third Floor Back*, she told how she had been there on the first night of its presentation, and went on to describe the story. Presently, warming to the subject, she really acted the leading part. I asked her how often she had seen the piece.

" Only once," she said.   " It was on the first night,

when I cried—oh, how I cried! At one of the intervals
Bogey went round to see Forbie in his dressing-room. I
was rather glad, as I could weep better by myself. It
turned out I wasn't alone. Looking up at the dress circle,
I saw a middle-aged man trying to look as if he wasn't
crying. That set me off again, and we kept it up together
till the curtain rose."

CHAPTER XXIV

SHORTLY after four o'clock this morning Sir Charles Dilke, home from a last visit to his beloved Provence, " slipped suddenly out of life." Busy to the last, he spent the day before in bed reading and marking Blue Books bearing upon the case of unorganised workers, whose cause he had long advocated.

I suppose I am one of the exceedingly few persons still connected with parliamentary life who heard the speech that first attracted public attention to him in the House of Commons. It was delivered on March 19, 1872, on a motion attacking the Civil List. A short time earlier, he had delivered an address at Newcastle, in which he frankly avowed opinions not far remote from republicanism. The result was a chorus of condemnation in the Press, and the severance of many personal friendships. With characteristic courage, he met this storm of obloquy by repeating his allegations and views from his place in the House of Commons upon a motion for papers amplifying information made in the estimates concerning the Civil List. In anticipation of a scene, and with determination to put down the young Member for Chelsea, the House was crowded in every part. Sir Charles rose from the corner seat below the gangway on the Ministerial side, a coign of vantage early seized with quick insight into its prominence. He was confronted by Lord Bury, who called upon the Speaker to refuse him a hearing on the ground that by declaration of republican principles he had violated the oath of allegiance. This appeal was backed up by a burst of tempestuous cheering, during which Sir Charles, having resumed his seat, ever careful to improve stray moments, studied his sheaf of notes.

The Speaker, with the jealousy of the rights of private Members that happily marks judgments delivered from the Chair of the House of Commons, declined to interfere, and Dilke, amidst renewed outburst of groans, began his speech. It was, as he himself frankly and truthfully admits, " studiously wooden, unutterably dull." But it was crowded with facts, and Members, partly because they had shouted themselves nearly hoarse, and partly from desire to hear the details put forward, abstained from further organised obstruction.

I noticed for the first time a curious mannerism which, in fainter degree, marked to the last Dilke's speeches delivered from his corner seat. Having the freedom of the gangway passage on his left and the floor before him, he, with monotonous regularity that finally got on the nerves, turned from left to right and from right to left, holding his manuscript in his left hand, and emphasising a particular passage by tapping it with the fingers of his right hand.

He resumed his seat amid dead silence. Gladstone, who followed, might have concluded the episode but for the interposition of Auberon Herbert, who had volunteered to second the motion for papers. The House had suffered Dilke. It would have none of an avowed sharer in his republican heresies. Having partly recovered its voice, it used it to howl at Herbert, who, going a step further than his temporary leader, utilised any moment of comparative silence by shouting avowal of republicanism. Lord George Hamilton, a man who, like Dilke himself, has gone far since those days of hot-headed youth, gave a new turn to affairs by spying strangers. Under the Standing Orders then in force the Speaker was bound forthwith to order strangers to withdraw.

Above the continued hooting, groaning, and shouting that beset Auberon Herbert when he attempted to continue his remarks, was distinctly heard the novel parliamentary sound of a cock crowing. Looking over the front of the Press Gallery, as with other strangers I withdrew, I observed Jemmy Lowther, standing just outside the range of the Speaker's eye, howling vociferously, and near him Cavendish Bentinck, with open hands held trumpet-wise by the sides of his mouth, emitting cock crows with a precision that might have deceived the morn. As I wrote at the time describing this historic scene, " Cavendish Bentinck went out behind the Speaker's chair and crowed thrice."

On a division Dilke's motion was defeated by 276 against 2. The two were Wilfrid Lawson and George Anderson, a Glasgow Member, in whose later compulsory withdrawal from parliamentary life in connection with a mining scandal good Tories recognised the avenging hand of Providence. Dilke and Herbert acted as tellers. Only once in the history of turbulent passages in the House of Commons has the minority been lessened. It happened when Major O'Gorman went into the " Aye " lobby to support a vote of censure on the judges in the Tichborne case moved by Dr. Kenealy. Political significance of the action was nullified by the admission, subsequently made by the physically stupendous Major, that he had taken this step because it was a sultry night and he thought there would be more room and fresher air in the " Aye " lobby.

This speech, delivered on the threshold of Dilke's parliamentary career, had a lasting effect upon its course. Queen Victoria never forgot, and grudgingly forgave, the attack on her Royal privileges. When Gladstone, emerging from a term of restless existence as an unofficial Member of the House of Commons, was, in 1880, returned by an overwhelming majority, and was practically forced against the Queen's wishes into the Premiership, he, recognising the indispensability of Dilke and Chamberlain as members of the Government, was disposed to offer Cabinet office to the former, inducting the latter into administrative office outside its circle. The Queen, however, objected to Dilke being placed in a position in which he must in turn come into personal communicaton with herself.

The perturbed Premier was spared further trouble in the matter by the action of the persons directly concerned. Dilke and Chamberlain, shortly after the arrival of the latter upon the parliamentary scene, formed an alliance, offensive and defensive, which, in its deliberate, detailed, and determined maintenance, finds no parallel in English political life. The nearest in ancient history is provided by the friendship of David and Jonathan. The reader must determine for himself which filled the part of Saul's son and which that of Jesse's. When young Members, having made a position for themselves in the House of Commons, contemplate the formation of a new Ministry, they doubtless have their idea of the place in it most suitable to their capacity and inclination. But they await the invitation of their leader and, as a rule, accept the seat proffered them. As soon as it became clear that Gladstone would be Prime Minister in succession to Lord Beaconsfield, Dilke and Chamberlain, in their well-ordered but strictly business fashion, met in consultation as to what course they should follow.

Imprimis, they decided that in appointment to office it should not be as happened, according to Scripture, to two men working in quite another field. One should not be taken and the other left. It must be both or neither. That settled, they proceeded to discuss the delicate question of Cabinet office. Whilst firmly decided that their party of two must be represented in the Cabinet, they revealed a latent spirit of moderation by agreeing that one seat would suffice. According to general opinion expressed after the event the honour was by preference due to Dilke. In the House of Commons he held a position superior to that at the period attained by Chamberlain. At this early crisis he, assuming the part of Jonathan rather than David, was willing to stand aside and let his friend pass on to promotion.

In accordance with this generous spirit it was Chamberlain who became a Cabinet Minister, Dilke contenting himself with the office of Under-Secretary for Foreign Affairs, a post for which he was by inclination and study specially fitted. It happened that, with respect to Cabinet advantages, he enjoyed an exceptional privilege. As a rule, Under-Secretaries know less of what passes at Cabinet Councils than does that omniscient person, the Man in the Street. It came to pass that Dilke became as fully and as regularly acquainted with what took place at successive Cabinet Councils as did anyone privileged to be present. Sanctity of the secretiveness of what passes in Cabinet Council is one of the props of the British Constitution. Chamberlain had a masterful way of dealing with prejudices of flimsy character. It was his habit to proceed straight from a Cabinet Council to Dilke's room in the House of Commons, or at his house in Sloane Street, and tell him everything said or done. Whatever may be thought by political purists of this arrangement, it evidently was of immense advantage to the Under-Secretary for Foreign Affairs in discharge of an onerous share in their direction left to him by his trusting chief, Earl Granville, constitutionally disposed towards indolence.

Thus, in the end the young men had their way, Chamberlain presiding over the Board of Trade with a seat in the Cabinet, Dilke going to the Foreign Office as Under-Secretary.

In the light of subsequent events two episodes in this arrangement are striking. Whilst, owing to the Queen's personal opposition, Dilke was impossible for the Cabinet, Gladstone objected to Chamberlain on the ground taken on an earlier occasion by Sir Robert Peel, that a man should not go straight into the Cabinet without having served an apprenticeship in non-Cabinet office. Possibly he

20

had prophetic instinct that Chamberlain would be a trouble-
some Cabinet colleague.   If that were so, apprehension
proved to be well founded.   The other noteworthy thing is
that at this early stage Chamberlain's desire was to be
Colonial Secretary.   Gladstone would not listen to the
proposal.

[When Chamberlain consented to join a Cabinet under
a Conservative leader he asked for the Colonial Secretaryship as the price of acquiescence, and obtained it, with
results of which the Empire finds the aftermath in the
magnificent rally of the Colonies to the help of their
Motherland fighting for her liberty and life.]

It was not long before Dilke's masterful management of
Foreign Office business made his admission to the Cabinet
incontestable.   The   Queen   not   further   pressing   her
objections he became President of the Local Government
Board with Cabinet rank.   The growth of his supremacy
in the House of Commons was not nurtured by wiles of
speech.   His frequent interposition in debate was not
illuminated by flashes of wit and humour, or by lofty
flights of eloquence.   He was there for business purposes,
and in accomplishing them was chiefly concerned to make
his meaning clear with the least expenditure of useful
time.   He was a master of the difficult art of answering
questions with brevity and lucidity.   This was in marked
contrast with the familiar example of the Prime Minister,
whose answers to questions, whether placed on the
paper or sprung upon him without notice, occasionally
reached the proportions of a speech.   This habit was the
subject of angry comment among his colleagues, more
especially by Lord Hartington.

[Among Sir Charles's papers was found a cutting from
a " Cross-bench " article, published in the *Observer*
during the session of 1881, in which this phase of his
parliamentary manner was noted :

" Sir Charles Dilke's answers," it was written, " are

perfect whether in regard of manner, matter, or style. A small grant of public money might be much worse expended than reprinting his answer to two questions put last night on the subject of Anglo-French commercial relations, having them framed and glazed and hung up in the bedroom of every Minister. . . . It occupies just twenty-eight lines of print, and it contains a clear and full account of an exceedingly intricate negotiation."]

Gladstone's Ministry of 1880, opening with the disastrous Bradlaugh affair, was in its internal relations not a happy one. Almost from the first it suffered from an epidemic of threatened resignations. From this indisposition Dilke was the most frequent sufferer, exceeding the number of attacks which shook the stalwart frames of Lord Hartington and Sir William Harcourt. " Nothing should be so sacred as a threat of resignation," Granville wrote to him in despair. Whenever he failed to get his own way in conducting his ministerial business he threatened resignation. In accordance with the covenant of the party of two, if one went the other must needs accompany him. Accordingly the distracted Premier, recognising the inevitable break-up of his Ministry if Dilke and Chamberlain withdrew, gave way, and there followed an interval of comparative quietness.

In the end the Premier himself caught the infection. Midway in the session of 1884 he plainly indicated his intention of resigning within the limits of its duration. It was generally agreed that Hartington should succeed. Thereupon David and Jonathan, in accordance with their custom, foregathered, discussed the situation, and decided upon what places they should take under the new *régime*. Somewhat to the disappointment of his affectionate colleagues, when the appointed time for resignation approached Gladstone changed his mind. Had he at this time carried into effect his first intention the history of England, and to some extent that of the universe, would have been altered. There would have been no immediate introduction of the Home Rule Bill, with consequent split of the Liberal party that led the bulk of it to wander with brief respite in the wilderness of opposition for a score of years ; no creation of the Unionist party and all it accomplished until it in turn was shattered at the General Election of 1905.

After experience of one year at the Foreign Office, with concurrent attendance at the House of Commons, throughout a prolonged session, Dilke found the necessity of resting on the seventh day of the week. He bought a piece of land at Dockett Eddy on the Thames, practically an island accessible from the river bank by punt. At first he built a bungalow, whither he retired on Saturdays, went to bed at eight o'clock, got up at five in the morning, had a swim in the Thames, breakfast at six o'clock, and so back to slavery at Westminster by early train on Monday morning. Whilst feeling the necessity of limiting acceptance of invitations to dine and sleep out, his instincts and habits of hospitality were not to be denied. After a short while he built another and larger house a few steps from the bungalow, and during his ministerial career, with fullest regularity after his resumption of parliamentary life as Member for the Forest of Dean, he had regular week-end parties.

Through a happy succession of autumns my wife and I were regular guests at Dockett. It was there one found Dilke at his best, and learned to like him with everincreasing affection and esteem. At the time I speak of he had gone through a crushing trouble, finding comfort and consolation in his wife. Lady Fussie, the pretty pet name bestowed upon her by her husband, was a remarkable woman. Dilke met her for the first time when, as he wrote in a " Memoir " prefixed to her *Book of the Spiritual Life*, he " loved to be patronised by her, regarding her with the awe of the hobbledehoy of sixteen or seventeen towards a beautiful girl of nineteen or twenty." Whilst still a girl she married Mark Pattison,

Rector of Lincoln College, a famous scholar, of whom, or of someone curiously like him, a portrait may be found sketched by George Eliot in *Middlemarch*. Left a widow in 1884, Mrs. Mark Pattison became privately engaged to Dilke. She was in India when news came of the cloud that suddenly, apparently irretrievably, overshadowed the life of her betrothed. As brave as she was loving she telegraphed to the *Times* making public announcement of an engagement hitherto kept secret, and set forth on her journey home to complete it.

Her married life was one long honeymoon. She was the queen of the island domain at Dockett, with the ever-busy statesman her attendant knight. In summer time, early and late, life was lived in the open air. Breakfast, luncheon, and dinner were served on the spacious verandah, which during Cecil Rhodes's first visit reminded him of the stoep of Groote Schuur, where under a blue star-speckled sky, lit by a moon brighter than the sun attempting to penetrate the atmosphere of smoky London, I have sat far through a South African night, listening to a man habitually reticent of speech enlarging on the glories of Ancient Rome and the story of some of its emperors. After dinner on Saturday and Sunday nights the guests at Dockett were accustomed to sit out on the verandah, a habit that demanded a generous supply of chairs. There was one which no visitor, however otherwise favoured, presumed to occupy. In Dilke's best handwriting, ordinarily rather lacking in legibility, was written "Lady Fussie's chair." Also he had built for her exclusive use a dinghy. After her death he was accustomed to row himself about the river. When he too was gone, Lady Dilke's niece, Miss Tuckwell, inseparable companion whether in Sloane Street or up the river, had the dinghy burned. To her faithful heart and spiritual mind it was too sacred a thing to be used by others when its owner and its donor had made their last river journey in another boat pulled by ferryman Charon.

Amongst the famous folk—British, continental and colonial—whom we frequently met during our visits to Dockett Eddy was Miss Tuckwell's father, the Rev. W. Tuckwell, from his bold advocacy of Liberal principles known to the newspaper reader as " the Radical parson." With an exceptionally wide range of reading, a marvellous memory that made its gems communicable, and a keen sense of humour, he was one of the most delightful men I ever met. When Dilke built the large cottage at Dockett Eddy he placed over the door a Latin inscription. Mr. Tuckwell's ready pen rendered it into breezy English :

> " 'Tis tiny, but it suits me quite,
>   Invades no jealous neighbour's right ;
>   'Tis neat and clean and—pleasant thought—
>   I earn the cash with which 'twas bought."

This last line is a reference to the fact that Sir Charles paid its cost out of his ministerial salary.

Shortly after Lady Dilke's death Sir Charles came to dine with us at Ashley Gardens. Familiar with his habit of punctuality that brought him to keep an engagement at the very moment for which it was fixed, I was surprised to find him in the drawing-room ten minutes before the dinner hour. Clasping my hand with a grip whose painful vigour I recall at this moment, he explained that he had called before other guests arrived, so that he might have an opportunity of thanking me for a brief notice appearing in *Punch* that week of Lady Dilke's *Book of the Spiritual Life*.

" It shows," he said with something suspiciously like tears in his eyes, " a singular insight to a complex character beautiful in all its varied aspects."

From his college days Dilke was in varied forms an athlete. One of his earliest achievements, of which he was not least proud, was winning the walking race in which he beat the University champion, covering the mile in eight minutes and forty-two seconds. A rapid pace of walking was a lifelong characteristic. His passage

through the lobbies of the House of Commons on his way
to his private room suggested a lap in the walking race
of the mid-'sixties. The pace gave a centrifugal movement to his coat-tails which caught the eye of the artist
who illustrated in *Punch* "The Diary of Toby, M.P."
He was therein frequently depicted crossing the Lobby
at a mile-a-minute pace with his coat-tails flying out
behind him. Another peculiarity of this nature was his
custom of being the first man out of the House when a
division was called and the first to return to his seat
when he had voted. Watching him take part in hundreds
of divisions I never saw him fail to achieve this distinction.

Whenever he stayed at Dockett Dilke occupied a
room in the smaller bungalow. My wife and I were
generally lodged in the same building. One Sunday
afternoon, going over to our room for a book, I found
prominently placed in the passage a shoe, with a half-sheet
of notepaper set in it bearing the strange device : "Don't
make a noise. I am sleeping." In accordance with his
habit of looking ahead and leaving nothing to chance,
this was Dilke's way of ensuring an hour's undisturbed
sleep, well earned by his early rising, his row on the
river, or his long ride ashore.

Mr. Tuckwell, who, like his daughter, long lived in
intimate relations with the household, tells how through
the last five years of Dilke's life he breakfasted alone with
him whenever he was at Pyrford, the Tuckwell country
home. "It was," he writes, "his softer hour, showing
him in a specially endearing light." As his companion
frankly and truly says, in large companies, such as frequently assembled at Dockett, Dilke "was occasionally
insistent, iterative, expressing himself, to use a term of
his own, with a fierceness corresponding to the strength
of his convictions. At our breakfasts he was gentle,
tolerant, talking and listening alternately."

This last was certainly a mood unfamiliar at Dockett.
When launched upon monologue, always interesting and

informing, if any of the listening circle ventured to inter-
polate a remark, Dilke had a trick of hurriedly responsing
" I know, I know," and forthwith the tide of talk surged
on. His knowledge was almost literally universal. It
was as detailed as it was extensive. Challenged on any
topic—literature, history, science or politics—he instantly
responded with a precision and fullness of knowledge
that suggested the subject was one he had exclusively
studied. He was equally at home with the birds of the
air, the running or creeping things on the earth, the fish
in the river, and the flowers in fields and gardens.

Oddly enough, the only slip he made in a long life
happened in one of these breakfast chats with Mr.
Tuckwell. Talking about Disraeli he quoted some of
his sayings. Among others a remark about Thomasson,
the deaf Member for Bolton, who, ear-trumpet in hand,
was wont to seat himself near any bore who might at the
moment be on his legs.

" No man," Dilke reported Dizzy as having said, " ever
so neglected his natural advantage."

The fact is the little quip was the invention of that
veracious parliamentary chronicler "Toby, M.P." One
night, in a nearly deserted House, Lord Sherbrooke,
entering the Peers' Gallery, discovered Thomasson, ear-
trumpet in hand, eagerly drinking in the flow of words
from a prosy Member who had otherwise almost succeeded
in emptying the House. It occurred to me that the
phrase in question was likely to express the feeling of
Bob Lowe, and it was accordingly put down to his
account. It was so frequently quoted in print and repeated in conversation that, in the end, Sherbrooke came
to believe it was his own. When his *Life* was written it
was so recorded. In a letter written to me by his bio-
grapher, in reply to one mentioning the fact of the case,
Mr. Patchett Martin informed me he had found among
Lord Sherbrooke's papers a note in his handwriting
" owning up " to the comment.

After the second trial in the divorce case there commenced in a section of the Press a venomous campaign
against Dilke, who found himself boycotted in the House
of Commons he had formerly dominated, and in society
once emulously competing for his company. At the
general election in the summer of 1886 Chelsea, accustomed to return him to Parliament by overwhelming
majorities, deserted him. For six years he remained
outside the place to which " his heart untravelled " ever
fondly turned. It was not that he lacked opportunities
of finding a seat. From time to time he was approached
by populous constituencies with invitation to represent
them at Westminster. He laid down as a primary
condition of acceptance of his candidature that there
must be " full and absolute belief " in him and in his
word. The Forest of Dean gave the required pledge
and, in 1892, returned him by a majority of two to one.
The seat proved invulnerable at subsequent elections, and
was held by him at the time of his death, the tie between
constituency and Member meanwhile steadily strengthening in esteem carried to the point of personal affection.

He went through a painful ordeal during the first
session of his return. A few old friends made a point
of openly welcoming him back. Mrs. Grundy, M.P.,
fearful of contamination, showed a disposition to draw
in her skirts as he passed by. What he suffered he never
told, except possibly in the closer and sustaining company
of his wife. He quietly set himself to live it down and,
slowly at first, completely as sessions followed each
other, he succeeded. For some time before he answered
the call which nightly, at the close of a House of Commons
sitting, resounds through the Lobby, " Who goes home ? "
he had reconquered the position attained by him in 1885,
a position which in the opinion of competent authorities
(including Gladstone) was a sure and certain stage on
the way to the Premiership.

CHAPTER XXV

THE House was shocked this afternoon to hear of the death of George Wyndham. He was leisurely returning from a holiday trip, stayed for a night at Paris, and there suddenly died.

The last time I saw him was in his wife's beloved home at Saighton. He came into the room late in the afternoon hot from a long run with the hounds, his scarlet coat freely speckled with November mud. With him was his son Percy, also a noted huntsman. [Percy went out to the Front with the First Hundred Thousand, and within three weeks of his reaching the firing-line followed his father into other and happier hunting grounds.]

Wyndham's sympathies with all things beautiful were widely diversified. No mean poet himself, he was familiar with all the best verse, ancient and modern. Next to poets and poetry, I think he most loved horses and riding, of which last art he was a master. " How beautifully you ride ! " Queen Alexandra said to him as his horse pranced in the cavalcade escorting King Edward and Her Majesty to the review in Phœnix Park, a principal pageant in Their Majesties' visit to Ireland in the summer of 1903, vividly described by the Chief Secretary in a letter to his sister.

Wyndham had an excellent training for the political and parliamentary life in which he came to play the part of *preux chevalier*. For six years he acted as private secretary (unpaid) to Arthur Balfour, at the time on the war-path in Ireland, holding the executive ministerial post to which his young friend later succeeded. Elected for Dover in 1889, a seat held at the time of his death,

he diligently set himself to win in the House of Commons
the place he habitually held in the hunting field.   At the
outset, indeed for some years, the House did not take
kindly to his style of oratory.   To tell the truth, he was
a little over-trained.   His style was ornate, his phrases
smelt of the lamp, and his delivery was marred by certain
mannerisms not wholly free from suspicion of practice
before the cheval glass.   It was a sore disappointment
when, in 1895, his dear friend and old chief, Arthur Balfour, became Leader of the House and found no place
for him on the Treasury Bench.   He told me at the time
that in this connection he had been grievously wounded
in the house of a friend.   Whilst struggling under a sense
of neglect, Balfour in friendly conversation advised him
to give himself up to the pursuit of literature.

   " That I perceived," Wyndham said, " meant that he
regarded me as hopeless for a political career."

   Opportunity came to him three years later and, as the
French say, he seized it by the hair.   Appointed to the
congenial office of Under-Secretary for War, he quickly
made his mark, justifying speedy promotion to the Irish
Office with Cabinet rank.   The Irish Members effusively
welcomed a lineal descendant of Lord Edward Fitzgerald.
It is true that in a brief period, finding him always
courteous but occasionally intractable according to their
view of the proper Government of Ireland, they genially
alluded to him as " the Smiling Assassin."   That was,
however, merely a variation upon the cognomen " Buck-
shot Forster," invented for a predecessor at the Chief
Secretary's Lodge in Phœnix Park.

   Wyndham's great legislative achievement was the
passing of the Irish Land Purchase Bill in the session of
1903, a measure to which is largely attributable the
prosperity that has comforted Ireland during the last
twelve years.   Since for the mutual benefit of Irish
landlord and tenant it pledged the credit of the British
taxpayer to the extent of one hundred millions sterling,

it was, naturally, popular in Ireland. The event marked
the apex of Wyndham's career. Had a dissolution or
his own resignation at that date terminated, or for a period
of two years interrupted, his ministerial engagement,
the otherwise unvaried happiness of his life would have
been undisturbed.

Shortly after his Bill was added to the Statute Book he
laughingly showed me a letter that had reached him from
a prominent and much-esteemed member of the Dublin
Casile staff. It advised him to retire from office whilst
the glimmer of success and personal popularity still shone
upon him. He was warned that if he stayed on another
two years, all he had done for Ireland would be forgotten,
and he would drift into some difficulty that would break
him down. Wyndham returned a sprightly confident
answer, assuring his colleague that he had other good
work to do for Ireland and would remain at his post until
it was accomplished. According to tradition at the
Irish Office, his mentor endorsed the letter " Wyndham's
a lost man," and locked it up in a private drawer of his
desk.

The prophecy was fulfilled almost to a month. In the
autumn recess of 1904 Wyndham, taking up his residence
at the Chief Secretary's Lodge, entered into communication with Lord Dunraven, engaged in framing a scheme
for the devolution of local legislation in Ireland, and the
decentralisation of its financial arrangements. Publication of the plan, understood to have been devised with
the knowledge, presumably the assent, of the Chief
Secretary, the Lord-Lieutenant, Earl Dudley, and the
Under-Secretary, Sir Anthony (now Lord) Macdonnell,
broke over Ulster like a thunderclap. Immediately upon
the meeting of Parliament in the following February the
Ulster Members, implacable, unrelenting, drove George
Wyndham out of office.

He bore the disaster with patience and courage, but
it broke his heart. He kept his seat for Dover, and

occasionally turned up at the House of Commons. The place was nevermore the same for him. In increasing measure he realised the aspiration of his cherished Horace, that he might, somewhere in the country, be " allowed to spend the time in sweet forgetfulness of busy life, now with books and now with sleep and lazy hours." One of his innumerable friends, Father John O'Connor, admirably sums up Wyndham's character : " He was," he writes, " humane as the Italian, vivacious and sympathetic as the Frenchman, straight and good-natured as the Englishman."

CHAPTER XXVI

He, single-handed, met and slew
Magicians, Armies, Ogres, Kings.
He lonely 'mid his doubting crew—
" In all the loneliness of wings "—
He fed the flame, he filled the springs,
He locked the ranks, he launched the van.

July 4, 1914.

LAST night the House of Commons, meeting as usual for the dispatch of public business, straightway adjourned. Joseph Chamberlain was dead.

Eulogies spoken across the table of the House of Commons honouring prominent Members who have died in harness are not uncommon. It is exceedingly rare that there should be added the last tribute of adjournment of the House. That it should have been paid to Chamberlain upon the motion of the Prime Minister, a political opponent of lifelong standing, adds to its value.

The scene presented the House in its best aspect. With one accord, Members uncovered when the Premier rose, and remained bareheaded through his speech. Chamberlain was a relentless foe, a mercilessly hard hitter. Having in the course of his career shattered in turn two great political parties, it was inevitable that he should have created a host of personal enemies. By his death-bed rancour was hushed. There was general, unqualified consent to Asquith's suggestion, clothed in one of the perfect sentences of an exquisite speech.

" It is," he said, " fitting that within these walls, where the echoes of his voice seem to many of us still to linger, we should suspend for a few hours the clash of controversy and conflict, while we all join in acknowledging our common debt to the life and example of a great Englishman."

At one point in this speech, Asquith incidentally referred to the fact that Chamberlain in the course of a brilliant career had never attained the Premiership, a position to which he seemed predestined. On this point I am able to supply interesting testimony of Chamberlain's personal views and aspirations on the subject. In the spring of 1900 I happened to sit next to him at a little dinner given by a mutual friend. He talked with the frankness, doubtless well considered, which sometimes startled people. He mentioned that he had that morning been reading a magazine article of mine published simultaneously in London and New York discussing his chances of succession to the Premiership.

" If," he said, " you want to know the truth about the matter, I will tell you. Never at any time in any circumstances do I intend to be Prime Minister of the Unionist party. I am ready to serve under Arthur Balfour or anyone else who may be preferred to the post. I confess it was different when I was on the other side. Fifteen years ago I was certainly resolved to be Prime Minister in the Liberal succession. If I had been, you would have seen established that condition of Liberal Imperialism of which Rosebery and others futilely talk to-day."

There were three crises in Chamberlain's career which, had they turned in a different direction, would have changed the history of England during two decades following on the year 1886. When, in 1882, W. E. Forster was driven out of the Irish Office, a feat the accomplishment of which was largely due to Chamberlain's action, the Member for Birmingham had marked succession to the Office as his own. At this epoch he, in conjunction with Charles Dilke, was the rising hope of turbulent Irish Nationalism clamouring for Home Rule. Forster had, at the risk of his life, attempted to stamp out the aspiration with the iron heel of Coercion

Acts. These Chamberlain opposed in Cabinet Council. Forster got out of the way, he was prepared to be installed in Dublin Castle with authority to attempt to cure Land Leagueism by kindness. In anticipation of the Chief Secretaryship being entrusted to him, he, in the early days of May 1882, took counsel with friends in the confidence of Parnell, friends not absolutely new to the Cabinet Minister.

With characteristic self-confidence, he counted without Gladstone, who passed him over in favour of Lord Frederick Cavendish. Incredible on the face of it, indisputable in fact, the first intimation of the appointment reached him when, seated on the Treasury Bench, he heard the Whip move for a writ for a new election in the West Riding of Yorkshire, " to fill the place of Lord Frederick Cavendish, who since his election has accepted the office of Secretary to the Lord-Lieutenant of Ireland."

That was adding insult to injury. It was probably the foundation for the personal animosity to his some time leader that marked their subsequent relations. Had he gone to Dublin in May 1882, he might have met the fate reserved for Lord Frederick; or he might have realised the strong desire possessing him at the time to give Home Rule to Ireland. In either case, the course of history at home and abroad would, as averred, have been altered.

The second crisis happened between the introduction of Gladstone's first Home Rule Bill and its second reading. Chamberlain, unaccustomed to the strange armour newly put on as an ally of Lord Salisbury, hankered after reconciliation with his old party. A principal objection taken by him against the Bill was the proposal to exclude Irish representation from Westminster. If that were withdrawn, he was prepared to abstain from opposition to the second reading, with the result that the Conservative onslaught would have been repulsed, the Bill would have gone into committee, and the earthquake that rent in twain the Temple of Liberalism would have been averted.

Largely through the agency of Labouchere, everything

was arranged to meet Chamberlain's views. In moving the second reading of the Bill, Gladstone was to announce the withdrawal of this part of the scheme. Chamberlain was to follow, declaring his objections removed. The quarrel would be patched up, and the Liberal party would live happily together ever afterwards. For inscrutable, never-explained reasons, Gladstone concluded his speech without making the stipulated announcement. In the ensuing division Chamberlain led his fifty-five followers into the Opposition lobby in line with the thirty-eight Whigs under the captaincy of Lord Hartington. The Home Rule Bill was rejected, and the Liberal party was driven out into the wilderness, where, with brief interval, they forlornly wandered for nineteen years.

The third crisis arose in connection with what is known in history as the Round Table conference. This final attempt at reconciliation had its origin in a speech addressed by Chamberlain to his Birmingham constituents, in which he let fall the significant remark that the differences between the severed sections of the Liberal party were such as might be settled by half a dozen men seated at a round table. As he thus summoned a conference on his own initiative, so he broke it up by an amazing letter, with strange irony addressed to a weekly religious paper. There is no doubt that when he entered upon the conference he hoped and believed it would lead to the closing up of sundered ranks. His frame of mind at this critical epoch is indicated in a passage from a letter written to me from Stornoway, dated April 21, 1887 : " I deplore with you the state of feeling now prevailing in the Liberal party. There has been nothing like it in our generation, and the outlook is very black. Like you, I wish I were out of it all, for politics have lost all charm for me."

As events turned out, he, then in his fifty-first year, halted on the threshold of a new departure in political life that led him to a pedestal from which he will through all time stand a dauntless epoch-maker.

21

It was assumed that Chamberlain's faculty for lucid, often dangerously sparkling speech was a gift of Nature, as reading and writing came to Dogberry. There was some foundation for this theory. But there was a secret behind his success unsuspected by the world. Talking on the subject at a comparatively early stage of his parliamentary career, he told me that what was apparently effortless was the result of painstaking practice. As everyone knows, he began by taking part in debate in the Town Council of Birmingham. He was, almost from the outset, successful in attracting and holding attention. Then, as was his custom in the House of Commons, a half-sheet of notepaper sufficed for the notes from which his speech was expanded.

The real work of preparation was done in his study. He wrote out his speech at length. If, on reading it, he was not satisfied, he wrote another on varied lines. Occasionally, if the issue were important, he tried the effect on a devoted friend, partly reading, partly reciting, his speeches in succession. When his choice was settled he got the speech off by heart, and it was so delivered. To those familiar with his later triumphs, whether in the House of Commons or on the platform, this story would be incredible if it were not recalled from his own utterance. Naturally, with lifelong practice the drudgery of his early Birmingham days was intermittent. But therein was laid the foundation of his supremacy.

At his best, and he remained at his best up to the last day he was seen in the House of Commons, Chamberlain was the most powerful of parliamentary debaters, not excepting Gladstone. Knowing the limits of his own capacity, he did not aim at oratory. Pre-eminently a man of business, he was endowed with the gifts of lightning-like acuteness of perception, consummately lucid expression. In charge of an intricate bill, he steered it through the shoals of committee with masterful hand. He was perhaps seen at his best when he stood with his

back to the wall, faced by a host of assailants. The
more noisy the interruption the cooler he grew, warding
off blows with deft parrying of his rapier, swiftly followed
up by telling thrust at his aggressor.

When in 1886 Gladstone nailed the Home Rule flag
to the Liberal masthead, and Chamberlain drifted into
the haven of Conservatism, he paid the penalty of his
supreme capacity as a phrasemaker. " He that maketh
others beware of his tongue," says Bacon, " let him
beware of other men's memory." During the last twenty
years of his active life Chamberlain, rising to address the
House of Commons, was ever faced by the ghost of his
dead self. Whatever questions might be to the front—
education, Ireland, Free Trade, or the place in the
political firmament held by the House of Lords—it turned
out that Chamberlain the Radical had said the thing
most damaging to the position at the moment taken up
by Chamberlain the colleague of Lord Salisbury. When
he had anything to say on any subject, whether the
averment were that a particular thing was black or white,
he said it in a clean-cut phrase that went straight home
to the understanding and lingered long in the memory.

There is abundant precedent for the circumstance that,
having commenced his political career in one camp, he
concluded it in another. In this respect he is in the good
company of Canning, Disraeli, and Gladstone. Canning
took the momentous step early in his political career,
crossing over from the Whig camp to join the Tories
when only twenty-three. This speciality in his case
was noted in an epigram written 120 years ago by Richard
Fitzpatrick :

> The turning of coats so common is grown,
> That no one would think to attempt it.
> But in no case until now was so flagrantly known
> Of a schoolboy turning his jacket.

Where Chamberlain's powerful individuality manifested
itself lies in the fact that, while in turn he dominated the

councils of the two great political parties of the State, he also, in turn rent them to their centre. The breaking up of the Liberal party on the question of Home Rule was followed seventeen years later by the disruption of the Unionists on the question of Free Trade. The hand that wrought the ruin was in both cases Chamberlain's.

It is small wonder that a man with such a history should have created many enemies. After 1886 they were divided in the House of Commons into two groups— the Irish Nationalists, whose early trust he had betrayed, and the Radicals, whom he deserted. The bitter feeling found outburst in the historical free fight on the floor of the House in the final stage of the Home Rule Bill of 1892. But if he had a cohort of enemies, he had a circle of warm friends, whose fidelity he was careful to reward.

The summit of his marvellous career was reached in the autumn of 1902, when, a passenger in the finest cruiser of the British Navy, the ex-Mayor of Birmingham, Secretary of State for the Colonies, sailed for the Cape, intent on binding up the wounds created by the ravages of war. The shout of Great Britain bidding him God-speed on his mission was drowned by the acclaim of South Africa welcoming him to its shore. He was at that time not only the most powerful, but the most popular man in England.

A companion picture presented five years later leaps to the eye. It shows a partly paralysed figure painfully making its way across a London railway station, with gallant but futile attempt to raise its hat in response to the greeting cheer. It was Joseph Chamberlain home from the Riviera, where he had passed some weeks in vain struggle with the effects of a blow that had stricken him down while, dauntless, hopeful to the last, he was counting on the achievement of his final campaign.

The incident suggested to one looker-on the idea of a wounded lion, long-time lord of the forest, returning to its lair to die.

CHAPTER XXVII

Hail and Farewell, dear Brother of the Pen,
Maker of sunshine for the minds of men.
Lord of bright cheer and master of our hearts—
What plaint is fit when such a friend departs ?
                              R. C. L. in *Punch*.

April 21, 1917.

" No flowers (of speech) by request," Frank Burnand
wrote to me in anticipation of his presiding for the last
time at the weekly *Punch* dinner.

In to-day's *Times* appears notification of his death in
his eighty-first year, concluding with the intimation " no
flowers." There were other coincidences in his passing
away. He died on a Saturday, the weekday which for
more than a quarter of a century he had been accustomed
to devote to the final preparations of *Punch* for the press.
He was buried on the following Wednesday, the day of
the week when, from time immemorial, the *Punch* dinner
has been held. He would, I fancy, like to have known
of this singular concatenation of dates.

In deprecating speech-making on his final appearance
in the editorial chair, Burnand was anxious to avoid
anything in the way of a scene at the close of an intimate
connection with colleagues some of whom had sat with
him at table through the full twenty-six years of his
editorship. His wish was respected in the matter of
refraining from anything in the form of formal speech-
making, a habit wholly foreign to Mr. Punch's board.
But it was impossible to carry on to the end the appearance of the ordinary weekly dinner. At the close of the
sitting some simple words were said across the table by
representative members of the staff, to which the retiring

captain made response, dignified and touching in its simplicity. Nothing could have been in better keeping with the terms on which the little companionship are accustomed to live and work than this final scene in a memorable career.

Although Burnand surrendered the chair to a younger man it was understood that he would not absolutely terminate his association with the table. When Thackeray resigned his place on the *Punch* staff he did not finally withdraw from the hospitable " Old Mahogany Tree " he lovingly sang. Up to the period of his death he occasionally dropped in at the dinner-hour, to meet with warm welcome from old friends. The same honorary membership was bestowed upon Sir John Tenniel when he finished his long labour, and it was heartily extended to Sir Frank Burnand. Once, and once only, after his retirement, Tenniel's beaming smile shone over the table and his old companions. Burnand " came back to Lochaber no more."

While he filled the editorial chair for nearly a quarter of a century, his connection with *Punch* as a contributor runs back for fifty-four years. Like Thackeray, he, at the outset of his career, " fancied himself " rather as an artist than a writer. In many of his letters to me he dropped in a sketch, hopelessly bad as to the drawing, but full of humour.

His principal achievement at Trinity College, Cambridge, where he graduated, was the founding of an amateur dramatic club, which still flourishes as the A.D.C. Casting about for a profession, he concluded he would take priestly orders. He made some formal preparation under the direction of Dr. Manning, but soon discovered that he was not born for the Church. The next best thing seemed to be the stage, which he trod for a brief time at Edinburgh. Next he thought of the Bar, and was actually " called," but, as he said, he " didn't come." His first appearance in the paper in whose life

later he filled a predominant part, was a sketch sent in
whilst he was an undergraduate at Cambridge.   The
idea was sufficiently attractive, but the drawing lacked
finish, as Disraeli said of Horsman's invective.   Leech
touched it up with the magic of his pencil, and it duly
appeared.   Burnand later became a regular contributor
to the pages of *Fun*, at the time, with the assistance of a
brilliant staff, attempting to dislodge *Punch* from the
pre-eminence of its popularity.

At that period, the mid-Victorian era when public
taste was bad in other respects than furniture and frocks,
sensationalism of a lurid kind pervaded the cheap press.
The *London Journal* was the principal, most prolific,
contributor to this fashion.   Burnand, closely following
the style of the original, wrote a fearsome story he called
" Mokeanna."   The proprietor of *Fun* saw no fun in it,
returning the contribution on the hands of the struggling
writer.   Burnand submitted it next to Mark Lemon,
then editor of *Punch*, who not only jumped at the idea,
but suggested means of carrying it out that contributed
to its immediate success.   Sir John Gilbert was engaged
to illustrate the story in a flamboyant style burlesquing
his own.   Type was used that presented a facsimile of
a page of the *London Journal*.   " Mokeanna " had a
great run, carrying on its back the author of its being
to fame and fortune.

Burnand well remembered his first *Punch* dinner.   It
was spread all on a summer day in an old inn at Dulwich.
Thackeray was there, and was kindly enthusiastic in his
reception of the recruit whose diploma work none had
admired more than he, to whom in some quarters it had
been attributed.   The custom of dining out in summer-
time, dating as far back as this occasion memorable to
Burnand, was observed during the life of William Bradbury, business manager of the firm of publishers into
whose possession *Punch* fell whilst in its teens and under
whose direction it greatly prospered.   In his hearty

cheeriness and his abounding hospitality, William Bradbury was personally a fitting embodiment of *Punch* in
genial mood.

In anticipation of my first dinner in Bouverie Street I
surmised a beef-steak, or possibly a joint, flanked by
tankards of stout or bitter. That was not William
Bradbury's idea of the fare to set before the company to
whom he affectionately alluded as " my boys." Nothing
was too good for them, whether in the way of meat or
drink, and, regardless of cost, they had both in abundance.
The dinner customarily served in the office in Bouverie
Street on the table on which are cut the names of men
famous during the last sixty years in literature and art,
was pleasantly varied by trips up the river to a famous
hostelry—the Mitre at Hampton Court for choice—or
a coach-and-four drive to Sevenoaks or other place where
rural beauty was supplemented by proximity of an inn
honourably known for its wine-cellar and its table traits.

At one period of Burnand's editorship there sprang up
the custom, soothing after hard labour, of ordering the
dinner for the following week. The cartoon settled, the
fagged company bent renewed energies on the menu for
the following Wednesday. In a note from Burnand, the
year as usual undated, he writes :

" The other night at Mrs. Jeune's [later Lady St. Helier]
we had wild duck and Bigarade sauce, which so much
astonished the Table when I ordered it on the bill of fare.
At Mrs. Jeune's it was done admirably. At the Table
it wasn't—all the difference. But you don't even know
of it, you, the Brillat-Savarin of the so-called nineteenth
century ! "

On this same topic of dinners, rather a favourite one,
he wrote, under date February 1, 1888 :

" Oh, you humbug ! You not dining out ! Marry
come up, forsooth go to. Go to——. Well, I hope you
will keep well. Yes, we'll dine with thee. Thou hast

asked us on the very day we can dine with you : couldn't
be better. I am Robsoning Rooseing. I was there
to-day, shall be there to-morrow. Too much dieting
will not suit me. But it will suit you and you must be
very careful. I have told Roose what a chap you are.
Don't have too many Marquises and Earls and Dukes
to meet me. Bless thee and thy wife. Yours ever."

The Robson Roose alluded to was the famous doctor
who at one time had the majority of Lord Salisbury's
Cabinet in his charge. He was Lord Randolph Churchill's
doctor through some anxious years, attending him to the
last.

Later in life, Burnand's once powerful constitution
showing signs of breaking up, he was placed under
Spartan restrictions with respect to diet. Of this
condition he as usual made fun. Writing from Ramsgate
on October 9, 1905, he says :

" I make progress in the Land of Lithia where the
Wiskivites live. There I fear I shall for some time dwell.
With all the Fleshmeat family I am dead cuts (cuts, not
cats). Priscilla Potage I now never press to my lips.
I find my truest friends in the firm Fish & Co., Billingsgate.
Peter Poultry is always with me."

Which all meant that his daily regime, omitting soup,
was limited to fish and poultry (not a poor provision),
his drink to lithia water, flavoured with a little whisky.

Burnand was a voluminous letter-writer. Rarely a
day, never a week, passed without receipt of a letter
written in his own hand. Present one day at the proceedings of the Parnell Commission, he dashed off the
following :

" What is the atmosphere of Bouverie Street compared
with that of the Court during the sitting of the Parnell
Commission ? Why, since it is ventilating the Irish
question, should it not itself be ventilated ? Biggar
delightful. You couldn't see him where you sat. Davitt

repressed Healy when the latter made an objectionable remark and was corrected by Hannen [President of the Court]. The usher is beautiful. He ought to be on the Bench. He was genuinely amused at everything. When there's likely to be a scene I shall look in again, but with a bagpipe full of pure air—pure air of Scotland—under my arm. Did you see Arthur à Beckett's umbrella ! ! [Here follows a pen-and-ink sketch showing an opened umbrella (obscuring the head of the owner), whereof Burnand not unnecessarily explained :] The white strips represent where it wanted mending."

The white strips were extravagantly wide.

Of more lasting fame than " Mokeanna " was the series of " Happy Thoughts " with which he made his next hit in the pages of *Punch*. It is one of the few contributions to periodical literature that have added a phrase to common conversation.

In the autumn of 1880, on the death of Tom Taylor, Burnand naturally succeeded him as editor. None of those present will forget the dinner in honour of his installation. It was held at the Albion, in the City, and, contrary to immemorial custom, outsiders were bidden to the feast. At the regular weekly *Punch* dinner the waiters before withdrawing from the room place on the table at the right hand of the editor pens, ink, and paper, and business forthwith begins. At the Albion dinner this custom was observed with added solemnity. The guests, who far outnumbered the habitual half-dozen who meet at the Wednesday dinner, being also supplied with writing materials, were invited to suggest a cartoon for the following week. There was full response, but none was adopted.

As editor of *Punch*, a writer of burlesques, a good friend, a cheery companion, the life and soul of any dinner party at which he might be present, Burnand's reputation was long established in diverse circles of social life in London. It was at the weekly dinner of

Punch that these qualities shone forth with fullest, most sustained lustre. He was literally at home with the little brotherhood, over which it can hardly be said he " presided " week by week through twenty-six years. He never assumed the editorial air, nor put on the presidential manner. The *Punch* staff realises in unique perfection the dream of Liberty, Equality, and Fraternity —especially fraternity. But as there is important business to be done at the dinner-table someone must direct the proceedings, and, without overt effort, the followers, unconscious of the kindly leash, Burnand led.

For many parliamentary sessions there appeared in the Sunday *Observer* an article purporting to be written " From the Cross-benches " of the House of Commons. It unintentionally but necessarily competed with the popularity of " The Diary of Toby, M.P." in *Punch*. Lord Rosebery, a sympathetic student of humour, preferred it. His late Majesty King Edward, whilst still Prince of Wales, told me that he " religiously had it served with his breakfast every Sunday morning." On the other hand, two potentates differing in character and position as did the late King of the Belgians and Mr. Roosevelt whilst President of the United States, made in curiously identical phrase the remark that their reading of reports of parliamentary proceedings at Westminster was limited to Toby, M.P.'s, Diary.

An editor, member of a veiled sect who, after all, are almost human, naturally would not like to have a contributor practising on slightly varied lines in the pages of a contemporary. There was nothing small about Burnand's nature. Above feelings of petty jealousy, he frequently wrote or spoke to me enthusiastically about the series. I have before me a letter written from his town residence, The Boltons, in October 1902, in which he says :

" Your Cross-bench article in the *Observer* this week

was exceptionally good. A record as a stirring description of an exciting scene, and absolutely dramatic in its treatment by you ; just on the border-line 'twixt farce and tragedy."

Some people were inclined to believe that *Punch* sorely drooped, was almost flattened, under the ponderosity of Tom Taylor. Burnand early succeeded in removing this reproach, the paper instantly feeling the impulse of his abundant vitality. He was ever on the look-out for new blood, and dolorously lamented the exceeding smallness of suitable supply. His painstaking patience was marvellously displayed on Wednesday nights during discussion over the subject and the treatment of the cartoon. Gentlemen of England who live at home at ease and, taking up their *Punch* on a Wednesday morning, study the cartoon, suppose it was settled, designed, drawn and printed during the previous night, with the latest telegrams and special editions of the evening papers at hand for suggestion and guidance. It is no criminal disclosure of secrets of the prison-house to say that the *Punch* cartoon is arranged in all its details a clear week before the day of publication. Considering that it chiefly deals with the rapidly revolving course of politics, and that it must needs hit on or about the centre of the target as it chances to be set up a week later, it will be seen that the task is one of no slight difficulty and delicacy.

Sometimes by happy inspiration, or by obvious direction of events, the work of the night may be disposed of in a quarter of an hour. There are times when two, even three, hours are occupied in close discussion. At such crises Burnand's clear-sightedness, his judicial frame of mind, his patience and perseverance were indomitable. He listened to every suggestion, quickly caught at any that seemed promising, had it beaten out till its quality was ascertained, and, if it proved a failure, began all over again on another tack.

When the cartoon was out of hand (it is known at the

dinner table as "the big Cut "), Burnand, with the abandon of a schoolboy freed for play after a morning's task, literally bubbled with jokes, which lost nothing of their effect from the contagion of his own hearty enjoyment. It was the same with his correspondence. Considering the pressure and amount of his literary work, it amazed me to receive from him at brief intervals letters of four, sometimes eight pages—not dictated or typewritten, but written by his own hand. Quip and crank gleamed on every page, absolutely unpremeditated, apparently born of the spluttering of his pen. In one letter received from him, a pencilled card written from a sick-bed, he concludes : " Now I think I'll doze ; sapientia doze-it." Not very good, you will say. Obvious when it is done. But there it is. The sick humorist, the tired punster, wearied with the effort of writing a few lines, flickering up with a final jest.

Burnand's humour was as spontaneous as it was inexhaustible. I remember one night talking with him amid the crush at the Foreign Office on a Birthday night. A be-starred and be-ribboned guest came up and warmly greeted him. With a puzzled look he did not reciprocate the recognition.

" Ah," said the stranger, " I see you don't know me from Adam."

" My dear fellow," replied Frank, " I didn't know Adam."

One time he appeared before the Income Tax Commissioners to protest against what he resented as a too liberal estimate of his income. In reply to searching inquiries he was a little hazy about particulars.

" Surely," said the presiding Commissioner, born and bred a man of business, " you must keep books."

" No, indeed," said Burnand. " I don't *keep* books. I write 'em."

A story, not his own, he hugely delighted in related to a driving tour to which some Bohemian friends treated

themselves.   On their way they put up at Stony Stratford.
One of the visitors passed a sleepless night, the bed being
liberally shared by entities who did not contribute to
the hotel charges.   When he came down to breakfast
next morning he ruefully remarked, " They may well call
this Stony Stratford.   I was never so much bitten in
my life."

Burnand claimed for this pre-eminence as a *non sequitur*.

When in April 1897 Sir William Agnew pressed upon
my acceptance the editorship of *Punch,* I confess it put
in my way a great temptation.   By reason of its historical
associations, its world-wide influence, and its personal
distinction, I regard the post as the blue ribband of
British journalism.   Acceptance meant the dislodgment
of Burnand, with consequences of financial ruin and,
possibly, heart-breaking.   In common with Owen Seaman, Lehrman, and Anstey Guthrie, I owed to him my
inclusion on the staff of the journal.   He was not merely
a colleague, but an old and intimate friend, trusted and
trusting.   To permit myself to be made the instrument
of his dethronement was unthinkable.   I have never
regretted the decision promptly arrived at.

Possessing the confidence of both parties, I had the
good fortune to be able to smooth away the differences
recently existing between the proprietors and the editor.
They were not renewed during the remaining lifetime
of Sir William Agnew and William Bradbury.

Enforced resignation of the editorship of *Punch,* nine
years later, came upon him as a staggering blow.   Having
filled the post with honour and distinction through a
period of twenty-six years he had come to regard himself
as indispensable.   He spoke and wrote very bitterly on
the subject, unadvisedly, as his best friends thought and
told him.   But for his own letters published in the Press
the pleasing fiction would have been kept up that he had
retired of his own accord on account of increasing years.
He certainly had no ground for complaint against the

proprietors, either in the matter of courtesy or of consideration. On vacating the editorial chair he received a substantial pension for life.

When the healing unction of Time was applied to the wound his former relations with the proprietors were happily renewed. Those with his old colleagues were never strained. They bade him farewell, or rather said *au revoir*, at a dinner made the occasion of the presentation of a token of their regard.

His old interlocutor among the Income Tax Commissioners would have said that, retiring from active work in his seventieth year, Burnand ought to have been at least comfortably off in the matter of worldly goods. Apart from his salary as editor of *Punch*, he had many outside sources of revenue. He reckoned that he had written over 120 plays, chiefly burlesques and light comedies. *The Colonel* alone, which had a prodigiously long run, must have heaped his pockets full of gold. But he was an open-handed man. If he earned money liberally, he spent it lavishly. Suddenly faced by the prospect of cessation of salary, he utterly broke down. He wrote to intimate friends pitiful letters deploring the prospect of the future. I had the good fortune, thanks to the hearty co-operation of Mr. Asquith, then Chancellor of the Exchequer, to obtain for him a pension on the Civil Service List. This in conjunction with his retiring allowance set him on his legs, and his doleful letters again beamed with humour.

"My dear Lucy," he wrote from Ramsgate, on August 1, 1906, " you set the ball a-rolling and it has at last tumbled into the right hole for it—my pocket. Very many thanks to you. I am now in comparative clover. I have only just discovered, on turning over the page, that this is but half a sheet. Quite enough in this weather when blankets are burdens."

He gallantly set himself to further increase his income

by undertaking a series of lectures, no slight task for a man of his age in failing health.

"My tour is for October," he wrote. "It occupies about half the month. Terms are very good, but whether 'twill be a success I haven't the faintest idea. If success, I doubt if I could continue the work. If not, then Fare thee well my trim-built wherry, and werry glad I shall be to have done with it."

In 1904 he had an illness of somewhat alarming character. The editor of a London morning paper, with the ghastly but necessary prevision in such cases, asked me to write a column *In memoriam*. When Burnand was quite better I told him of this.

"A column!" he cried, with twinkling eyes. "I never thought I should get so much. Why, that's what they gave to Nelson in Trafalgar Square and the Duke of York on the top of the steps overlooking the Horse Guards."

His record of a genial, hard-working life which added much to the gaiety of nations is loftier than the average column.

CHAPTER XXVIII

October 31, 1917.

IN his *Recollections,* just published, Lord Morley makes no reference to his maiden speech in the House of Commons. I happened to hear it, and across the waste of twenty-four years retain vivid memory of the scene. In accordance with the chivalrous custom of the House of Commons, he as a new Member had choice of the moment when he desired to join in debate. He rose immediately after questions were disposed of, and, contrary to its custom of an afternoon, the crowded House remained to hear the new-comer whose fame as a literary man preceded him. It happened that after the interval of a night, he followed Mr. Joseph Gillis Biggar, who had been in the primest mood of his quaint unconscious humour. Fluent, self-possessed, never at a loss for a word, not particular as to its relevance, he chattered for a full half-hour. Next day came John Morley with his carefully prepared treatise couched in polished sentences gleaming from profound depths of thought. The House vigorously cheered when he rose, and sat in silent sympathy as he struggled through his opening sentences.

It was a striking contrast, not without a note of sadness, to think of Joseph Gillis saying nothing with easy fluency, and to look on at this embodiment of culture, this man teeming with great thoughts, this master of perfect literary style, standing with parched lips and strained eyes stumbling through recitation of his sedulously prepared essay.

On his entry into parliamentary life John Morley was handicapped by two conditions ordinarily fatal to supreme success. He was in his forty-sixth year, a splendid age,

22   327

the very prime of manhood, but, except in rare cases—
Chamberlain's the most prominent—too far advanced
in years for entrance upon a term of apprenticeship in
that complex, inscrutable assembly, the House of Commons. In addition, he had made a wide reputation
outside the walls of Westminster, a thing interesting and
attractive in itself, but not of a character to be maintained
in the course of parliamentary procedure. In course of
time, by sheer force of character, he overcame these draw-
backs, and took his place among debaters of the first rank.

The position was slowly acquired. From the first, he
had in him the gift of ordered persuasive speech, but for
some time he could not be induced to let himself go in its
delivery. To his ascetic literary taste the looser style
of expression more fitting when addressing a public
audience, was repellent. He found salvation in accidental
circumstances. Called upon to address a conference of
Liberal delegates gathered at Leeds, contagion of their
high spirits in anticipation of success at the coming
general election was communicated to the austere
statesman on the platform. Cutting himself adrift from
the trammels of notes prepared in the chilling atmosphere
of his study, he talked to his enthusiastic audience in a
frank, hearty manner which delighted them and probably
astonished himself.

The speech was a marked success not only with the
representative audience, but with the wider circle that
read a verbatim report in the newspapers. He never
turned aside from the departure thus made by chance.
It was as if a man floating on the water, by accident
deprived of his life-belt, discovered that he could swim
very well without it Morley never plunged into the
stream of debate in the House of Commons with the
boisterous joyousness displayed by Harcourt. But he
improved session by session, maintaining his supremacy
in the alien atmosphere of the House of Lords whither
he was, to the amazement of his friends, translated.

Amazement is deepened when we learn that the change of scene and status was not the result of friendly action from outside, but on the initiative of the lifelong Radical and sometimes scorner of the Peerage caste. With habitual frankness Morley relates how, shortly after the death of Campbell-Bannerman, Asquith, entering his official room at the House of Commons, informed him of his call to the Premiership, and asked if he had any views as to his own place in the Ministry.

" If you approve," was the unexpected reply, " I will stay at the India Office and go to the House of Lords."

" Why on earth should you go there ? " asked the master of stately eloquence, startled into colloquialism. Morley explained that he would better do his work, literary and political, " in the comparative leisure of the other place." So it was settled.

Seated on the red-leather cushion of the House of Lords, in comforting contiguity to the bench of surpliced archbishops and bishops, Lord Morley among his *Recollections* may have recalled a description upon which he once ventured of the august body to which he has been recruited. It was, to the uproarious delight of his audience, embodied in a speech delivered at Manchester shortly after the Lords had by overwhelming majority thrown out Gladstone's second Home Rule Bill. " With the House of Lords," said the Commoner of those distant days, " you are dealing with a vast, overwhelming preponderance, a huge dead weight of prejudice and passion, of bigotry, of party spirit, immovable by discussion, impenetrable to argument, beyond the reach of reason, to be driven from its hereditary and antiquated entrenchments not by arguments or by reason, but by force."

Lord Morley's *Recollections*, by chance published a few weeks after the admirable *Life of Sir Charles Dilke* was given to the world, cover much the same period of time. They supplement the Dilke memoir mainly in respect of the vicissitudes of the Home Rule question. Dilke and

Chamberlain in the early stage of their alliance were
Home Rulers. Dilke remained so to the end, though
his personal interest more directly lay in the field of
foreign politics. Chamberlain became the bitterest
and most powerful opponent of his early creed. He
marshalled and successfully led the Liberal revolt which
destroyed Gladstone's first Home Rule Bill. He became
the mainstay of the Unionist party ranged under the
titular leadership of Lord Salisbury, and thereafter, to
the tragic close of his life, enjoyed the companionship
and confidence of the class he, before finding salvation
denounced as those " who toil not, neither do they spin."
Faithful to the last, John Morley fought for Home Rule,
and more than any man since Gladstone preserved it from
permanent wrecking.

Morley's personal relations with Parnell before the
downfall of the Irish leader were habitually intimate.
Parnell, who kept his own followers in the House of
Commons at a distance they bitterly resented, unbosomed
himself to the Englishman with rare frankness. I
remember being in the Lobby in the House of Commons
late on a night shortly before the O'Shea divorce case
came into court, when Parnell, making his first appearance
at the sitting, crossed the floor with rapid footsteps.
Seeing me, he stopped and conversed for a few minutes.
When he resumed his passage to the Library, Dick Power,
the Parnellite Whip, asked me if I could tell him whether
his chief proposed to take part in the debate then going
forward. Considering the intimate relations ordinarily
subsisting between a party leader in the House of
Commons and his Chief Whip, this incident, trifling in
itself, throws a flood of light upon Parnell's treatment
of his followers when in the plenitude of his power.

During Morley's first term of service at the Irish Office,
and later when he sat on the Front Opposition Bench,
Parnell frequently visited him, and conversed on current
phases of the Irish question. In violation of his vow

never to break bread in the house of a Saxon, he even
occasionally dined with him.   One such occasion—it must
have been the last—happened when Morley was staying
at Brighton in the winter of 1890.   As soon as his guest
left, he made a note of their prolonged conversation.
At that time the Unionist Government, buttressed by
the adhesion of Chamberlain and Hartington, was
tottering to a fall.   So imminent was a general election,
and so certain of its result was Gladstone, optimistic to
the last, that he, in consultation with Morley, occupied
himself in drafting a Liberal Cabinet.   Doubtless not
without knowing Gladstone's feeling in the matter, Morley
" guilelessly," as he says, asked Parnell would it be
possible for him to accept the post of Chief Secretary to
the Lord-Lieutenant ?   The Irish leader, without show
of the amazement that would have filled the House of
Commons had it known that such a dramatic turn of
events was ever dreamt of, emphatically declined to
consider the suggestion.   A week later the co-respondent
in the O'Shea divorce case was adjudged guilty by the
Court, and Parnell's career as leader of a party that
sometimes arbitrarily held the balance between British
Liberals and Conservatives, finally closed.

This idea of Irish home affairs being committed to the
care and control of an Irishman was not new in Liberal
circles.   Whilst still a member of Gladstone's Ministry
Chamberlain advocated it.   In the spring of 1882, when
the Government of Ireland had broken down in the
hands of Forster, he wrote to the editor of the *Pall Mall
Gazette* (Mr. Morley) :

" I wish you would openly advocate Shaw as Chief
Secretary.   It would be an appeal to the electors to aid
in the creation of a new policy, and they might rise to
the occasion.   If they did not, at least the English
Government would be free from reproach, and would
have tried to rule Ireland by the Irish."

The Shaw referred to was an Irish Home Rule Member

who, after Parnell was ousted from leadership of the Nationalists, for a short time attempted to fill his place.

When Morley entered the House of Commons he was promptly taken by the hand of Chamberlain, who recognised in him a promising recruit to a party which at the time solely consisted of Dilke. Friendship, political and social, existed for some years. It was severed by lack of docility on the part of Morley, which in similar circumstances Chamberlain resented in Dilke. The Member for Birmingham was what, to Charles Dickens's delight, by way of parting shot in an angry controversy about a fare, a cabman called Foster, " a harbitry gent." His ideal of a colleague and companion was realised in the case of Jesse Collings and Powell Williams, who were ready to follow his political divigations whithersoever they led him. They applauded his " Unauthorised Programme," and faithfully followed his footsteps when they led him into Society and the advocacy of principles of which that historic document was the scourge. In conversation on controversial topics he desired in an interlocutor full measure of the acquiescence of Polonius in conversation with Hamlet :

Ham. Do you see yonder cloud that's almost in shape of a camel ?
Pol. By the mass, and 'tis like a camel indeed !
Ham. Methinks it is like a weasel.
Pol. It is backed like a weasel.
Ham. Or like a whale.
Pol. Very like a whale.

Morley and Dilke, though closely drawn to Chamberlain by bonds of personal affection, susceptible to his commanding personality, were not of the breed of Polonius or Jesse Collings. When crisis was reached he accordingly, in letters curiously alike in tone, warned each of them that, howsoever reluctantly, he must terminate an intimacy with which they had hitherto been favoured above ordinary men. Towards the close of 1885 he was

drifting apart from Gladstone and the majority of the
Liberal party on the question of Home Rule. Morley,
faithful to convictions at one time shared by his friend,
went to his constituents and delivered a speech which
committed him to some form of Home Rule. Chamberlain forthwith wrote :

" I do not blame you for holding your opinion. Possibly
you are right and I am wrong. But do not let us attempt
to blind ourselves to the fact that on the most important
issue which has arisen since you were in Parliament we
are working against each other, and not as allies."

Regardless of this solemn warning of the consequences
of his action, Morley went his headstrong way, accepting
office under Gladstone, and playing a leading part in the
desperate crusade under the Home Rule flag. In subsequent relations Chamberlain modified something of the
implacable attitude assumed towards the rest of former
colleagues who followed Gladstone. But he was never
again friendly on the old terms of intimacy.

After the general election that made an end of Lord
Salisbury's brief administration—named by Chamberlain
in one of his happy phrases "the Stop-gap Government"—
it was evident that John Morley would be offered by
Gladstone a post with Cabinet rank. How this expectation was realised is vividly related. Under date Sunday,
January 31, 1886, Lord Morley noted in his diary :

" Was writing an article peaceably at home when
telegram arrived from Mr. G. asking me to call on him
at Carlton House Terrace at two. I got there to the
moment, and found him at his writing-table, with no
sign of fuss or hurry. He had to make to me, he said, an
important proposition, and it was that I should accept
the office of Irish Secretary. . . . In a pretty tense frame
of mind I walked slowly down to the Athenæum, had
some tea, noted down seven separate strong reasons
against my fitness for the Irish office, and went across
to Mr. Gladstone."

In the meanwhile, Morley had seen Chamberlain and communicated to him the great news. " For an instant he changed colour, and no wonder. My going to Ireland was the sudden arrival of long-apprehended peril to a cherished private intimacy."

I happen to know something about that leading article penned midway in the career of John Morley, leading him on to high offices of State, a Peerage, and the jealously exclusive Order of Merit. My personal relations with him were in one respect unique. For a time he was my editor. Subsequently I was, *longo intervallo*, his. Whilst he was in charge of the *Pall Mall Gazette* he did me the honour to invite me to contribute a series of weekly articles on doings at Westminster. When in this same momentous month—January 1886—I reluctantly obeyed a call to the editorship of the *Daily News*, I obtained his valuable assistance as writer of the leading article. He was engaged upon what proved to be his last contribution when interrupted by the summons from Gladstone. It is characteristic of him that, his world being suddenly changed, he looked in at his club, finished his article, and dispatched it to the editor with intimation that nothing more in the journalistic line was to be expected from him.

Particulars of Gladstone's final retirement from the Premiership Morley relates with full frankness. It is not a pretty tale, amounting to the hustling off the boards of the commanding figure that had dominated the parliamentary scene for more than half a century. With the defeat in 1894 of his second Home Rule Bill, Gladstone began to talk of retirement. His Cabinet colleagues had, with well-concealed regret, heard of this before. This time it really might be true. Its accomplishment was hastened by an incidental influence. Lord Spencer, First Lord of the Admiralty, submitted naval estimates for the coming year which the Premier declared to be grossly excessive. The majority of the Cabinet backed up the First Lord, who literally stood to his guns and his ships.

His colleagues, including Morley, were perhaps more insistent in support of him since, as the Irish Secretary put it in a memorandum made at the time, " It would be against Mr. G.'s honour to remain at the head of the Government whilst the estimates of which he disapproved were actually being framed."

One evening at a time when it was secretly decided that Gladstone must go, the only question remaining being whether action should forthwith be taken or whether it should be delayed by a month, Morley, at his chief's invitation, went to dine in Downing Street. " Mr. G.," he notes, " not in his gay mood, but still perfectly cheerful and full of talk, only no flow." After dinner, in the drawing-room the Prime Minister sat down to a game of backgammon with his old friend and faithful servitor George Armitstead. Mrs. Gladstone, seeing her opportunity, drew Morley aside and asked how things stood. " I told her that the reign was over, and that the only question was whether the abdication should be now or in February."

" What a curious scene," the diarist muses, " the breaking to her that the pride and glory of her life was at last to face eclipse, that the curtain was falling on a grand drama of fame, power, acclamation ; the rattle of the dice on the backgammon board and the laughter and chuckles of the two long-lived players sounding a strange running refrain ! "

The end, however, was not yet. Gladstone went to Biarritz, where he stayed for nearly a month. On February 17, there was a Cabinet dinner which his colleagues, every one of whom had found opportunity of reaching Cabinet rank bestowed by his hand, hopefully attended. Now or never ! But the old fox was not yet run to earth.

" We ate our dinners expectantly," moans Morley, " the coffee found the oracle still dumb, and in good time a crestfallen flock departed."

Six days later there was another Cabinet at which Gladstone casually remarked that " when the Prorogation speech was settled the moment would have come to end his co-operation with the Cabinet." More delay.   It meant that the Premier intended to hold office throughout the session.

" The words fell like ice on men's hearts," the chronicler records.   " There was an instant's hush, and we broke up in funereal groups."

Everything comes to the men who wait.   A week later —what happened in the interval is not told—the last Cabinet of a series of unparalleled length attended by Gladstone was held.   Lord Kimberley, as senior, was deputed to say words of farewell.   Emotion overcame him, and his utterance was broken by tears.   Harcourt, more successful in mastering his feelings, voiced the grief with which he recognised that the congenial task of lightening his beloved chief's toil was at an end. Gladstone, who had sat composed, still as marble, closed the scene in an eloquent speech of four or five minutes, the sentences of moving cadence, the voice unbroken and serene, the words and tones low, grave, and steady.   Concluding in a tone hardly above a breath, but every accent heard, he said " God bless you all."

History repeats itself.   Probably a diarist, eye and ear-witness, will relate for future generations particulars of the scene happening some years ago, in which another Liberal Prime Minister (Asquith), long time regarded as indispensable, received a visit from his colleagues and straightway resumed his former status of a private Member of the House of Commons.   It is reasonable to suppose that he did not dismiss his morning callers with the benediction that, under analogous circumstances, fell from Gladstone's lips.

Whilst Gladstone, with habitual magnanimity, uttered no reproach, he thoroughly understood the situation, and in his heart deeply resented it. Conversing with him four years later, Morley notes in his diary : " Mr. Gladstone talked much about his having been turned out by Spencer and Harcourt—turned out of the Cabinet."

A side-blow that assisted in bringing to a climax the fall of Lord Rosebery's Government in 1895, was dealt in connection with the proposal to vote £500 for a statue of Oliver Cromwell. The Irish Nationalists, under the temporary leadership of Justin McCarthy, rose in angry protest. Prolonged, acrid, debate followed. The Unionist party, perceiving opportunity of making an end of the Government, joined in the fray. It was evident that if the proposal were persisted in, this alliance would repeat earlier achievements on the same lines by defeating the Government in the division lobby. In these circumstances, " I had," Lord Morley writes, " the agreeable duty of withdrawing our vote on the specious ground that, in face of opposition so varied and apparently so hot, it no longer meant a really national recognition of the Protector's grandeur."

News of this new danger besetting his former colleagues reached Gladstone, one of a hundred of Sir Donald Currie's guests on board the *Tantallon Castle* on her historic voyage to Kiel for the opening of the Canal, which, in connection with surrendered Heligoland, has played so important a part in the Great War. The fact that his son Herbert, First Commissioner of Works, had charge of the project of erecting the statue, lent it special interest in his eyes. The more he thought of it, the more the subject possessed him. For fully a day he talked of nothing else. The topic effusively came up when Viscount Peel, long-time honoured Speaker of the House of Commons, came aboard the *Tantallon Castle* at Kiel, paying an afternoon call upon his illustrious father's former colleague and his own old friend.

" And what do you think we talked about ? " Lord Peel asked me when he left the state-room on deck, where for fully half an hour Gladstone had fervently conversed with him. " Why, about Oliver Cromwell ! "

Lingering at the dinner-table the same evening Gladstone, reverting to the subject, expressed surprise that the Government, having carried the vote on account of the statue through Committee of Supply, should subsequently have abandoned the project.

" I am not sure," he added, " that, had I been in the House, I should have voted for the statue. I admit Cromwell to have been one of the biggest men who ever wielded power in this country. Though never actually King, no crowned monarch has exceeded the measure of his autocracy. The blot on his character I cannot forgive was the Irish massacres. The Irish Members were fully justified in their opposition, and I drink to the health of Justin McCarthy."

Which he forthwith did.

On March 2, 1894, Gladstone went down to Windsor to tender his resignation. Assuming that, in accordance with custom, the Queen would ask him for advice as to his successor, he consulted Morley on the point. Morley named Lord Rosebery. " I shall advise Spencer," Gladstone responded. Presumably advice was not sought, Her Majesty losing no time in calling Lord Rosebery to the helm. On his return from Windsor, having kissed hands on his high appointment, the new Premier joined his colleagues at an official dinner given by Kimberley in his capacity as Lord President.

" The meal was not convivial," Lord Morley reports. " We were out of a prolonged severe ordeal ; and even those of us whose view of life was never to look back upon action that could not be revoked, may have mused over the chances of a future ordeal severer still."

The difficulty was Harcourt. When the Parliament of 1892 opened with Gladstone as Premier, Harcourt's colleagues had, Lord Morley testifies, " cherished every good feeling towards him." As the senior, the most experienced, and, for parliamentary purposes, the most competent of all the men sitting with him on the Treasury Bench, his succession in due course to the Premiership was naturally expected, and in anticipation conceded. Now, when the contemplated hour had struck they, fully recognising the obvious disadvantage of a Premier not being seated in the House of Commons, could not agree to take service under him.

" How," asks Lord Morley, " came such gifts, claims, and work as his to miscarry just when the prospects of natural ambition were so promising ? The short answer is that, though he was a large-hearted man, and a warm-hearted man, and a man of commanding parliamentary power, he was daily liable to moods that made him difficult."

So, as Gladstone had been dismissed, Harcourt was shunted. But his colleagues in the Cabinet had quite another man to deal with. Morley's gloomy vaticinations of what should have been the joyous birthday dinner celebrating Lord Rosebery's accession to the Premiership were immediately and persistently realised. As Chancellor of the Exchequer Harcourt grumbled his way through the short chapter of Lord Rosebery's Government. The Parliament was not to his mind, still less was the size of the majority ; he was not sustained by enthusiasm for his own arduous task in framing an historic Budget ; he missed old stable companions and did not take to all of the new. He varied continuous complaints with frequent threats of resignation. Meeting Lord Morley at a party at Brook House given by that peerless hostess, Lady Tweedmouth, to celebrate the opening of the session of 1895, I asked whether there was any truth in the recurrent rumour.

" Well," said the harassed Minister, with what for him was a rare burst of bitterness, " if Harcourt doesn't resign very soon, the rest of us will."

Harcourt, who, amid the petty friction of the time,

had carried his epoch-making Budget of 1894, regarded these rumours with grim humour. Talking to me in this same month of February 1895, he said with a big chuckle, " There is hardly a night when I go to bed in Downing Street that I am not called up by the representative of some news agency wanting to know if it is true I have resigned. It reminds me of Louis XVI when, after his flight from Paris, he was captured and interned at the Tuileries. Every night, soon after the poor man had turned into bed, the mob, suspicious of fresh escape, assembled before the palace windows and demanded to see him. The hapless King, yielding to necessity, got out of bed, slipped on his dressing-gown, put on the night-cap of Liberty, and, popping his head out of the window, cried, ' *Me voici, citoyens.*' Whereupon the crowd went home content. So the news agency man comes to me in the dead of night to assure himself and his employers that I have not slipped out of Downing Street by the back door. Meanwhile, *me voici.*"

In these conditions, harassed in his inner councils, hampered by the dwindling smallness of his majority in the Commons, Lord Rosebery gallantly carried on till, on a June night in the same year, came joyful deliverance by the agency of a puff of cordite ignited by St. John Brodrick.

Printed by Hazell, Watson & Viney, Ld., London and Aylesbury, England.